It's another Quality Book from CGP

This book is for anyone doing AQA Modular GCSE Maths at Foundation Level.

It contains lots of tricky questions designed to make you sweat — because that's the only way you'll get any better.

It's also got some daft bits in to try and make the whole experience at least vaguely entertaining for you.

What CGP is all about

Our sole aim here at CGP is to produce the highest quality books — carefully written, immaculately presented and dangerously close to being funny.

Then we work our socks off to get them out to you — at the cheapest possible prices.

Contents

Don't panic! We haven't forgotten about Modules Two and Four — they're coursework modules, so you don't need to revise them for the exams.

Module One

Module Three

Module Five

Published by Coordination Group Publications Ltd.
Illustrated by Ruso Bradley, Lex Ward and Ashley Tyson

Coordinated by June Hall and Mark Haslam

Contributors:
Philip Wood
Margaret Carr
Barbara Coleman
John Lyons
Gordon Rutter
Claire Thompson

Updated by:
Tim Major
Mark Moody

ISBN 1 84146 098 2

Groovy website: www.cgpbooks.co.uk

Printed by Elanders Hindson, Newcastle upon Tyne.
Clipart sources: CorelDRAW and VECTOR.

Questions on Mode and Median

Remember the GOLDEN RULE — put things IN ORDER OF SIZE first.

The MODE or MODAL value is the one that occurs most often in a set of data.

Q1 Find the MODE for each of these sets of data.

a) 3, 5, 8, 6, 3, 7, 3, 5, 3, 9, Mode is ....

b) 52, 26, 13, 52, 31, 12, 26, 13, 52, 87, 41 Mode is ....

Q2 The temperature in °C on 10 Summer days in England was:

25, 18, 23, 19, 23, 24, 23, 18, 20, 19

What was the Modal temperature? Modal temperature ....°C.

Q3 The time it takes twenty pupils in a class to get to school each day in minutes is:

18, 24, 12, 28, 17, 34, 17, 17, 28, 12
23, 24, 17, 34, 19, 32, 15, 31, 17, 9
17, 32, 15, 17, 21, 29, 34, 17, 12, 17

What is the modal time? Modal time.............mins.

The MEDIAN is the middle value when the data has been put in order of size.

Q4 Find the median for these sets of data.

a) 3, 6, 7, 12, 2, 5, 4, 2, 9

.... Median is ....

b) 14, 5, 21, 7, 19, 3, 12, 2, 5

.... Median is ....

Q5 These are the heights of fifteen 16 year olds.

162cm 156cm 174cm 148cm 152cm
139cm 167cm 134cm 157cm 163cm
149cm 134cm 158cm 172cm 146cm

What is the median height? Put it in the shaded box.

														Median

Questions on Mean and Range

Yikes — MEAN questions... well, they're not as bad as everyone makes out. Remember to include zeros in your calculations — they still count.

The mean of a set of data is the total of the items ÷ the number of items

Q1 Find, without a calculator, the mean for each of these sets of data:

a) 5, 3, 7, 3, 2 =...........

b) 18, 6, 12, 4 =...........

c) 7, 3, 9, 5, 3, 5, 4, 6, 2, 6 =..............

d) 5, 4, 0, 3, 0, 6 =...............

Q2 Now you can use a calculator to find the mean. If necessary, round your answers to 1 decimal place:

a) 13, 15, 11, 12, 16, 13, 11, 9 =..............

b) 16, 13, 2, 15, 0, 9 =..............

c) 80, 70, 80, 50, 60, 70, 90, 60, 50, 70, 70 =..............

Q3 a) Stephen scored a mean mark of 64 in four Maths tests. What was his total marks for all four tests?

....

b) When he did the next test, his mean mark went up to 66. What mark did he get in the fifth test?

....

Q4 The number of goals scored by a hockey team over a period of 10 games is listed below.

0, 3, 2, 4, 1, 2, 3, 4, 1, 0.

What is the range in the number of goals scored? ....

Q5 Sarah and her friends were measured and their heights were found to be:

1.52m, 1.61m, 1.49m, 1.55m, 1.39m, 1.56m.

What is the range of the heights? ....

Q6 Here are the times 6 people took to do a Maths test:

1 hour 10 mins, 2 hours 10 mins, 1 hour 35 mins,
1 hours 55 min, 1 hour 18 mins, 2 hours 15 mins.

What is the range of these times? ....

Questions on Averages

Geesh — as if it's not enough to make you work out all these boring averages, they want you to write stuff about them as well. Oh well, here goes nothing.

Q1 These are the mathematics marks for John and Mark.

John	65	83	58	79	75
Mark	72	70	81	67	70

Calculate the mean and range for each pupil. Who do you think is the better maths student? Why?

....

....

Q2 The shoe sizes in a class of girls are:

3 3 4 4 5 5 5 5 6 6 6 7 8

Calculate the mean, median and mode for the shoe sizes.

....

....

If you were a shoe shop manager, which average would be most useful to you, and why?

....

Q3 A house building company needs a bricklayer. This advert appears in the local newspaper. The company employs the following people.

Position	Wage
Director	£600
Foreman	£260
Plasterer	£200
Bricklayer	£150
Bricklayer	£150

What is the median wage? ....

What is the mean wage? ....

Which gives the best idea of the average wage?

....

Is the advert fair? .... Why? ....

Write a fairer advert.

Questions on Averages

Q4 The number of absences for 20 pupils during the spring term were:

0 0 0 0 0 0 1 1 1 2 3 4 4 4 7 9 10 10 19 22

Work out the mean, median and modal number of absences.

....

....

....

If you were a local newspaper reporter wishing to show that the local school has a very poor attendance record, which average would you use and why?

....

If you were the headteacher writing a report for the parents of new pupils which average would you use and why?

....

Q5 On a large box of matches it says "Average contents 240 matches".
I counted the number of matches in ten boxes.
These are the results:

241 244 236 240 239 242 237 239 239 236

Is the label on the box correct? Use the mean, median and mode for the numbers of matches to explain your answer.

....

....

....

Q6 Jane has a Saturday job. She earns £2.20 an hour. She thinks that most of her friends earn more. Here is a list of how much an hour her friends are paid.

Lisa	£2.10	Scott	£3.00
Kate	£2.75	Kylie	£1.90
Helen	£2.51	Kirsty	£2.75
Ben	£2.75	Ruksana	£2.40

Work out the mean, median and mode for her friends' pay.

....

....

Jane's employer offers her a rise to £2.52 because she claims that this is the average hourly rate. Which average has her employer used?

....

Which average should Jane use to try to negotiate a higher pay rise?

....

The big trick with wordy questions is to IGNORE THE WAFFLE... you only need the numbers to work out the averages, so why worry about the rest of it...

Questions on Tally/Frequency Tables

Q1 At the British Motor Show 60 people were asked what type of car they preferred. Jeremy wrote down their replies using a simple letter code.

Saloon - S Coupe - C Hatchback - H 4x4 - F MPV - M Roadster - R

Here is the full list of replies.

H	S	R	S	S	R	M	F	S	S	R	R
M	H	S	H	R	H	M	S	F	S	M	S
R	R	H	H	H	S	M	S	S	R	H	H
H	H	R	R	S	S	M	M	R	H	M	H
H	S	R	F	F	R	F	S	M	S	H	F

Fill in the tally table and add up the frequency in each row. Draw the frequency graph of the results.

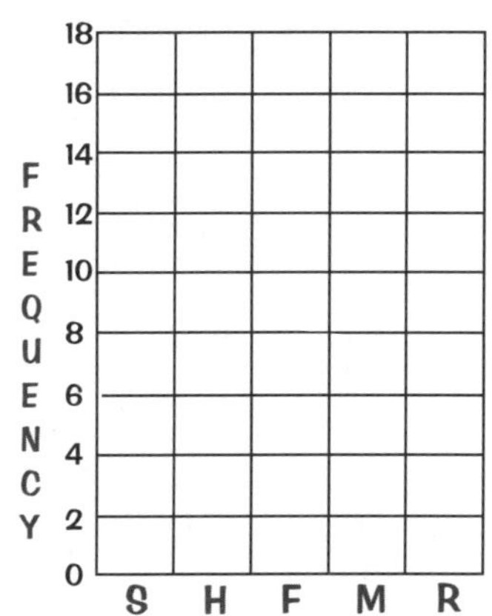

TYPE OF CAR	TALLY	FREQUENCY
Saloon		
Hatchback		
4 × 4		
MPV		
Roadster		

Q2 Last season Newcaster City played 32 matches.
The number of goals they scored in each match were recorded as shown.

2	4	3	5
1	0	3	2
4	2	1	2
0	2	3	1

1	0	0	1
1	1	1	0
1	3	2	0
1	1	0	4

Complete the tally chart and draw the frequency graph of the scores.

GOALS	TALLY	FREQUENCY
0		
1		
2		
3		
4		
5		

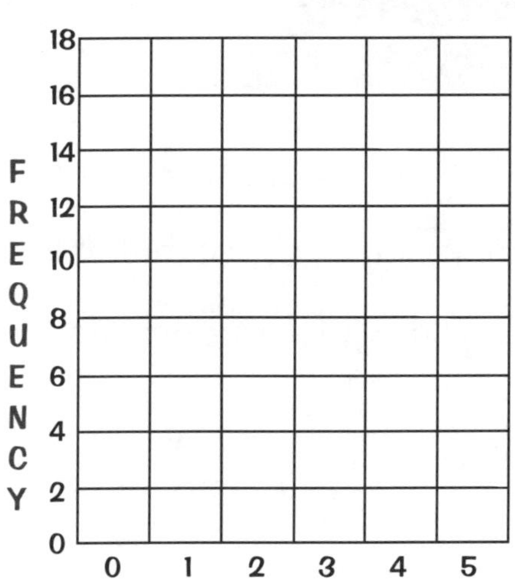

Go through the data in the <u>same order</u> as it's written and <u>cross off</u> each one as you put it in the list.

Questions on Tally/Frequency Tables

Q3 Here is a list of marks which 32 pupils gained in a History test:

65	78	49	72	38	59	63	44
55	50	60	73	66	54	42	72
33	52	45	63	65	51	70	68
84	61	42	58	54	64	75	63

Complete the tally table making sure you put each mark in the correct group. Then fill in the frequency column.

MARKS	TALLY	FREQUENCY
31-40		
41-50		
51-60		
61-70		
71-80		
81-90		
	TOTAL	

Q4 The frequency table below shows the number of hours spent Christmas shopping by 100 people surveyed in a town centre.

Number of Hours	0	1	2	3	4	5	6	7	8
Frequency	1	9	10	10	11	27	9	15	8
Hours × Frequency									

a) What is the modal number of hours spent Christmas shopping? ....

b) Fill in the third row of the table.

c) What is the total amount of time spent Christmas shopping by the all the people surveyed?

....

d) What is the mean amount of time spent Christmas shopping by a person?

....

Don't forget to group your tally scores in 5's, using the 5 bar tally — 𝍸. Makes it all nice and tidy, doesn't it — and quicker to count.

Questions on Bar Charts and Sample Sizes

Q1 Here is a horizontal bar chart showing the favourite colours of a class of pupils.

a) How many like blue best? ....

b) How many more people chose red than yellow? ....

c) How many pupils took part in this survey? ....

d) What fraction of the class prefer green? ....

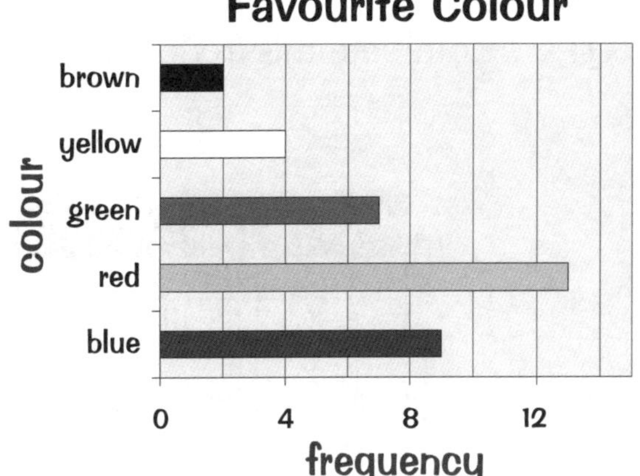

Q2 This bar chart shows the marks from a test done by some students:

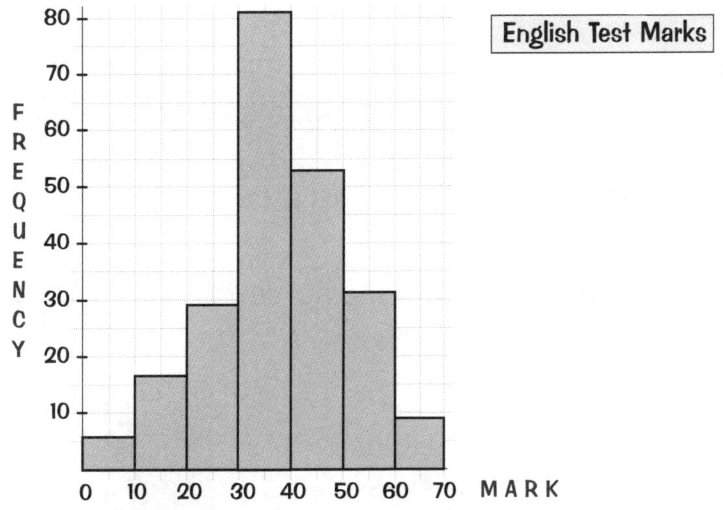

a) How many students scored 20 marks or less? ....

b) The pass mark for this test was 30. How many students passed the test? ....

c) How many students took the test? ....

Q3 Carol was asked to find out if most people have a calculator in their Maths lessons. She asked the people she liked in her Maths set if they had brought a calculator to school, 2 said yes, 3 said no. From this she claims most people do not have a calculator. Give 3 criticisms of Carol's survey.

....

....

Questions on Tables, Charts and Graphs

Bar charts are a bit of a breeze — the bars' heights are just proportional to the frequencies they represent...

Q1 Complete this frequency table, and then draw a bar chart for the results.

TEST SCORE	TALLY	FREQUENCY
1 - 5	~~IIII~~ I	6
6 - 10	~~IIII~~ III	
11 - 15	III	
16 - 20	~~IIII~~	
21 - 25	III	

FREQUENCY

TEST SCORE

Q2 One hundred people were asked in a survey what colour eyes they had. Use this two-way table to answer the following questions.

a) How many people in the survey had green eyes? ....

b) How many women took part in the survey? ....

c) How many women had blue eyes? ....

d) How many men had brown eyes? ....

	Green eyes	Blue eyes	Brown eyes	Total
Male	15			48
Female	20		23	
Total		21		100

Q3 This pictogram shows the favourite drinks of a group of pupils.

Favourite Drinks	Number of Pupils
Lemonade	✧✧✧✧✧✧✧✧✧
Coke	✧✧✧✧✧✧✧✧✧✧✧
Tango	✧✧✧✧✧✧
Orange Squash	✧✧✧
Milk	✧

✧ Represents 2 pupils.

a) How many pupils were questioned?................ pupils.

b) How many pupils prefer non-fizzy drinks?.............. pupils.

c) 18 pupils liked lemonade best. How many more liked coke best?.............pupils.

d) Make one general comment about the information given................

Questions on Stem & Leaf Diagrams and Line Graphs

Q1 This stem and leaf diagram shows the ages of people in a cinema showing 'The Lord of The Things'.

Stem	Leaf
1	2 2 4 8 8 9 9
2	0 1 1 2 5 6
3	0 0 0 5
4	2 5 9
5	
6	8

Key: 2 | 5 means 25

a) How many people in the cinema were in their twenties? ....

b) Write out the ages of all of the people in the cinema below.

Q2 I've been measuring my friends' noses. Here are the lengths in millimetres:

12	18	20	11	31
19	27	34	19	22

Complete the stem and leaf diagram on the right to show the results above.

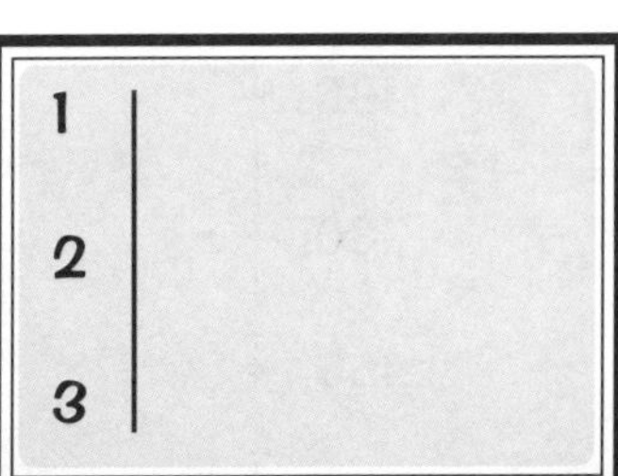

Key: 2 | 2 means 22

Q3 A baby was weighed every 5 days. The results are given below. Draw a graph to show how the baby's weight changed.

DAY N°	0	5	10	15	20	25	30
WEIGHT KG	5.3	5.2	5.9	6.4	6.6	6.7	6.8

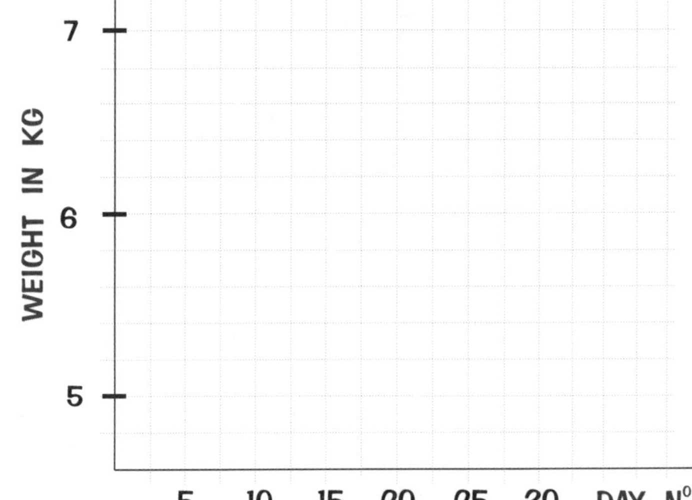

In your own words describe how the baby's weight changed:

....

....

....

....

Questions on Scattergraphs

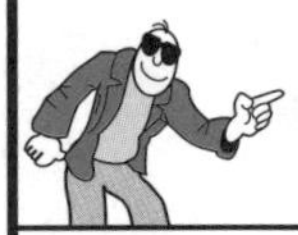

Scatter graphs aren't supposed to make a nice line — they're always a bit messy. Just a load of points scattered round all over the shop.

Q1 These are the shoe sizes and heights for 12 pupils in Year 11.

Shoe size	5	6	4	6	7	7	8	3	5	9	10	10
Height (cm)	155	157	150	159	158	162	162	149	152	165	174	178

On the grid below draw a scattergraph to show this information.

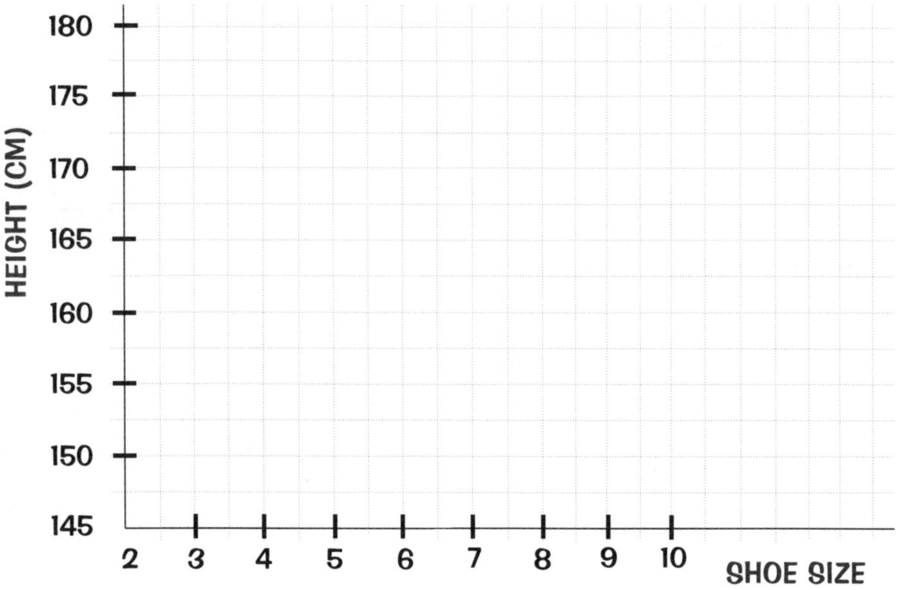

What does the scattergraph tell you about the relationship between shoe size and height for these pupils?

....

Q2 The scattergraphs below show the relationship between:

a) The temperature and the amount of ice cream sold.
b) The price of ice cream and the amount sold.
c) The age of people and the amount of ice cream sold.

a)

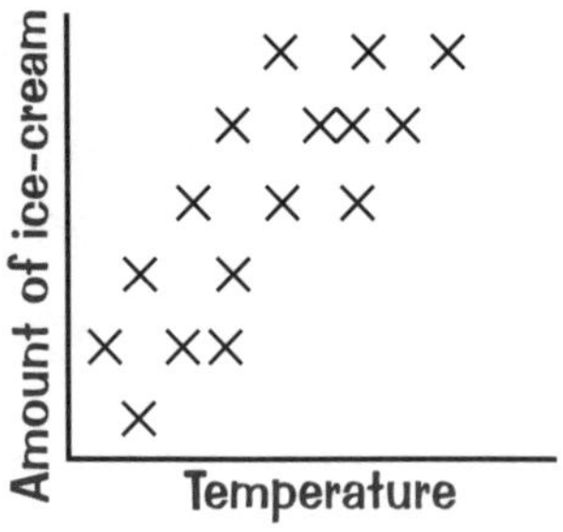

b)

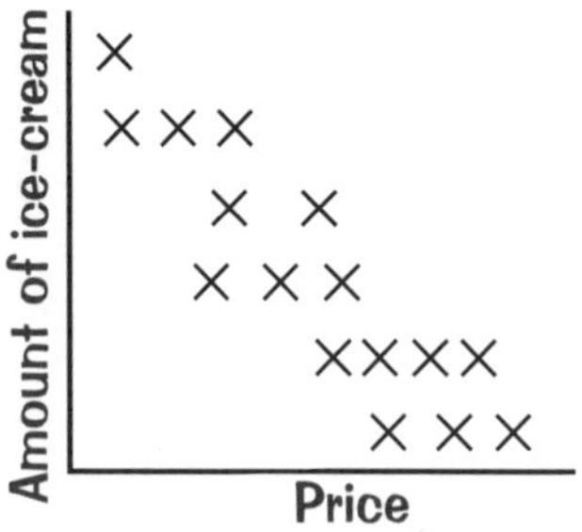

c)

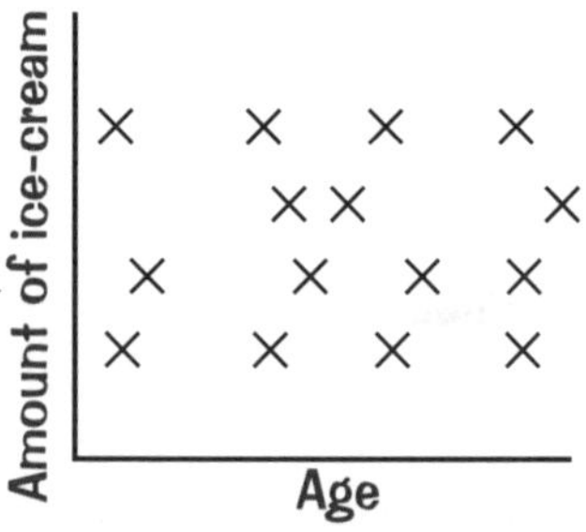

Describe the correlation of each graph and say what each graph tells you.

a) ....

b) ....

c) ....

Questions on Pie Charts

Q1 In a University department there are 180 students from different countries.

Country	UK	Malaysia	Spain	Others
Number of students	90	35	10	45

To show this on a Pie chart you have to work out the angle of each sector. Complete the table showing your working. The UK is done for you.

COUNTRY	WORKING	ANGLE in degrees
UK	90 ÷ 180 × 360 =	180°
MALAYSIA		
SPAIN		
OTHERS		

Now complete the Pie chart using an angle measurer. The UK sector is done for you.

Q2 On TV, programmes of different types have the amount of air time as shown in the table.

Programme	Hours	Angle
News	5	
Sport	3	
Music	2	
Current Affairs	3	
Comedy	2	
Other	9	
Total	24	

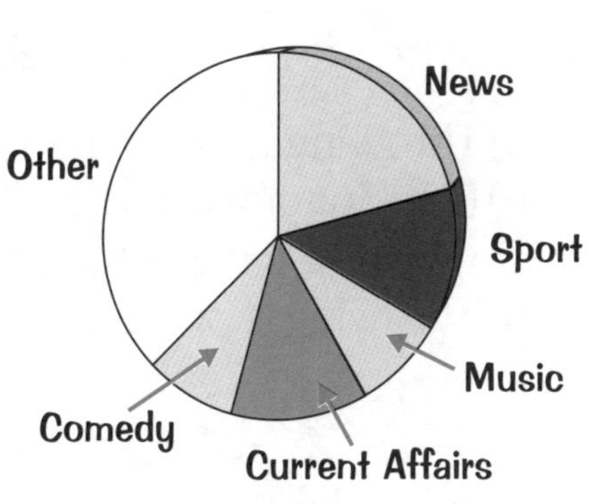

Complete the table by finding the size of the angle represented by each type of programme. Use an angle measurer or calculation method.

The full circle (that's all 360° of it) represents the total of everything — so you shouldn't find any gaps in it, basically.

Questions on Probability

Probability always has a value between 0 and 1 — if it's 0, the thing's DEFINITELY NOT going to happen... if it's 1, it DEFINITELY IS going to happen.

Q1 Write down whether these events are impossible, unlikely, even, likely or certain.

a) You will go shopping on Saturday. ....
b) You will live to be 150 years old. ....
c) The next person who comes into the room is female. ....
d) There will be a moon in the sky tonight. ....

Q2 Mike and Nick play a game of pool. The probability of Nick winning is 7/10.

a) Put an arrow on the probability line below to show the probability of Nick winning. Label this arrow N.

b) Now put an arrow on the probability line to show the probability of Mike winning the game. Label this arrow M.

0 ——————————————————— 1

Q3 Write down the probability of these events happening...

a) Throwing an odd number with a dice. ....
b) Drawing a black card from a pack. ....
c) Drawing a Black King from a pack of cards. ....
d) Throwing a prime number with a dice. ....

Q4 A bag contains ten balls. Five are red, three are yellow and two are green. What is the probability of picking out:

a) A yellow ball. ....
b) A red ball. ....
c) A green ball. ....
d) A red or a green ball. ....
e) A blue ball. ....

Questions on Probability

Q5 The outcome when a coin is tossed is head (H) or tail (T). Complete this table of outcomes when two coins are tossed together.

a) How many possible outcomes are there? ....

b) What is the probability of getting 2 heads? ....

c) What is the probability of getting a head followed by a tail? ....

		2nd COIN	
		H	T
1st COIN	H		
	T		

Q6 Two dice are rolled together. The scores on the dice are added. Complete the table of possible outcomes below.

How many possible outcomes are there? ....

		SECOND DIE					
		1	2	3	4	5	6
FIRST DIE	1						
	2	3					
	3						
	4						
	5			8			
	6						

What is the probability of scoring:

a) 2 ....

b) 6 ....

c) 10 ....

d) More than 9 ....

e) Less than 4..........................

f) An even number ....

g) More than 12 ....

Q7 Two spinners are spun and the scores are multiplied together.

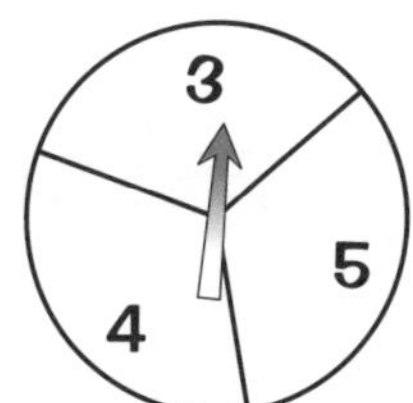

Fill in this table of possible outcomes.

What is the probability of scoring 12?.....................

To win you have to score 15 or more. What is the probability of winning ?

....

		SPINNER 1		
		2	3	4
SPINNER 2	3			
	4			
	5			

You're always better off using a table to put down the "possible outcomes" — you can't miss any out that way.

Questions on Probability

Well, OK, the probability is that you'd rather not be doing these at all... still — this is the last page, so I'm sure you'll cope for a bit longer.

Q8 One day Sarah did a survey in her class on sock colour. She found out that pupils were wearing white socks, black socks or red socks. Jack said "If I pick someone at random from the class, then the probability that they are wearing red socks is 1/3." Explain why Jack might be wrong.

....

....

Q9 Imagine you have just made a 6-sided spinner in Design and Technology. How could you estimate the probability that it was a fair spinner?

....

....

....

Q10 How could you estimate the probability that it is going to snow on Christmas Eve this year?

....

....

....

Q11 "There is a 50% chance that it will rain tomorrow because it will either rain or it won't rain." Is this statement true or false? Explain your answer.

....

....

....

Questions on Writing Numbers

Q1 Write these words as numbers.

a) Twenty six ....

b) Seventy three ....

c) Eight hundred and sixty ....

d) Five thousand seven hundred and ninety two ....

e) Twenty seven thousand and fifty two ....

f) Four hundred and sixty three thousand and four ....

g) Mr U. N. Lucky won three hundred and fourteen pounds on the Lottery. Write this in the space on his cheque.

Royal Bank of CGP Today

PAY Mr. U. N. Lucky

Three hundred and fourteen pounds £

Signature L.OTerry.

Q2 Put these numbers in ascending, smallest to biggest, order.

a) 23 117 5 374 13 89 67 54 716 18

....

b) 1272 231 817 376 233 46 2319 494 73 1101

....

Q3 Write down the value of the number 4 in each of these...

For example 408 *hundreds*

a) 347 .... **b)** 41 .... **c)** 5478 ....

d) 6754 .... **e)** 4897 .... **f)** 6045 ....

g) 64098 .... **h)** 745320 .... **i)** 405759 ....

j) 2402876 .... **k)** 4987321 .... **l)** 6503428 ....

Questions on Multiplying by 10, 100, etc.

Fill in the missing numbers. Do not use a calculator for this page.

Q1 6 × ☐ = 60 0.07 × ☐ = 0.7

6 × ☐ = 600 0.07 × ☐ = 7

6 × ☐ = 6000 0.07 × ☐ = 70

Q2 Which number is ten times as large as 25? ....

Q3 Which number is one hundred times as large as 93? ....

Q4 8 × 10 = ... 34 × 100 = ... 52 × 100 = ...

9 × 1000 = ... 436 × 1000 = ... 0.2 × 10 = ...

6.9 × 10 = ... 4.73 × 100 = ...

0.65 × 1000 = ... 3.7 × 1000 = ...

Q5 For a school concert chairs are put out in rows of 10. How many will be needed for 16 rows? ....

Q6 

How much do 10 chickens cost? ....

Q7 A shop bought 1000 bars of chocolate for £0.43 each. How much did they cost altogether?

....

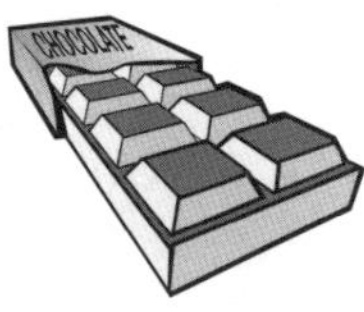

Q8 

A school buys calculators for £2.45 each. How much will 100 cost? ....

Q9 20 × 30 = ... 40 × 700 = ... 250 × 20 = ...

6000 × 210 = ... 18000 × 500 = ...

Multiplying by 10, 100 or 1000 moves each digit 1, 2 or 3 places to the left — you just fill the rest of the space with zeros.

Questions on Dividing by 10, 100, etc.

Keep track of which way that decimal point's moving.

Q1 Work these out without a calculator:

a) 30 ÷ 10 = ...
b) 43 ÷ 10 = ...
c) 5.8 ÷ 10 = ...
d) 63.2 ÷ 10 = ...
e) 0.5 ÷ 10 = ...
f) 400 ÷ 100 = ...
g) 423 ÷ 100 = ...
h) 228.6 ÷ 100 = ...
i) 61.5 ÷ 100 = ...
j) 2.96 ÷ 100 = ...
k) 6000 ÷ 1000 = ...
l) 6334 ÷ 1000 = ...
m) 753.6 ÷ 1000 = ...
n) 8.15 ÷ 1000 = ...
o) 80 ÷ 20 = ...
p) 860 ÷ 20 = ...
q) 2400 ÷ 300 = ...
r) 480 ÷ 40 = ...
s) 860 ÷ 200 = ...
t) 63.9 ÷ 30 = ...

Q2 Ten people share a Lottery win of £62.
How much should each person receive?

....

Q3 Blackpool Tower is 158m tall. If a model of it is built to a scale of 1 : 100 , how tall would the model be?

....

Q4 If 1000 identical ball-bearings weigh 2100g, what is the weight of one of the ball-bearings?

....

Q5 Mark went on holiday to France. He exchanged £100 for 891 francs to spend while he was there. How many francs did he get for each £1?

....

Questions on Adding & Subtracting

NO CALCULATORS HERE! ALWAYS put the numbers in COLUMNS when you're adding... and check the UNITS, TENS & HUNDREDS line up.

Q1 Do these questions as quickly as you can, writing the answers in the spaces provided:

a) 5 + 9 = ...
b) 26 + 15 = ...
c) 34 + 72 = ...

d) 238 + 56 = ...
e) 528 + 173 = ...
f) 215 + 2514 = ...

Q2 Now try these:

a) 63 +32

b) 75 +48

c) 528 +196

Q3 Add the rows and add the columns:

a)

2	6	7	
8	6	4	
4	2	9	

b)

8	3	7	
2	6	9	
7	3	4	

c)

2	7	1	
6	5	8	
3	6	2	

Q4 Subtract the following without a calculator:

a) 36 – 13 = ...
b) 45 – 23 = ...

c) 89 – 24 = ...
d) 25 – 8 = ...

e) 80 – 42 = ...
f) 72 – 19 = ...

Q5 Fill in the missing digits:

a) 65 −3• = •4

b) 73• −2•4 = •25

c) 87• −•32 = 2•9

d) •56 −278 = 1••

Q6 At the beginning of the day a supermarket had 462 tins of beans. By the end of the day 345 had been sold. How many were left? ....

Q7 Scafell Pike is 979m high. Ben Nevis is 1344m high. What is the difference in height between the two mountains?

....

Questions on Adding and Subtracting Decimals

Q1 Work out the answers without using a calculator.

a) 2.4 + 3.2

b) 3.5 + 4.6

c) 6.2 + 5.9

d) 7.34 + 6.07

e) 9.08 + 4.93

f) 15.73 + 25.08

g) 26.05 + 72.95

Q2 Write these out in columns and work out the answer without using a calculator.

a) 3.6 + 7.3 **b)** 21.4 + 13.8 **c)** 0.9 + 5.6 **d)** 9.98 + 6.03 **e)** 2.9 + 7

f) 4.36 + 7.1 **g)** 9.8 + 1.05 **h)** 6 + 6.75 **i)** 0.28 + 18.5 **j)** 47.23 + 6.7

Q3 Work these out <u>without</u> a calculator:

a) 9.6 – 4.3 = ... **b)** 10.8 – 3.5 = ... **c)** 8.4 – 6.4 = ...

d) 9.8 – 3.1

e) 7.3 – 2.3

f) 6.2 – 1.5

g) 8.6 – 3.9

h) 7.0 – 1.6

i) 13.6 – 12.7

j) 14.65 – 4.7

k) 8.34 – 4.65

Q4 Put the following in columns first then work them out:

a) 8.5 – 1.6 **b)** 18.3 – 5.9 **c)** 24.1 – 16.3

d) 9 – 3.6 **e)** 40 – 2.3 **f)** 51 – 18.32

Some questions don't have the decimal point, so you'll have to put it in yourself — you'll have to add some zeros, too... careful now.

Questions on Multiplying and Dividing

Don't forget to put a zero under the units when you multiply by that extra number in the tens column.

Q1 Multiply the following <u>without</u> a calculator:

a) 23 × 2 = ... **b)** 40 × 3 = ... **c)** 53 × 4 = ...

d) $\begin{array}{r} 18 \\ \underline{\times\ 2} \end{array}$ **e)** $\begin{array}{r} 54 \\ \underline{\times\ 3} \end{array}$ **f)** $\begin{array}{r} 75 \\ \underline{\times\ 5} \end{array}$ **g)** $\begin{array}{r} 93 \\ \underline{\times\ 4} \end{array}$

Q2 What is the total cost of 6 pens at 54p each?

....

Q3 How many hours are there in a year (365 days)?

....

Q4 Do these divisions without a calculator:

a) 46 ÷ 2 You may wish to set the sum out like this $2\,\overline{)\,46}$ with 23 on top

b) 86 ÷ 2 **c)** 96 ÷ 3 **d)** 76 ÷ 4

e) 85 ÷ 5 **f)** 96 ÷ 6 **g)** 91 ÷ 7

Q5 Seven people share a lottery win of £868.00. How much did each person get?

....

Q6 A chocolate cake containing 944 calories is split into 8 slices. How many calories are in each slice?

....

OK they're easier with the calulator, but even without it they're a bit of a doddle — just make sure you set the sum out neatly.

Questions on Multiplying and Dividing Decimals

Ignore the decimal point to start with — just multiply the numbers. Then put the point back in and CHECK your answer sounds sensible.

Q1 **a)** 3.2 × 4 = ... **b)** 8.3 × 5 = ... **c)** 6.4 × 3 = ...

d) 21 × 0.3 = ... **e)** 35 × 0.4 = ... **f)** 263 × 0.2 = ...

g) 2.4 × 3.1 = ... **h)** 5.3 × 2.4 = ... **i)** 1.7 × 6.8 = ...

Q2 At a petrol station, each pump shows a ready reckoner table. Complete the table when the cost of unleaded petrol is 64.9p per litre.

Litres	Cost in pence
1	64.9
5	
10	
20	
50	

Q3 Divide these without a calculator.

a) 8.4 ÷ 2 You may wish to set the sum out like this

$$2\overline{)8.4}\ = 4.2$$

b) 7.5 ÷ 3 **c)** 8.5 ÷ 5 **d)** 26.6 ÷ 7

e) 4.75 ÷ 5 **f)** 8.28 ÷ 9 **g)** 0.944 ÷ 8

Q4 Eight people share £9.36. How much does each get?

....

Q5 A plank of wood 8.34m long is cut into 6 equal pieces. How long is each?

....

Questions on BODMAS

Remember this old chap — he tells you which order to work things out. The most important bit is that brackets have priority over everything else.

Brackets Over Division Multiplication Addition Subtraction

Q1 **a)** $4 + 3 \times 2 =$ .... **b)** $4 \times 3 + 2 =$ .... **c)** $4 - 3 \times 2 =$ ....

d) $9 \div 3 + 5 =$ .... **e)** $12 \div 4 + 5 =$ .... **f)** $7 - 10 \div 2 =$ ....

Q2 **a)** $7 \times (3 + 5) =$ .... **b)** $6 - (8 \div 2) =$ .... **c)** $15 \div (9 - 4) =$ ....

d) $(6 + 7) \times 3 =$ .... **e)** $(18 - 6) \div 3 =$ .... **f)** $(21 - 7) \times 2 =$ ....

Q3 **a)** $14 - (2 + 5) =$ .... **b)** $(14 - 2) + 5 =$ .... **c)** $(14 \div 2) + 5 =$ ....

d) $20 - (10 \div 2) =$ .... **e)** $(20 \div 10) - 2 =$ .... **f)** $20 + (10 - 2) =$ ....

Q4 Three cards are picked from a pack. These are: 4, 3, 6.

Put ÷, ×, +, – or ( ) in each sum to make it true.

a) 4 6 3 = 6 **b)** 4 6 3 = 30

c) 4 6 3 = 27 **d)** 4 6 3 = 13

Q5 **a)** $4 + 6 \times 5 - 3 =$ .... **b)** $4 \times 6 + 5 \times 3 =$ ....

c) $12 \div 3 + 4 \times 2 =$ .... **d)** $7 \times 4 \div 2 - 3 =$ ....

Questions on Estimating

An estimate isn't just a wild guess — you've usually got to do SOME work.

Q1 Estimate the answers to these questions...

For example: 12 × 21 <u>10 × 20</u> = <u>200</u>

a) 18 × 12 .... × .... = ...

b) 23 × 21 .... × .... = ...

c) 57 × 46 .... × .... = ...

d) 98 × 145 .... × .... = ...

e) 11 ÷ 4 .... ÷ .... = ...

f) 22 ÷ 6 .... ÷ .... = ...

g) 97 ÷ 9 .... ÷ .... = ...

h) 147 ÷ 14 .... ÷ .... = ...

i) 195 × 205 .... × .... = ...

j) 545 × 301 .... × .... = ...

k) 901 ÷ 33 .... ÷ .... = ...

l) 1207 ÷ 598 .... ÷ .... = ...

Q2 Andy earns £12,404 a year. Bob earns £58,975 a year. Chris earns £81,006 a year.

a) Estimate how much Andy will earn over 3 years. £............

b) Estimate how many years Andy will have to work to earn as much as Chris does in one year. ....

c) Estimate how much Bob earns per month. £............

Q3 Estimate the following lengths then measure them to see how far out you were:

<u>OBJECT</u>	<u>ESTIMATE</u>	<u>ACTUAL LENGTH</u>
a) Length of your pen or pencil	....	....
b) Width of your thumb nail	....	....
c) Height of this page	....	....
d) Height of the room you are in	....	....

Round off to NICE EASY CONVENIENT NUMBERS, then use them to do the sum. Easy peas.

Questions on Powers

Q1 Work out the square of these numbers.

a) 3 .... **b)** 12 .... **c)** 15 ....

Q2 What is the cube of these numbers?

a) 4 .... **b)** 7 .... **c)** 20 ....

Q3 Find the value of these:

a) 4^2 = ... **b)** 16^2 = ... **c)** 3^3 = ...

d) 6^3 = ... **e)** 2^5 = ... **f)** 5^4 = ...

g) 1^7 = ... **h)** 2^7 = ... **i)** 3^5 = ...

Q4 Write these in index notation.

a) 5 × 5 × 5 × 5 = ... **b)** 3 × 3 × 3 = ...

c) 7 × 7 = ... **d)** 11 × 11 × 11 × 11 × 11 × 11 = ...

e) six squared = ... **f)** eight cubed = ...

Q5 Work out:

a) $7^2 - 6^2$ = ... **b)** $8^2 - 7^2$ = ...

c) $9^2 - 8^2$ = ... **d)** $10^2 - 9^2$ = ...

What do you notice? ....

Use your last answer to work out $30^2 - 29^2$ without using a calculator. ....

Q6 Complete this number pattern:

1^3 = ...

$1^3 + 2^3$ = ...

$1^3 + 2^3 + 3^3$ = ...

$1^3 + 2^3 + 3^3 + 4^3$ = ...

What do you notice about your answers? ....

....

Q7 Your calculator may have a button for working out powers.
It looks like this X^y .
e.g. 5^3 On your calculator key in 5 X^y 3 = .
You should get the answer 125.

Try these:

a) 7^9 = ... **b)** 2^{12} = ...

c) 23^5 = ... **d)** 13^7 = ...

Questions on Squares and Cubes

Q1 Work out without a calculator:

a) 5^2 = ... **b)** 7^2 = ... **c)** 2^3 = ... **d)** 4^3 = ...

e) 6^2 = ... **f)** 5^3 = ... **g)** 9^2 = ... **h)** 10^3 = ...

Q2 Do these with a calculator:

a) 1.4^2 = ... **b)** 3.5^2 = ... **c)** 5.95^2 = ... **d)** 7.63^3 = ...

e) $3^2 + 6^2$ = ... **f)** $7^3 - 5^3$ = ... **g)** $6^3 - 14^2$ = ...

Q3 Put a ring round the square numbers in the following list:

17 6 9 15 4 16 21 11 20 1 50

Q4 Put a ring round the cube numbers in the following list:

8 25 27 1 100 125 42 10 16 30 18

Q5 Work out:

a) 10 squared = ... **b)** 4 cubed = ...

Q6 What is the next square number after 64? ....

Q7 What is the next cube number after 216? ....

Q8 Work out with or without a calculator:

a) $2^3 \times 5^2$ = ... **b)** $3^2 \times 1^3$ = ... **c)** $3^3 \times 2^2$ = ...

Q9 Write down two square numbers which are also cube numbers.

Q10 A block of flats with 20 floors has 20 windows on each floor. How many windows does the building have altogether?
If it takes 20 minutes to clean each window, how many minutes does it take to clean the block?

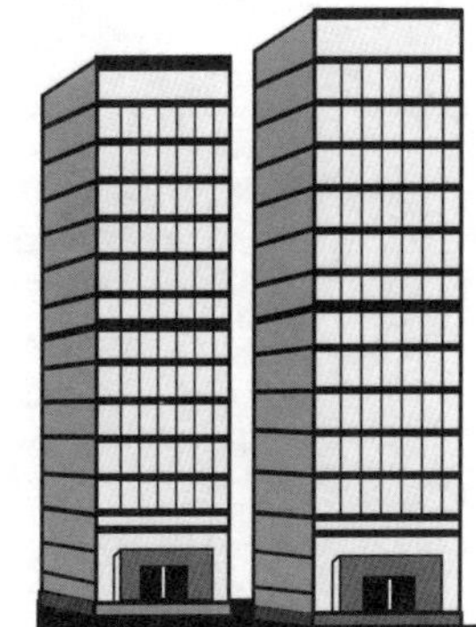

....

**These aren't as bad as they seem — "three squared" = $3^2 = 3 \times 3 = 9$.
Same with cubes — "ten cubed" = $10^3 = 10 \times 10 \times 10 = 1000$.**

Questions on Square Roots

Q1 What are the answers to the following...

a) $\sqrt{16}$ = ... **b)** $\sqrt{49}$ = ... **c)** $\sqrt{81}$ = ...

d) $\sqrt{100}$ = ... **e)** $\sqrt{1}$ = ... **f)** $\sqrt{144}$ = ...

Q2 The square root of 10 must be between the square root of 9, which is 3, and the square root of 16, which is 4. Therefore $\sqrt{10}$ is between 3 and 4. Complete the following...

a) $\sqrt{1}$ = ... , $\sqrt{4}$ = ... , so $\sqrt{2}$ is between .... and ....

b) $\sqrt{16}$ = ... , $\sqrt{25}$ = ... , so $\sqrt{20}$ is between .... and ....

c) $\sqrt{50}$ is between .... and ....

d) $\sqrt{115}$ is between .... and ....

e) $\sqrt{150}$ is between .... and ....

Q3 Use your calculator to answer the following. Give your answers correct to two decimal places.

a) $\sqrt{41}$ = ... **b)** $\sqrt{75}$ = ... **c)** $\sqrt{106}$ = ...

d) $\sqrt{137}$ = ... **e)** $\sqrt{181}$ = ... **f)** $\sqrt{200}$ = ...

g) $\sqrt{225}$ = ... **h)** $\sqrt{250}$ = ... **i)** $\sqrt{1000}$ = ...

Q4 If a square has an area of $64cm^2$, what is the length of its sides?

Area = $side^2$
$side^2 = 64$
so, side = ... cm

A square root just means WHAT NUMBER TIMES ITSELF GIVES... It's just the reverse of squaring, in fact.

Questions on Negative Numbers

Q1 Write these numbers in the correct position on the number line below:

a) –4 3 2 –3 0 –5 1

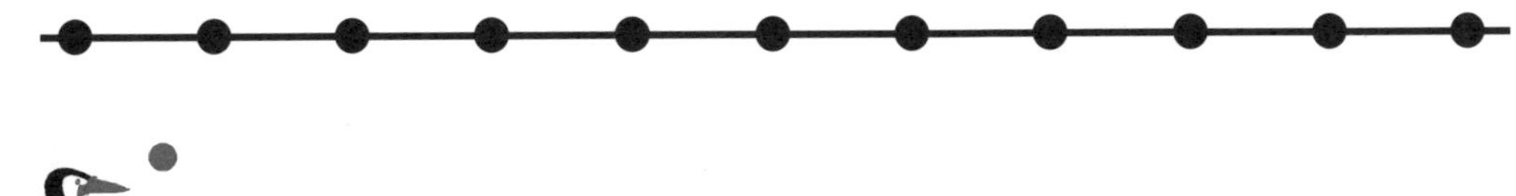

b) Which temperature is lower (colder), 8°C or –4°C ? ....

c) Which temperature is 1° warmer than –24°C ? ....

Put the correct symbol, < or >, between the following pairs of numbers:

d) 4 –8

e) –6 –2

f) –8 –7

g) –3 –6

h) –1 1

i) –3.6 –3.7

j) Rearrange the following numbers in order of size, largest first:

–2 2 0.5 –1.5 –8 = ...

k) If the temperature is 6°C but it then gets colder and falls by 11°, what is the new temperature?

....

l) One day in winter the temperature at 0600 was –9°C.
By midday, it had risen to –1°C.
How many degrees did the temperature rise by?

....

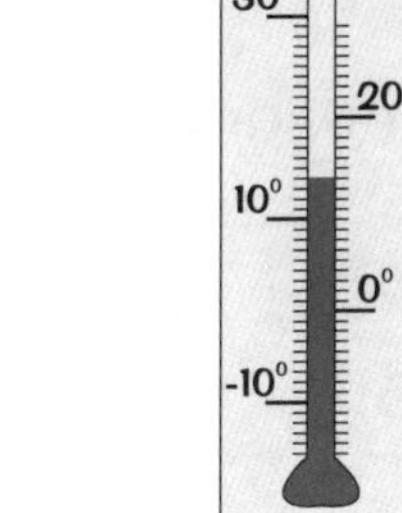

Always draw a number line to count along, so you can see what you're doing.

Questions on Negative Numbers

When you've got really big numbers, just mark off the tens (or even just the hundreds) — you'll be there all day otherwise.

Q2 Work out:

a) 2 – 7 = ... **b)** 4 – 18 = ... **c)** 1 – 20 = ...

d) 12 – 14 = ... **e)** 72 – 77 = ... **f)** 3 – 100 = ...

Q3 Work out:

a) -6 + 1 = ... **b)** -10 + 2 = ... **c)** -8 + 8 = ...

d) -70 + 3 = ... **e)** -100 + 13 = ... **f)** -1000 + 1 = ...

Q4 Work out:

a) -3 – 2 = ... **b)** -3 – 6 = ... **c)** -13 – 3 = ...

d) -50 – 4 = ... **e)** -2 – 19 = ... **f)** -7 – 96 = ...

Q5 Work out:

a) -4 + 6 = ... **b)** -4 – -6 = ... **c)** -6 – -20 = ...

d) -18 – -9 = ... **e)** -30 – -6 = ... **f)** -25 – -25 = ...

Q6 Work out:

a) -8 + 2 = ... **b)** -8 + -2 = ... **c)** -10 + -5 = ...

d) -31 + -3 = ... **e)** -4 + -27 = ... **f)** -47 + -29 = ...

If you minus a negative number, it's the same as adding a positive one. Isn't it great...

Questions on Equivalent Fractions

Q1 Shade in the correct number of sections to make these diagrams equivalent...

$\frac{1}{4} =$ 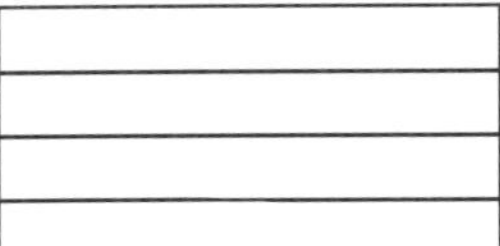 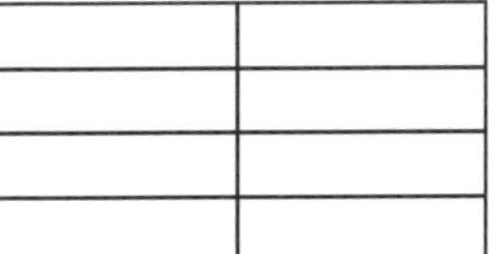 

$\frac{1}{3} =$ 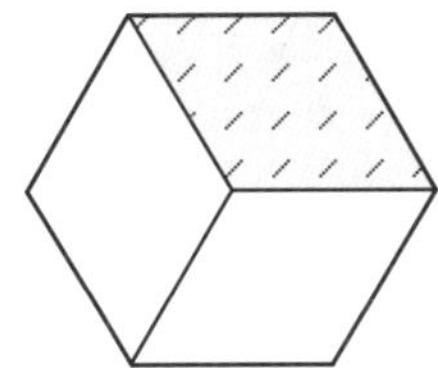 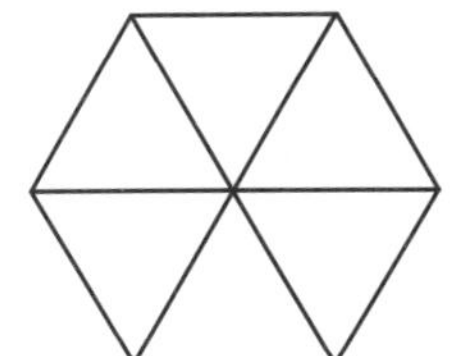 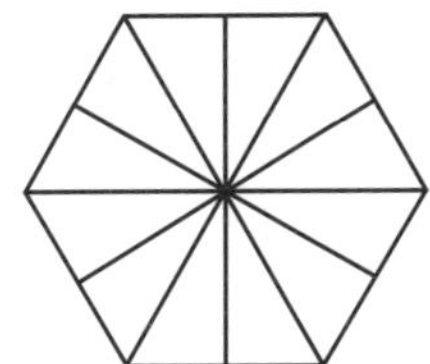 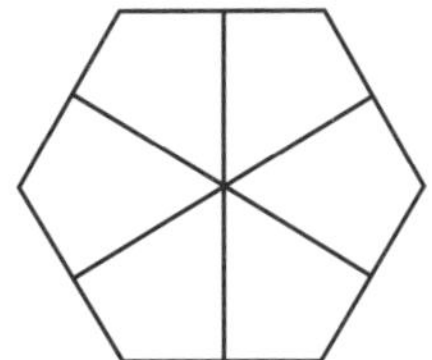

Q2 Write in the missing numbers to make these fractions equivalent.

For example: 1/2 = 7/14

a) 1/4 = 4/........ **b)** 3/4 = 9/........ **c)** 1/3 = ... /6

d) 2/3 = 8/........ **e)** 2/7 = 6/........ **f)** 6/18 = 1 /........

g) 8/16 = ... /2 **h)** 24/32 = 3/........ **i)** 10/60 = 5/........

Q3 Write in the missing numbers to make each list equivalent.

a) 1/2 = 2/...... = ... /6 = ... /8 = 5/10 = 25/...... = ... /70 = ... /100

b) 200/300 = 100/ ...... = ... / 15 = 40/ ...... = 120/180 = ... / 9 = .../3

c) 7/10 = 14/ ...... = ... / 30 = 210/ ...... = 49/ ...... = ... /20

d) 19/20 = ... /80 = 38/ ...... = 57/ ...... = ... /100 = ... /1000

e) 500/600 = 250/ ...... = 50 / ...... = ... / 150 = 1000/ ....

Q4 Which is bigger?

a) 1/5 or 2/10 .... **b)** 3/7 or 6/21 ....

c) 10/15 or 4/6 .... **d)** 1/3 or 33/100 ....

To make an EQUIVALENT fraction, you've got to multiply the TOP (numerator) and BOTTOM (denominator) by the SAME THING.

Questions on Fractions of Quantities

Q1 Write down the fractions of the following quantities...

a) Half of 12 = ... **b)** Quarter of 24 = ... **c)** Third of 30 = ...

d) 1/4 of 44 = ... **e)** 3/4 of 60 = ... **f)** 2/3 of 6 = ...

Q2 Calculate the fractions of the following ...

e.g. 1/3 of 18 = 18 ÷ 3 = <u>6</u>

a) 1/8 of 32 = ... ÷ 8 = ... **b)** 1/10 of 50 = ... ÷ 10 = ...

c) 1/12 of 144 = ... ÷ .... = ... **d)** 1/25 of 75 = ... ÷ .... = ...

e) 1/30 of 180 = ... ÷ .... = ... **f)** 1/27 of 540 = ... ÷ .... = ...

Q3 Calculate the fractions of the following...

e.g. 2/5 of 50 50 ÷ 5 = 10 2 × 10 = <u>20</u>

a) 2/3 of 60 60 ÷ 3 = ... 2 × .... = ...

b) 4/5 of 25 25 ÷ .... = ... 4 × .... = ...

c) 7/9 of 63 .... ÷ .... = ... × .... = ...

d) 3/10 of 100 .... ÷ .... = ... × .... = ...

e) 12/19 of 760 .... ÷ .... = ... × .... = ...

f) 6/9 of £1.80 .... ÷ .... = ... × .... = £....... or ....p

g) 10/18 of £9.00 .... ÷ .... = ... × .... = £..........

h) 2/3 of one day (24 hours) .... ÷ .... = ... × .... = ...hours

i) 5/6 of one year (12 months) .... ÷ .... = ... × .... = ...months

j) 2/5 of one kilogram (1000 grams) .... = ...g

DIVIDE BY THE BOTTOM, TIMES BY THE TOP — and suddenly fractions don't seem so bad...

Questions on Fractions, Decimals, %

Q1 Change these fractions to decimals:

a) $\frac{1}{2}$........ **b)** $\frac{3}{4}$........ **c)** $\frac{7}{10}$........ **d)** $\frac{19}{20}$........

e) $\frac{1}{100}$........ **f)** $\frac{3}{8}$........ **g)** $\frac{2}{1000}$........ **h)** $\frac{1}{3}$........

Q2 Change these fractions to percentages:

a) $\frac{1}{4}$........ **b)** $\frac{3}{10}$........ **c)** $\frac{4}{5}$........ **d)** $\frac{12}{25}$........

e) $\frac{8}{100}$........ **f)** $\frac{2}{40}$........ **g)** $\frac{7}{8}$........ **h)** $\frac{11}{30}$........

Q3 Change these decimals to percentages:

a) 0.62 .... **b)** 0.74 .... **c)** 0.4 .... **d)** 0.9 ....

e) 0.07 .... **f)** 0.02 .... **g)** 0.125 .... **h)** 0.987 ....

Q4 Change these decimals to fractions (in their lowest terms if possible):

a) 0.5 .... **b)** 0.8 .... **c)** 0.19 .... **d)** 0.25 ....

e) 0.64 .... **f)** 0.06 .... **g)** 0.125 .... **h)** 0.075 ....

Q5 Change these percentages to fractions (in their lowest terms if possible):

a) 75% .... **b)** 60% .... **c)** 15% .... **d)** 53% ....

Q6 Change these percentage to decimals:

a) 25% .... **b)** 49% .... **c)** 3% .... **d)** 30% ....

A FRACTION IS A DECIMAL IS A PERCENTAGE — they're all just different ways of saying "a bit of" something.

Questions on Percentages

Only use the % button on your calculator when you're sure you know what it does — or things will just go pear-shaped.

Q1 Try these without a calculator:

a) 50% of £12 =...........

b) 25% of £20 =...........

c) 10% of £50 =...........

d) 5% of £50 =...........

e) 30% of £50 =...........

f) 75% of £80 =...........

g) 10% of 90cm =...........

h) 10% of 4.39kg =...........

Now you can use a calculator:

i) 8% of £16 =...........

j) 15% of £200 =...........

k) 12% of 50 litres =...........

l) 85% of 740kg =...........

m) 40% of 40 minutes =...........

n) 17½% of £180 =...........

A school has 750 pupils.

o) If 56% of the pupils are boys, what percentage are girls? ....

p) How many boys are there in the school? ....

q) One day, 6% of the pupils were absent. How many pupils was this? ....

r) 54% of the pupils have a school lunch, 38% bring sandwiches and the rest go home for lunch. How many pupils go home for lunch?

....

Questions on Percentages

1% is just 1 out of 100 — that's all there is to it... and it's worth learning — someday you'll be interested in working out what a 7% pay rise gives you...

Q2 Car workers at the Fiort plant are given a pay rise. Each grade of worker gets a different percentage (%) increase.

a) Complete the table to show what each worker will now earn.

	Current Pay	% Rise	Extra Pay	New Pay
Manager	£35,000	7%		
Skilled	£24,000	5%		
Unskilled	£18,000	3%		

At another company things are going badly. Sales have fallen and the workers are asked to take a pay cut of 8% to save their jobs.

b) Complete the table to show how much money each worker will lose.

	Current Pay	% Cut	Pay cut in £
Manager	£35,000	8%	
Skilled	£24,000	8%	
Unskilled	£18,000	8%	

Q3 VAT (value added tax) is charged at a rate of 17.5% on many goods and services. Complete the table showing how much VAT has to be paid and the new price of each article.

Article	Basic price	VAT at 17.5%	Price + VAT
Tin of paint	£6.75		
Paint brush	£3.60		
Sand paper	£1.55		

Q4 A company claims that its insulation material will cut home heating bills by 40%. The Coalman family currently pay £480 per year for heating their house. How much will they save each year if they buy this new insulation material?

Savings made each year ....

Questions on Percentages

Q5 Express each of the following as a percentage. Round off if necessary...

a) £6 of £12 = ...

b) £4 of £16 = ...

c) 600kg of 750kg = ...

d) 6 hours of one day = ...

e) 1 month of a year = ...

f) 25m of 65m = ...

Q6 Calculate the percentage saving of the following:

e.g. Trainers: Was £72 Now £56 Saved **£16** of £72 = **22.2%**

a) Jeans: Was £45 Now £35 Saved .... of £45 = ...%

b) CD: Was £14.99 Now £12.99 Saved .... of .... = ...%

c) Shirt: Was £27.50 Now £22.75 Saved .... of .... = ...%

d) TV: Was £695 Now £435 Saved .... = ...%

e) Microwave: Was £132 Now £99 Saved .... = ...%

Q7 a) In their first game of the season, Nowcastle had 24,567 fans watching the game. By the final game there were 32,741 fans watching. What is the percentage increase in the number of fans? ....%

b) If Tim Hangman won 3 out of the 5 sets in the Wimbledon Men's Final, what percentage of the sets did he not win? ....%

c) Jeff went on a diet. At the start he weighed 92kg, after one month he weighed 84kg. What is his percentage weight loss? ....%

d) Of Ibiza's 25,000 tourists last Summer, 23,750 were between 16 and 30 years old. What percentage of the tourists were not in this age group? ....%

Divide the new amount by the old, then × 100... or if you've been practising on your calc, you'll know you can just press the % button for the 2nd bit...

Questions on Ratio

Ratios compare quantities of the same kind — so if the units aren't mentioned, they've got to be the same in each bit of the ratio.

Q1 What is the ratio in each of these pictures?

a)

Circles to Triangles

.... to ....

Triangles to Circles

.... : ....

b)

Small stars to big stars

.... to ....

Big stars to small stars

.... : ....

Q2 Write these ratios in their simplest form. The first one is done for you.

a) 4 to 6

2 : 3

b) 15 to 21

...... : ......

c) 14 to 42

.... : ......

d) 72 to 45

.... : ......

e) 24 cm to 36 cm

...... : ......

f) 350 g to 2 kg

...... : ......

g) 42 p to £1.36

...... : ......

Q3 In 'The Pink Palace' The walls are painted a delicate shade of pink using 2 tins of red paint to every 3 tins of white paint.

Write this as a ratio.
Red tins .... to White tins ....

R........... : W...........

How much white paint is needed to mix with 12 red tins? .... White tins.

Questions on Ratio

Q4 To make grey paint, black and white paint are mixed in the ratio 5:3. How much black paint would be needed with:

a) 6 litres of white ....

b) 12 litres of white ....

c) 21 litres of white ....?

Q5 To make orange squash you mix water and concentrated orange juice in the ratio 9:2. How much water is needed with:

a) 10 ml of concentrated juice ....

b) 30 ml of concentrated juice ....

c) 42 ml of concentrated juice ....?

Q6 The ratio of men to women at a football match as 11:4. How many men were there if there were:

a) 2000 women ....

b) 8460 women ....?

How many women were there if there were:

c) 22000 men ....

d) 6820 men ....?

I think I can spot a Golden Rule lurking here: DIVIDE FOR ONE, THEN TIMES FOR ALL.

Questions on Ratio

Q7 Split the following quantities into the given ratio.

For example:

£400 in the ratio 1 : 4 $\quad$ 1 + 4 = 5 $\quad$ 400 ÷ 5 = 80

<u>1 × £80 = £80 and 4 × 80 = £320</u>

<u>£80 : £320</u>

a) 100 g in the ratio 1 : 4 $\quad$ .... + ... = ... $\quad$ .... ÷ .... = ...

.... × .... = ... and .... × .... = ...

= .... : ....

b) 500 m in the ratio 2 : 3 = ... : ....

c) £12,000 in the ratio 1 : 2 = ... : ....

d) 6.3 kg in the ratio 3 : 4 = ... : ....

e) £8.10 in the ratio 4 : 5 = ... : ....

Q8 Now try these...

a) Adam and Mags win £24 000. They split the money in the ratio 1 : 5. How much does Adam get?

....

b) Sunil and Paul compete in a pizza eating contest. Between them they consume 28 pizzas in the ratio 3 : 4. Who wins and how many did they eat?

.... eats .... pizzas

c) The total distance covered in a triathlon (swimming, cycling and running) is 15 km. It is split in the ratio 2 : 3 : 5. How far is each section?

Swimming = ... Cycling = ... Running = ...

A great way to check your answer works is to add up the individual quantities — they should add up to the original amount.

Questions on Best Buys

Start by finding the AMOUNT PER PENNY — the more of the stuff you get per penny, the better value it is.

Q1 Which of these boxes of eggs is better value for money?

60p £1.10 ....

Q2

The small bar of chocolate weighs 50g and costs 32p.
The large bar weighs 200g and costs 80p.

a) How many grams do you get for 1p from the small bar?

....

b) How many grams do you get for 1p from the large bar?

....

c) Which bar gives you more for your money?

....

Q3 The large tin of tuna weighs 400g and costs £1.05.
The small tin weighs 220g and costs 57p.

a) How many grams do you get for 1p in the large tin?

....

b) How many grams do you get for 1p in the small tin?

....

c) Which tin gives better value for money?

....

Questions on Metric and Imperial Units

km m cm mm tonne kg g mg l ml

Q1 Which metric units from the box would you use to measure these in?

a) The length of your bedroom ....

b) Your weight ....

c) The distance to Paris ....

d) The amount of water in the bath ....

e) The weight of a packet of crisps ....

f) The length of your finger ....

g) The amount of medicine in a teaspoon ....

h) The thickness of a coin ....

i) The weight of a bus ....

j) The weight of a butterfly ....

APPROXIMATE CONVERSIONS

1kg = 2.2lbs 1gall = 4.5l 1in = 2.5cm

Q2 Change each of these weights from kilograms to pounds.

10kg = ... lbs 16kg = ... lbs 75kg = ... lbs

Change each of these capacities in gallons to litres.

5galls = ... l 14galls = ... l 40galls = ... l

Q3 Convert the measurements of the note book and pencil to centimetres.

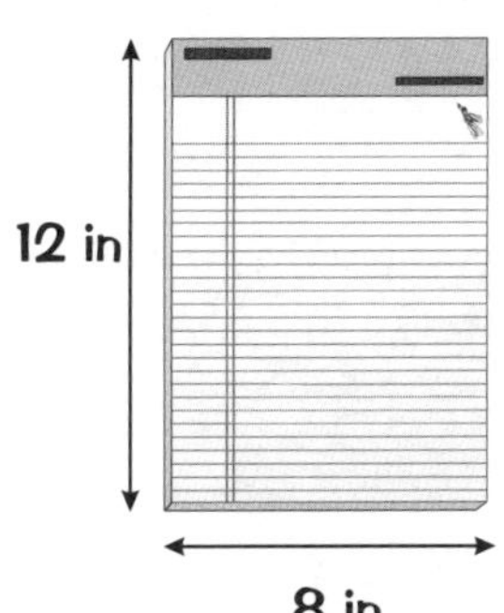

12in = ... cm

8in = ... cm

5in = ... cm

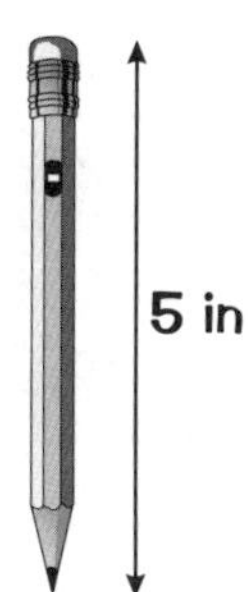

Questions on Speed, Distance, Time

Q1 A car travels a total distance of 300 miles in 6 hours. What is the average speed for the journey?

Speed = Distance ÷ Time

Speed = ... ÷............. = ... miles per hour.

Q2 It takes John 15 minutes to cycle to school, he lives 8 kilometres from the school. At what speed, in kilometres per hour, does he cycle?

15 minutes = 0.25 hours

Speed = ... = ... kph.

Q3 Hannah walks to the youth club, it takes her 20 minutes to walk 2 miles. Her friend Jess lives 6 miles away from the club, she gets there by car, going at an average speed of 30 miles per hour.

a) At what speed does Hannah walk? ....

b) How long does it take Jess to get to the club? Time = Distance ÷ Speed.

Time = ... ÷ .... = ... hours, which is .... × 60 = ... minutes.

Q4 The World Record for swimming 50m freestyle is 17.4 secs. What average speed is this?

....

Q5 The speed of light is 300,000,000 metres per second. How many kilometres would light travel in 4 seconds?

....

Q6 a) If I leave my house to go to a party 18 miles away at 7.35pm, and I need to be at the party for 8.05pm. At what average speed would I have to drive?

....

b) Rob catches a train at 4.30pm to go to the same party, 150 miles away. Assuming that there are no delays and the train travels at an average speed of 75 mph. What time will Rob arrive at the party?

....

Questions on Conversion Factors

Here are some conversions that you've got to learn — these are easy marks, so get memorising...

10 mm = 1 cm	1000 mg = 1 g
100 cm = 1 m	1000 g = 1 kg
1000 m = 1 km	1000 ml = 1 l

Q1 Complete this crossnumber using the conversion factors above.

ACROSS
1) 2cm in mm
2) 3500cm in m
4) 1.02m in cm
5) 0.5kg in g
6) 6.7km in m
7) 890 000g in kg

DOWN
1) 2.4m in cm
2) 3l in ml
3) 5.2kg in g
4) 1.57kg in g
6) 69 000ml in l

Q2 Fill in the gaps using the conversion factors:

20mm = ... cm   82mm = ... cm   ....mm = 6cm

142cm = ... m   .... cm = 2.5m   2550mm = ... m

9000m = ... km   3470m = ... km   .... m = 2km

3km = ... cm   .... mm = 3.4m   .... cm = 0.5km

6200mg = ... g   8550g = ... kg   2.3kg = ... g

12 000 000mg = ... kg   7.5kg = ... mg

1.2l = ... ml   4400ml = ... l   6.75l = ... ml

Questions on Scale Drawings

Q1 The scale on this map is 1cm : 4km.

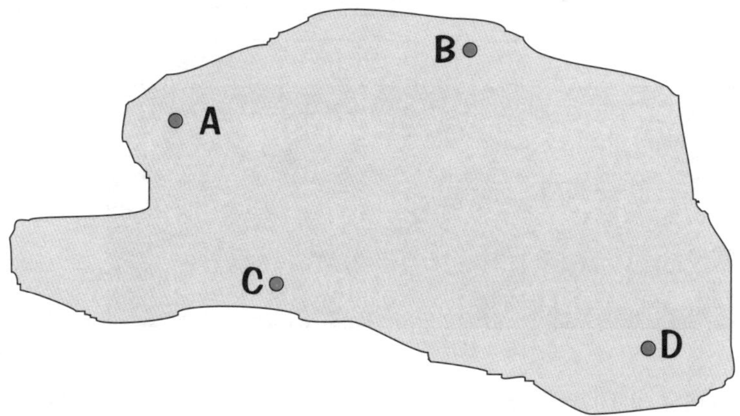

a) Measure the distance from A to B in cm. ....

b) What is the actual distance from A to B in km? ....

c) A helicopter flies on a direct route from A to B, B to C and C to D. What is the total distance flown in km?

....

Q2 Here is a plan of a garden drawn to a scale of 1 : 50.

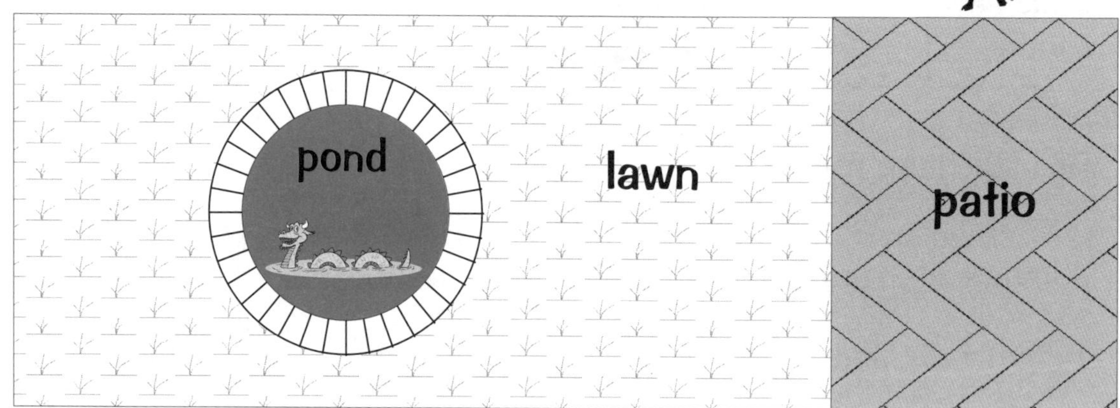

a) Measure the full length of the garden in mm: ....

b) What is the actual length of the garden in mm? ....

c) What is the actual length of the garden in metres? ....

If the scale doesn't say what units it's in, it just means that both sides of the ratio are the same units — so _1 : 1000_ would mean _1cm : 1000cm_.

Questions on Scale Drawings

Watch out for those units... there's quite a mixture here — you'll have to convert some of them before you can go anywhere.

Q3 A room measures 20m long and 15m wide. Work out the measurements for a scale drawing of the room using a scale of 1cm = 2m.

Length = ...; Width = ...

Q4 Katie drew a scale drawing of the top of her desk. She used a scale of 1:10. This is her drawing of the computer keyboard. What are the actual dimensions of it?

Length = ...; Width = ...

Q5

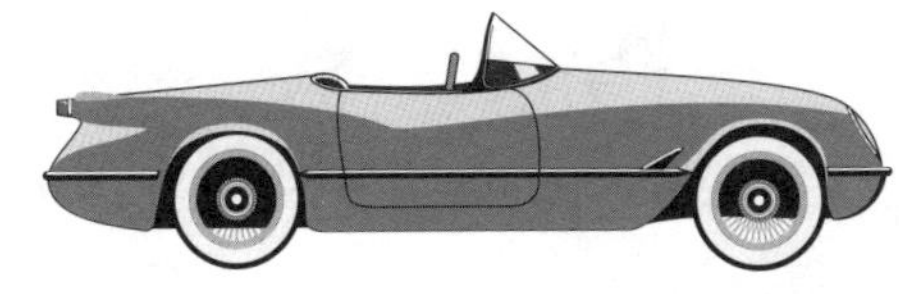

This is a scale drawing of Paul's new car. Measure the length of the car. ....cm. If the drawing uses a scale of 1:90, work out the actual length of the car.

....

Q6 A rectangular field is 60m long and 40m wide. The farmer needs to make a scale drawing of it. He uses a scale of 1:2000. Work out the measurements for the scale drawing. (Hint — change the m to cm)

....

....

Q7 A rectangular room is 4.8m long and 3.6m wide. Make a scale drawing of it using a scale of 1cm to 60cm. First work out the measurements for the scale drawing.

Length = ...
Width = ...

On your scale drawing mark a window, whose actual length is 2.4m, on one long wall and mark a door, actual width 90cm, on one short wall.

Window = ...
Door = ...

Questions on Rounding Off

You always round off to the NEAREST NUMBER. It's a bit more tricky if it's exactly 1/2 WAY between 2 numbers — and then you just round UP.

Q1 Give these amounts to the nearest pound:

a) £4.29 ....
b) £16.78 ....
c) £12.06 ....
d) £7.52 ....
e) £0.93 ....
f) £14.50 ....
g) £7.49 ....
h) £0.28 ....

Q2 An average family has 2.3 children, how many children is this to the nearest whole number?

....

Q3 Round the following to the nearest whole number:

a) 2.9 ....
b) 26.8 ....
c) 2.24 ....
d) 11.11 ....
e) 6.347 ....
f) 43.5 ....
g) 9.99 ....
h) 0.41 ....

Q4 By the time she is 25, the average woman will have driven 4.72 cars. What is this to the nearest whole number?

....

Q5 Give these amounts to the nearest hour:

a) 2 hours 12 minutes ....
b) 36 minutes ....
c) 12 hours 12 minutes ....
d) 29 minutes ....
e) 100 minutes ....
f) 90 minutes ....

Questions on Rounding Off

Q6 Round off these numbers to the nearest 10:

a) 23 = ... **b)** 78 = ... **c)** 65 = ... **d)** 99 = ...

e) 118 = ... **f)** 243 = ... **g)** 958 = ... **h)** 1056 = ...

Q7 Round off these numbers to the nearest 100:

a) 627 = ... **b)** 791 = ... **c)** 199 = ... **d)** 450 = ...

e) 1288 = ... **f)** 3329 = ... **g)** 2993 = ...

Q8 Round these off to the nearest 1000:

a) 5200 = ... **b)** 8860 = ... **c)** 9870 = ...

Q9 Crowd sizes at sports events are often given exactly in newspapers. Round off these exact crowd sizes to the nearest 1000:

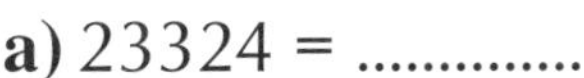

a) 23324 = ...

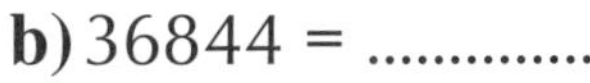

b) 36844 = ...

c) 49752 = ...

Q10 The number of drawing pins in the box has been rounded to the nearest 10.

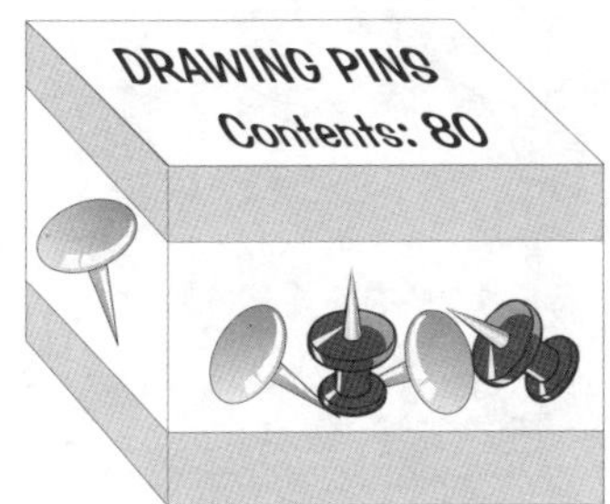

What is the least number of drawing pins in the box? ....

What is the greatest number? ....

Q11 The population of Whichtown is given as 1300 to the nearest 100. What is the smallest number the population could be? ....

What is the largest it could be? ....

When you round numbers off to the nearest unit, the ACTUAL measurement could be up to HALF A UNIT bigger or smaller...

Questions on Rounding Off

Q12 Round off these numbers to 1 decimal place (1 d.p.):

a) 7.34 = ... **b)** 8.47 = ... **c)** 12.08 = ... **d)** 28.03 = ...

e) 9.35 = ... **f)** 14.618 = ... **g)** 30.409 = ...

Q13 Round off the following to 2 d.p.

a) 17.363 = ... **b)** 38.057 = ... **c)** 0.735 = ...

d) 5.99823 = ... **e)** 4.297 = ... **f)** 7.0409 = ...

Q14 Now round these to 3 d.p.

a) 6.3534 = ... **b)** 81.64471 = ... **c)** 0.0075 = ...

d) 53.26981 = ... **e)** 754.39962 = ...

f) 0.000486 = ... **g)** 121.607593 = ...

Q15 Seven people have a meal in a restaurant. The total bill comes to £60. If they share the bill equally, how much should each of them pay? Round your answer to 2 d.p.

....

Q16 A 5m length of wood is cut into 12 equal pieces. How long is each of the pieces? Round your answer to 3 d.p.

....

Remember rounding to whole numbers... well this exactly the same — only slightly different.

Questions on Multiples

Q1 What are the first five multiples of:

a) 4 ....

b) 7 ....

c) 12 ....

d) 18 ....

Q2 Find a number which is a multiple of:

a) 2 and 6 ....

b) 7 and 5 ....

c) 2 and 3 and 7 ....

d) 4 and 5 and 9 ....

Q3 **a)** Find a number which is a multiple of 3 and 8 ....

b) Find another number which is a multiple of 3 and 8 ....

c) Find another number which is a multiple of 3 and 8 ....

Q4 Which of these numbers 14, 20, 22, 35, 50, 55, 70, 77, 99 are multiples of:

a) 2 ....

b) 5 ....

c) 7 ....

d) 11 ....

The multiples of a number are its times table — if you need multiples of more than one number, do them separately then pick the ones in both lists.

Questions on Factors

Factors multiply together to make other numbers

E.g. 1 × 6 = 6 and 2 × 3 = 6, so 6 has factors 1, 2, 3 and 6.

Q1 **a)** I am a factor of 24.
I am an odd number.
I am bigger than 1.
What number am I?

....

b) I am a factor of 30.
I am an even number.
I am less than 5.
What number am I?

....

Q2 Circle all the factors of 360 in this list of numbers.

1 2 3 4 5 6 7 8 9 10

Q3 A perfect number is one where the factors add up to the number itself.
For example, the factors of 28 are 1, 2, 4, 7 and 14 (not including 28 itself).
These add up to 1+2+4+7+14 = 28, and so 28 is a perfect number.

Complete this table, and circle the perfect number in the left hand column.

Number	Factors	Sum of Factors
2		
4	1, 2	3
6		
8		
10		

The sum of the factors is all the factors added together.

Q4 **a)** What is the biggest number that is a factor of both 42 and 18? ....

b) What is the smallest number that has both 4 and 18 as factors? ....

Q5 Fill in the missing numbers in the factor trees.
The first one has been done for you.

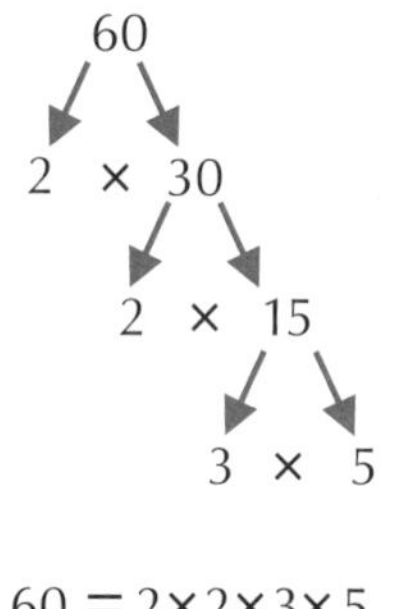

60 = 2×2×3×5

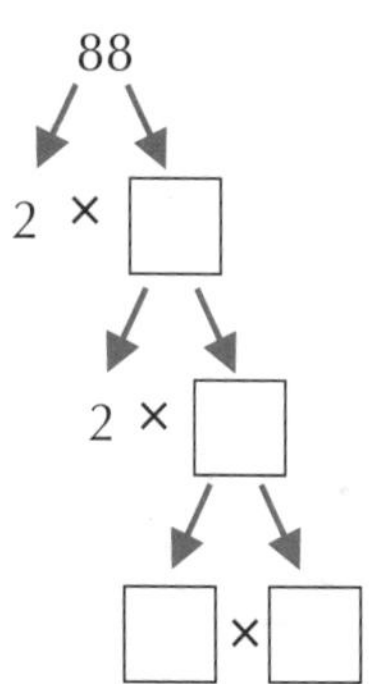

88 = 2×2×..........×..........

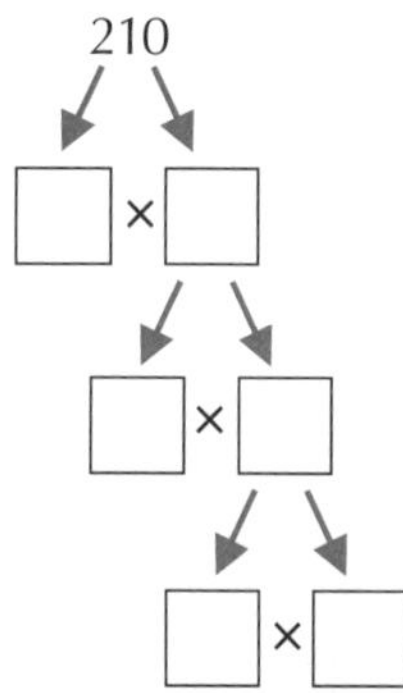

210 = ...×..........×..........×..........

Questions on Substitution

Don't forget the rules about negative numbers when you're substituting.

Q1 Find the value of $n + 5$ when n is:

a) 3 .... **b)** 17 .... **c)** 6.7 .... **d)** -9 ....

Work out the value of $3w + 2$ when w is:

e) 4 .... **f)** 1.5 .... **g)** -5 .... **h)** $\frac{1}{4}$ ....

If $x = 4$ and $y = 2$, find the value of:

i) $x^2 + y =$ .... **j)** $3x - y =$ .... **k)** $2x - 4y =$ ....

l) $\frac{6x}{2} =$ .... **m)** $\frac{4x - 3y}{5} =$ .... **n)** $x^2 \times y^2 =$ ....

Here is a formula $A = c - d^2$

o) Work out A when $c = 50$ and $d = 6$

....

A formula for the cost in £ of repairing an Easiwash dishwasher is $C = 35 + 18 \times n$, where n = number of hours.

p) How much would it cost if it took 3 hours to repair? ....

q) How much would it cost if it took half an hour to repair? ....

r) If the repair cost was £80, how long did it take to repair it? ....

Questions on Formulas

Q1 Mrs. Jones works out the weekly pocket money for each of her children. She uses the formula:

Pocket money = Age in years × 20
(in pence)

Work out the pocket money for:

a) Joe, aged 10 years ....

b) Paul, aged 8 years ....

c) Sara, aged 5 years ....

Q2 The formula to work out the cooking time for a turkey is:

Cooking time = Weight × 20 + 30
(in mins) (in pounds)

How long will it take to cook:

a) a 12 pound turkey ....

b) a 15 pound turkey ....

Q3 The formula to find the speed of a car is S = D ÷ T where S is the speed, D is the distance and T is the time. Use the formula to find the speed if:

a) D = 200 miles, T = 4 hours ....

b) D = 350 miles, T = 5 hours ....

Q4 The formula to work out the cost of hiring a carpet cleaner is C = 3d + 2 where C is the cost in £ and d is the number of days. Use the formula to find:

a) the cost of hiring the cleaner for 3 days ....

b) the cost of hiring the cleaner for a week ....

Q5 A formula to find the area of a rhombus is A = pq ÷ 2 where A is the area and p and q are the lengths of the diagonals. Use the formula to find

a) A when p = 6cm and q = 4cm. ....

b) A when p = 9.6cm and q = 6.4cm. ....

Show *every stage* of your working — write the *formula in words*, then again with the *numbers in*, then the *answer* — each bit could be worth something.

Questions on the Language of Algebra

It's no big mystery — algebra is just like normal sums, but with the odd letter or two stuck in for good measure.

Q1 Write the algebraic expression for these:

a) Three more than x ....

b) Seven less than y ....

c) Four multiplied by x ....

d) y multiplied by y ....

e) Ten divided by b ....

f) A number add five ....

g) A number multiplied by two ....

h) Two different numbers added together ....

Q2 Steven is 16 years old. How old will he be in:

a) 5 years .... **b)** 10 years .... **c)** x years ....?

Q3 Tickets for a football match cost £25 each. What is the cost for:

a) 2 tickets ....
b) 6 tickets ....
c) y tickets ....

Q4 There are n books in a pile. Write an expression for the number of books in a pile that has:

a) 3 more books ....

b) 4 fewer books ....

c) Twice as many books ....

Q5 **a)** I have 6 CDs and I buy 5 more. How many CDs have I now? ....

b) I have 6 CDs and I buy *w* more. How many CDs have I now? ....

c) I have x CDs and I buy *w* more. How many CDs have I now? ....

Q6 **a)** This square has sides of length 3cm.
What is its perimeter? ....
What is its area? ....

b) This square has sides of length d cm.
What is its perimeter? ....
What is its area? ....

Questions on Basic Algebra

Q1 Collect the like terms together.

a) $2x + 3x =$ ....

b) $5x - 4x =$ ....

c) $6x + 2y - 3x + y =$ ....

d) $10x + 3y + 2x - 3y =$ ....

e) $5x + 3y - 2z - 6y =$ ....

f) $-4z + 6x - 2y + 2z - 3y =$ ....

g) $15x - 4y + 3z - z - 11x + 5y - y - 4x + z =$ ....

Q2 Remember that $x \times x = x^2$. Collect like terms in the following...

a) $y \times y \times y =$ ....

b) $y \times x =$ ....

c) $x \times 2x =$ ....

d) $y \times y + x \times x \times x =$ ....

e) $p \times p + 2q \times q \times q =$ ....

f) $r \times r \times r + q^2 \times q \times 3p^2 =$ ....

Simplify by multiplying out the brackets, then collecting the like terms.
The first one is done for you:

Q3 **a)** $3(a - 1) + 2(a - 2)$
$3a - 3 + 2a - 4$
$5a - 7$

b) $7(2b - 1) - (5b - 1)$

....

c) $-2(4c + 3) + 5(2c - 3)$

....

d) $-4(d - 5) - 3(2d - 3)$

....

To solve these equations multiply out the brackets first.
The first one is done for you.

Q4 **a)** $2(x + 5) = 6$
$2x + 10 = 6$
$2x = -4$
$x = -2$

b) $3(x - 2) = 12$

....

c) $4(2x + 3) = 20$

....

Remember that when a letter's stuck to a number there's a hidden times sign, in other words $2y = 2 \times y$ so $2y + 3y = y + y + y + y + y = 5 \times y = 5y$

Questions on Conversion Graphs

Q1 This graph can be used to convert the distance (miles) travelled in a taxi to the fare payable (£). How much will the fare be if you travel:

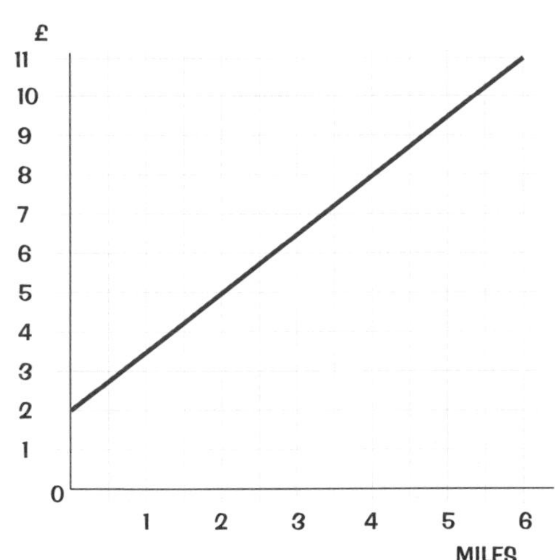

a) 2 miles ....

b) 5 miles ....

c) 10 miles ....

How far would you travel if you paid:

d) £5 ....

e) £11 ....

f) £14 ....

Q2 80km is roughly equal to 50 miles, use this information to draw a conversion graph on the grid. Use the graph to estimate the number of miles equal to:

a) 20 km ....

b) 70 km ....

c) 90 km ....

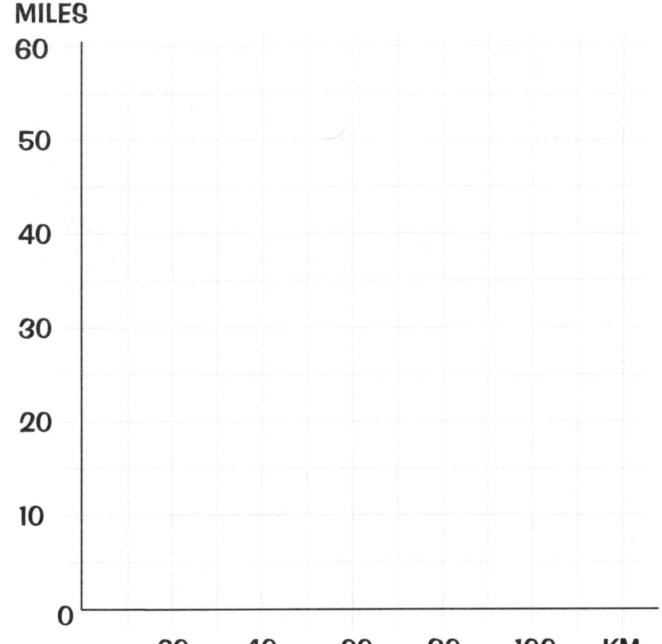

Q3 How many km are equal to:

a) 40 miles ....

b) 10 miles ....

c) 30 miles ....

Remember conversion graphs can be read 2 ways — you can convert from one thing to the other and back again.

Questions on Making Formulas from Words

Q1 Write down the number I first thought of in each of these...

a) I multiply by 3 and then take away 5. The answer is 19.

My number was ....

b) I add 10 then double the number. The answer is 26.

My number was ....

c) I half it then add 9. The answer is 24.

My number was ....

d) I divide by 5 then add 12. The answer is 32.

My number was ....

e) I subtract 15 then divide by 3. The answer is 20.

My number was ....

Q2 Now try this...
I think of a number, multiply it by itself, add 5, divide by 2 then add 10. The answer is 25.

My original number was ....

Hint: the opposite to multiply by itself or squaring is $\sqrt{\ }$.

The trick is to work backwards from the answer, doing the opposite of each step (add instead of subtract, divide instead of times, that sort of thing).

Questions on Equations

Q1 Solve these equations:

a) $a + 6 = 20$ ....

b) $b + 12 = 30$ ....

c) $48 + c = 77$ ....

d) $397 + d = 842$ ....

e) $e + 9.8 = 14.1$ ....

f) $3 + f = 7$ ....

Q2 Solve these equations:

a) $\frac{t}{3} = 5$ ....

b) $u \div 6 = 9$ ....

c) $\frac{v}{11} = 8$ ....

d) $\frac{w}{197} = 7$ ....

e) $x \div 1.8 = 7.2$ ....

f) $\frac{y}{-3} = 7$ ....

Q3 Solve these equations:

a) $3x + 2 = 14$

b) $5x - 4 = 31$

c) $8 + 6x = 50$

d) $20 - 3x = -61$

Q4 Solve these equations:

a) $3(2x + 1) = 27$

b) $2(4x + 1) + x = 56$

c) $5x + 3 = 2x + 15$

d) $2(x + 7) = 6x - 10$

You've got to get the letter on its own (x = ...). You can add, divide... well, anything really — but you gotta do it to both sides or it'll all go horribly wrong.

Questions on Real Life Equations

Write an equation which describes each of the situations given. Solve each equation.

Q1 I have 3 bags of sweets, each with the same number of sweets (call this s). I eat 7 sweets. I now have 29 sweets left. How many sweets were in each bag (s) to start with?

....

Q2 The number of peanuts in a bag (call this p) is shared between 5 friends, each friend gets 6 peanuts with 3 peanuts left over. How many peanuts were in the bag (p)?

....

Q3 A rectangle is x cm long, the height of the rectangle is 5cm more than this. The perimeter of the rectangle is 40cm. Find the length (x).

....

Q4 Tom's age (call this t) when multiplied by 6 is 10 less than his father's age. His father is 28. How old is Tom (t)?

....

Don't forget to check your answers by putting the numbers back in. If it doesn't work you've messed up somewhere, so try again.

Questions on Number Patterns

Q1 Draw the next two pictures in each pattern. How many match sticks are used in each picture?

a) 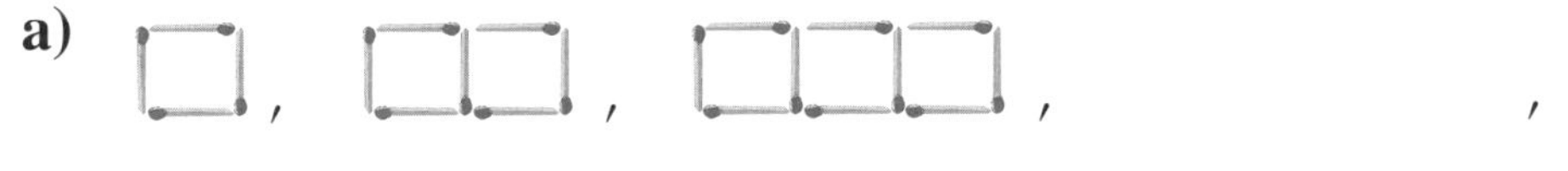

....

b) 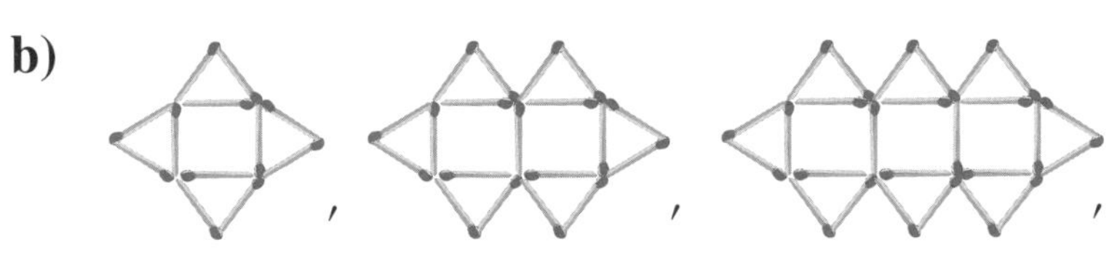

....

c) 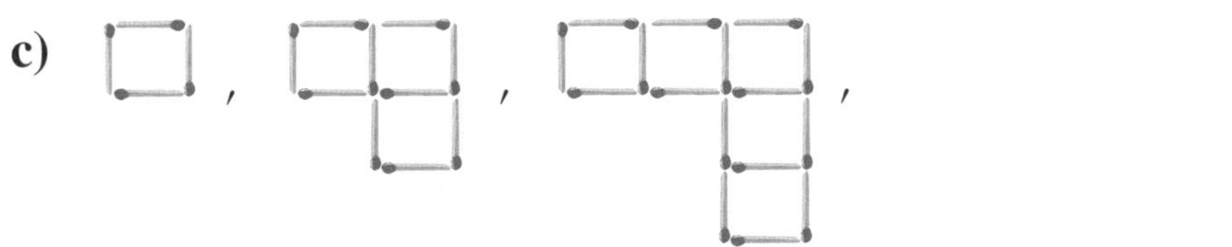

....

d) 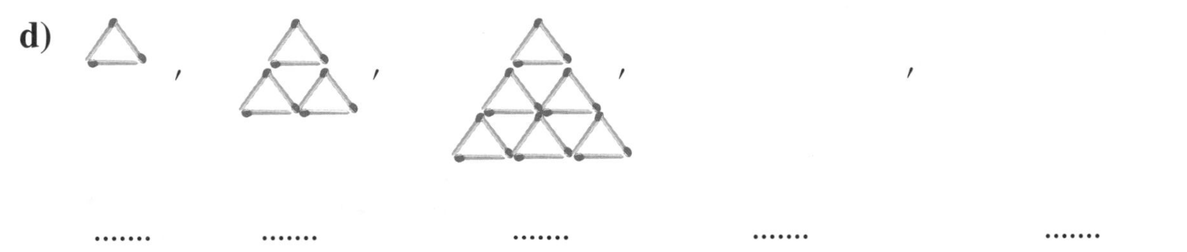

....

Q2 Look for the pattern and then fill in the next three lines. Some of the answers are too big to fit on a calculator display so you must spot the pattern.

a)

7 × 6 = 42
67 × 66 = 4422
667 × 666 = 444222
6667 × 6666 = ...
66667 × 66666 = ...
666667 × 666666 = ...

b)

1 × 81 = 81
21 × 81 = 1701
321 × 81 = 26001
4321 × 81 = 350001
54321 × 81 = ...
654321 × 81 = ...
7654321 × 81 = ...

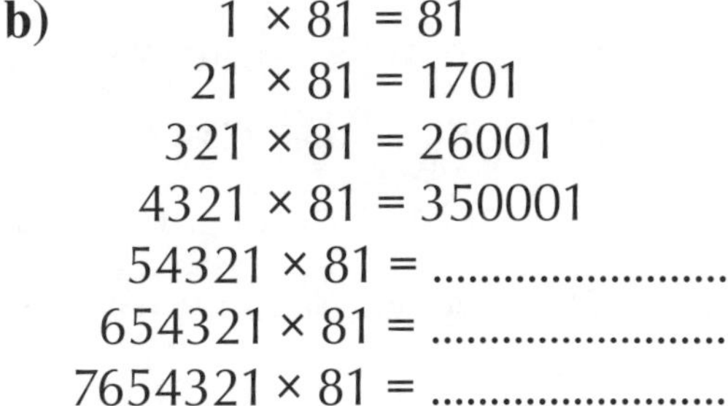

Look for patterns in the numbers as well as pictures.

Questions on Number Patterns

Q3 In each of the questions below, write down the next three numbers in the sequence and write the rule that you used...

a) 1, 3, 5, 7, ... , ... , ... Rule ....

b) 2, 4, 8, 16, ... , ... , ... Rule ....

c) 3, 30, 300, 3000, ... , ... , ... Rule ....

d) 3, 7, 11, 15, ... , ... , ... Rule ....

e) 6, 15, 24, 33, ... , ... , ... Rule ....

f) 19, 14, 9, 4, –1, ... , ... , ... Rule ....

Q4 The letter n describes the position of a term in the sequence. For example, if $n = 1$, that's the 1st term...if $n = 10$ that's the 10th term and so on.
In the following, use the rule given to generate (or make) the first 5 terms.

a) $3n + 1$ so if $n = 1$ the 1st term is $\underline{(3 \times 1) + 1} = \underline{4}$

$n = 2$ the 2nd term is .... = ...

$n = 3$ .... = ...

$n = 4$ .... = ...

$n = 5$ .... = ...

b) $5n - 2$, when $n = 1, 2, 3, 4$ and 5
produces the sequence ...., ..., ..., ..., ...

c) n^2, when $n = 1, 2, 3, 4$, and 5
produces the sequence ...., ..., ..., ..., ...

d) $n^2 - 3$, when $n = 1, 2, 3, 4$, and 5
produces the sequence ...., ..., ..., ..., ...

e) $(n + 2) \div 2$, when $n = 1, 2, 3, 4$, and 5
produces the sequence ...., ..., ..., ..., ...

Q5 Find the next two terms in this sequence: 8 13 18 23 ....
What is the difference between the terms? ....
Subtract the difference between the terms from the first term. ....
Write down the rule for finding the 'n'th term. ....
What is the 20th term in the sequence? ....

Once you've worked out what you think the next numbers should be, go back and write down exactly what you did — that will be the rule you're after.

Questions on Determining Angles

Estimating angles is easy once you know the 4 special angles: 30°, 45°, 60° and 90° — you can use them as reference points.

For each of the angles below write down its name, estimate its size (before you measure it!) and finally measure each angle with a protractor. The first one has been done for you.

Angle	Name	Estimated Size	Actual Size
a	acute	40°	43°
b			
c			
d			
e			
f			

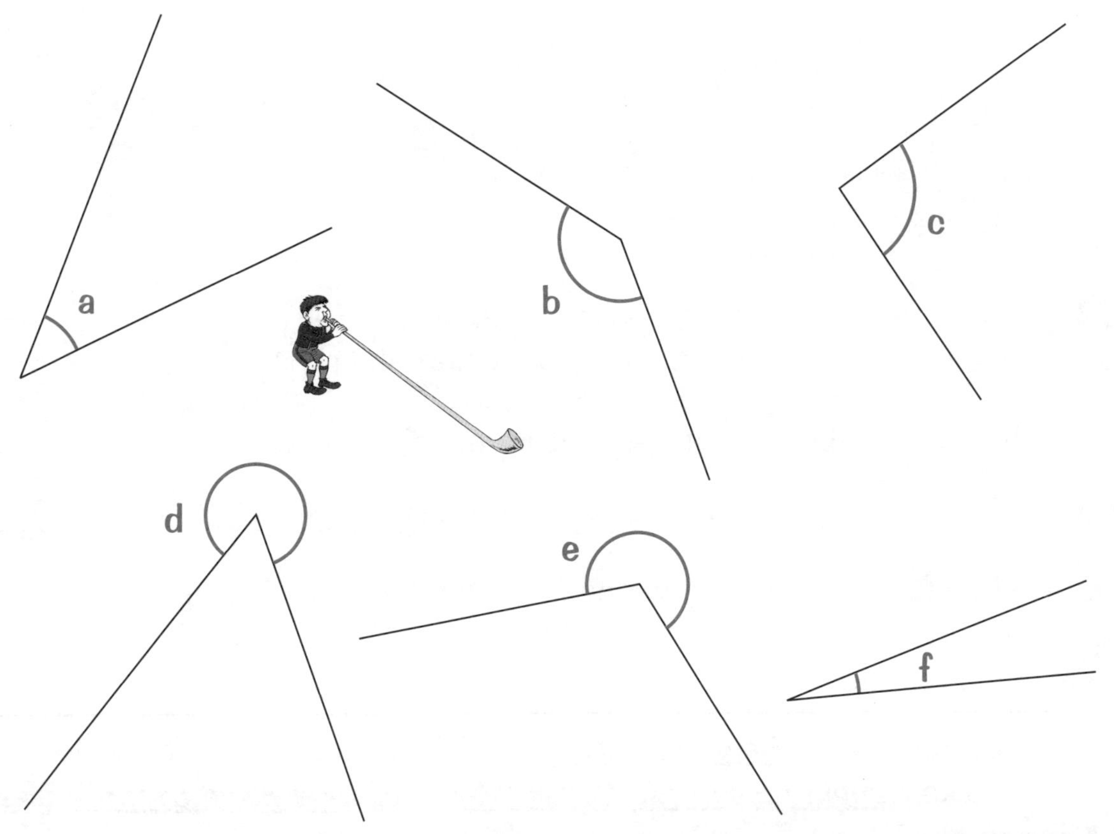

Questions on Compass Directions

Q1

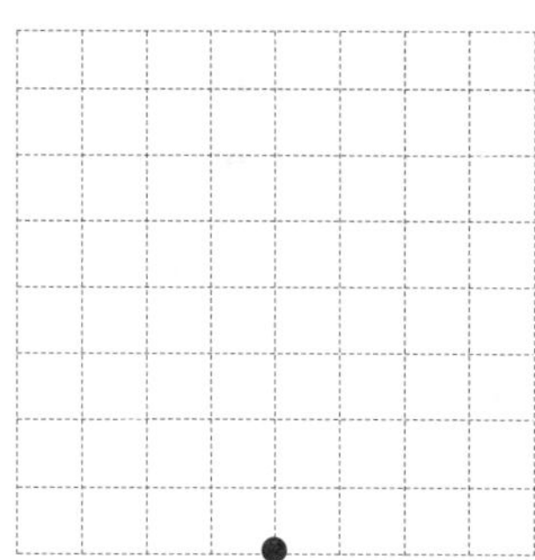

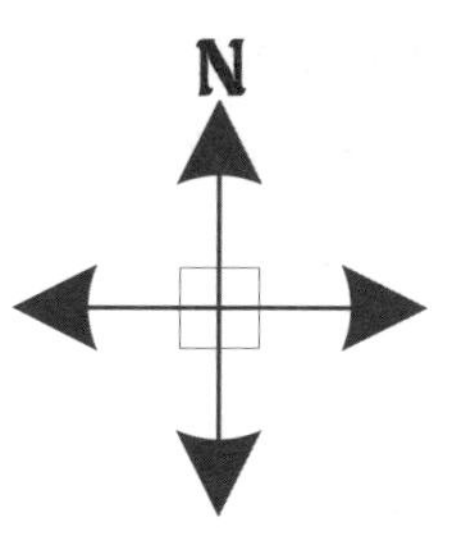

Start at the dot in the middle of the bottom line and follow the directions. What shape have you drawn? ....

a) West 4 squares.
b) North 4 squares.
c) East 4 squares.
d) South 4 squares.
e) North East through 2 squares.
f) North 4 squares.
g) South West through 2 squares.
h) West 4 squares.
i) North East through 2 squares.
j) East 4 squares.

This is a map of part of a coastline. The scale is one cm to one km.

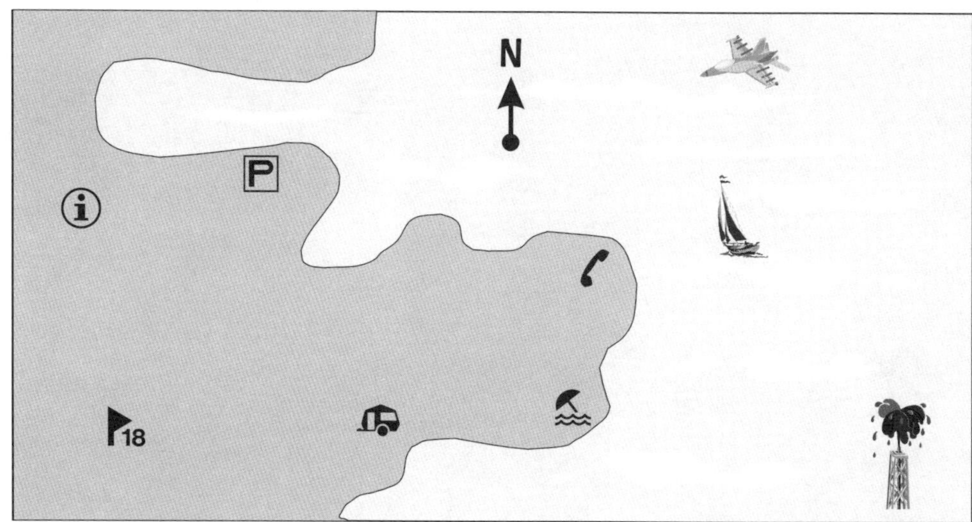

Q2 The water ski centre, , is on a bearing of 050° from the golf course, , and at a distance of 4.5 km. Put a star where the ski centre is.

Q3 What is the bearing of the P from the ? ....

Q4 What is the bearing of the from the ⓘ? ....

Q5 How far and on what bearing is the boat from the oil rig?

....

You could use *"Never Eat Shredded Wheat"* but it's more fun to make one up — like *Naughty Elephants Squirt Water*, or *Nine Elves Storm Wales*... (hmm)

Questions on Drawing Angles

These instruments are used to measure angles.

An angle measurer.

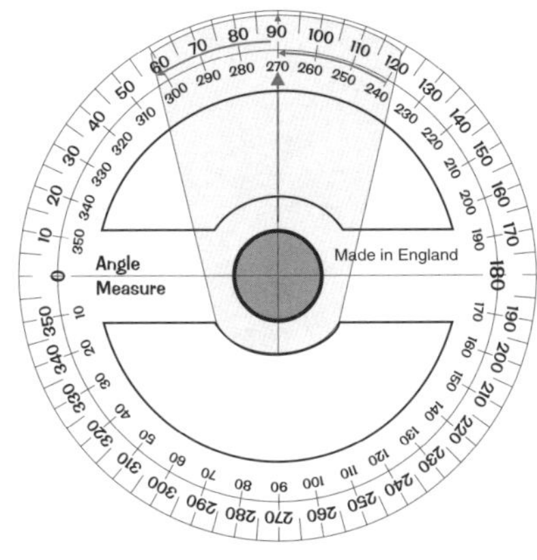

A protractor.

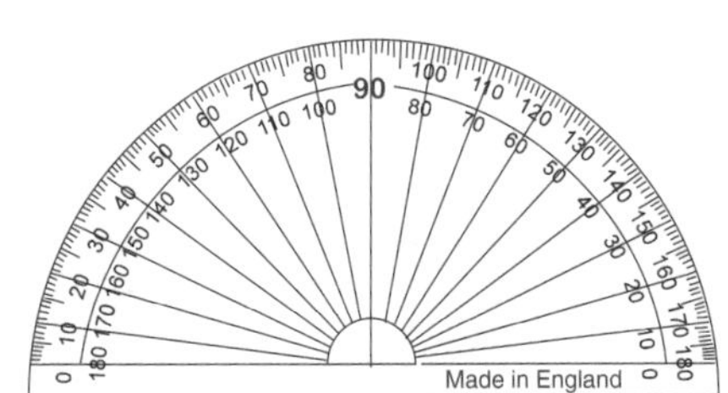

Q1 Use an angle measurer or protractor to help you to draw the following angles.

a) 20° **b)** 65° **c)** 90°

d) 136° **e)** 225° **f)** 340°

Q2 a) Draw an acute angle and measure it. **b)** Draw an obtuse angle and measure it.

Acute angle measures ....° Obtuse angle measures ....°

c) Draw a reflex angle and measure it.

Reflex angle measures ....°

Don't forget protractors have two scales — one going one way and one the other... so make sure you measure from the one that starts with 0°, not 180°.

Questions on Angles

Hope you've learnt those angle rules for a straight line and round a point...

Q1 Work out the angles labelled:

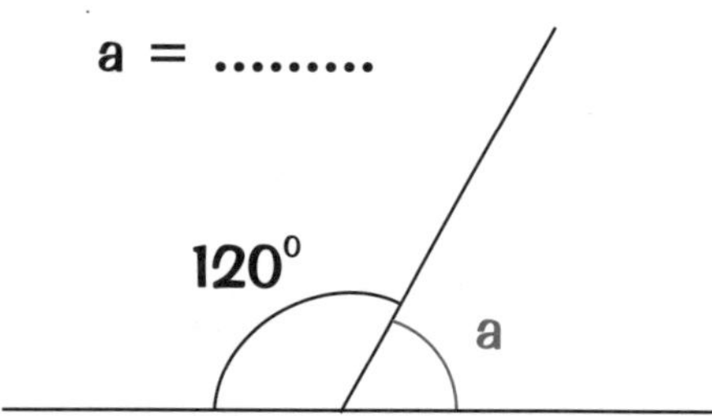

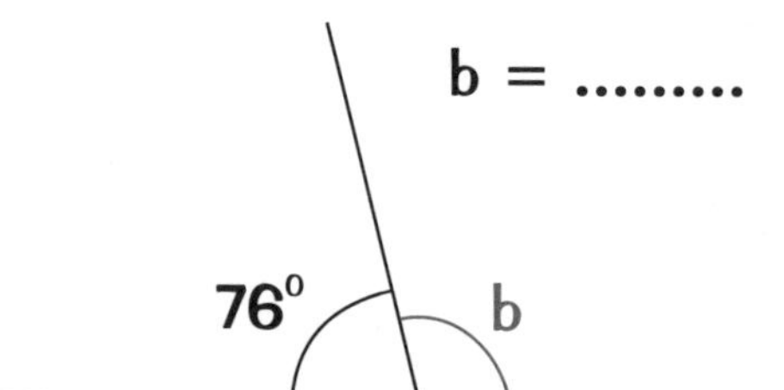

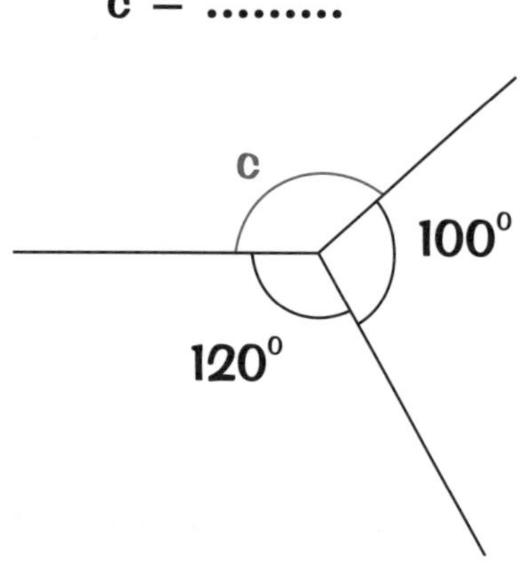

d = ...

87°
d
118°
125°

e = ...

f = ...

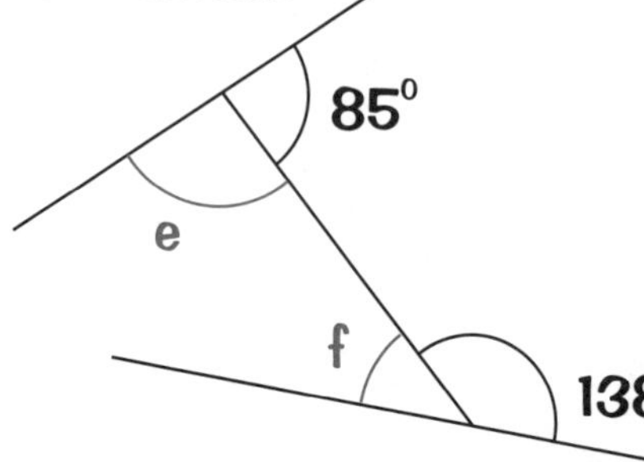

g = ...

h = ...

i = ...

g
41°
h
53°
i

Questions on Angles

Q2 The three angles inside a triangle always add up to 180°

Work out the missing angle in each of these triangles. The angles are not drawn to scale so you cannot measure them.

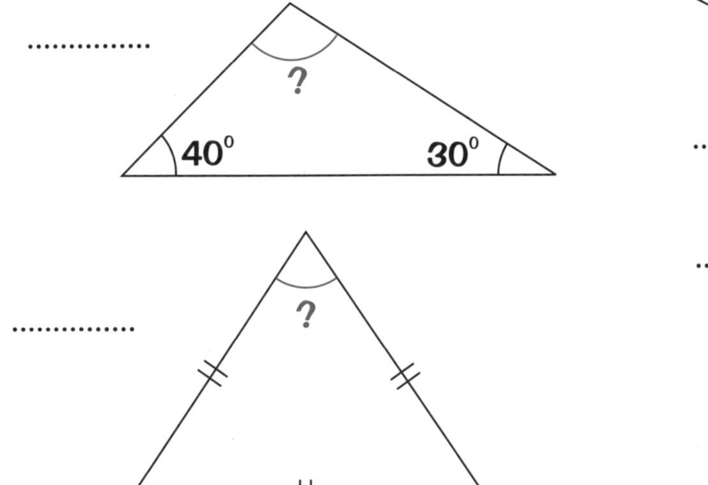

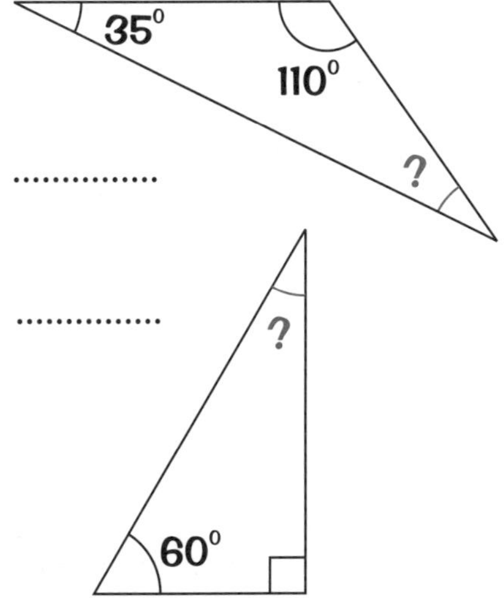

The angles in a quadrilateral always add up to 360°

Q3 Work out the missing angles in these quadrilaterals.

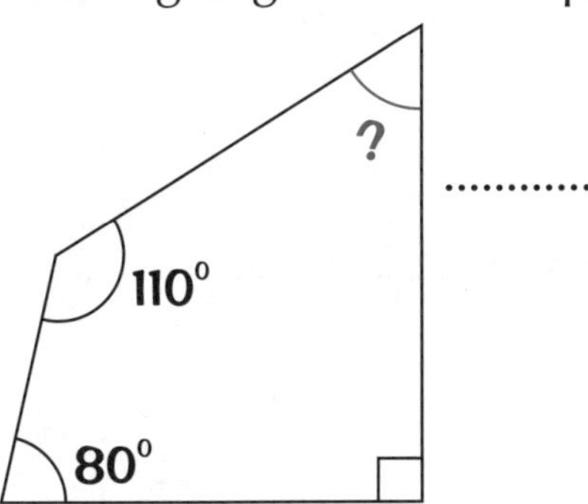

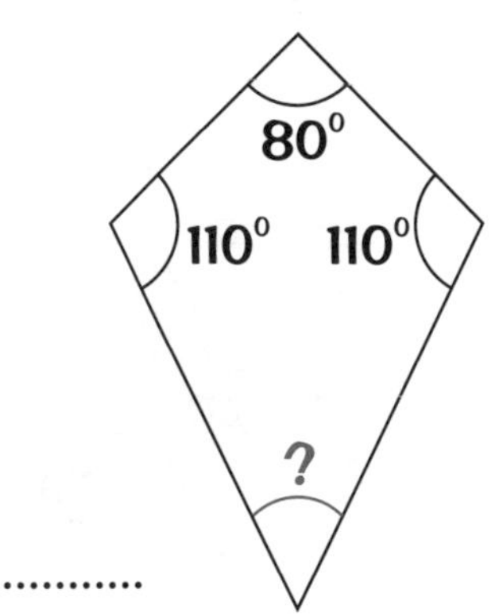

Q4 Work out the missing angles in these diagrams.

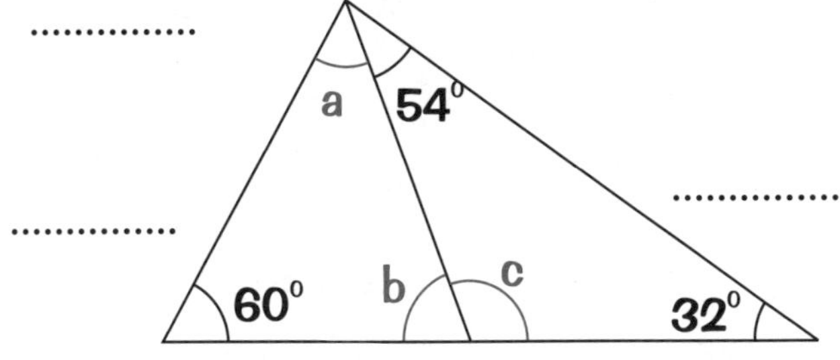

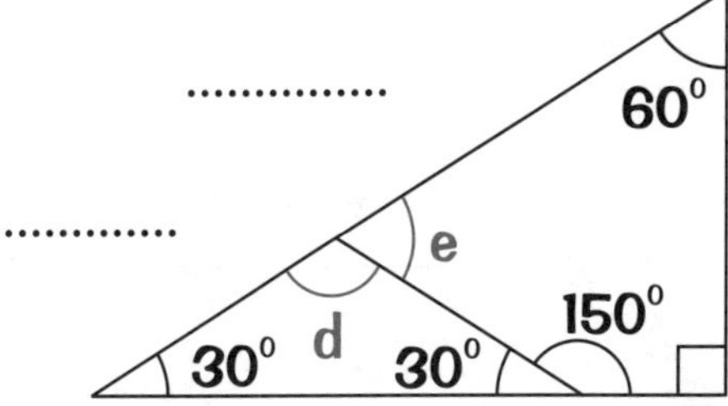

You'd better get learning these rules too — they're not that hard, and you'll be well and truly stumped without them.

Questions on Angles

More rules... once you know the 3 ANGLE RULES for parallel lines, you can find all the angles out from just one — ah, such fun...

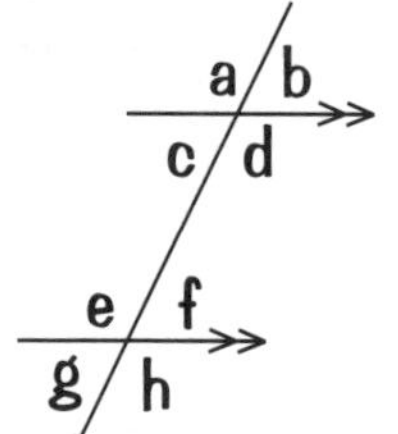

c = f and d = e — Alternate angles
a = e, c = g, b = f and d = h — Corresponding angles
$d + f = 180^0$, $c + e = 180^0$ — Supplementary angles

Q5 Find the sizes of the angles marked by letters in these diagrams. Write down which rule applies in each case.

NOT DRAWN TO SCALE

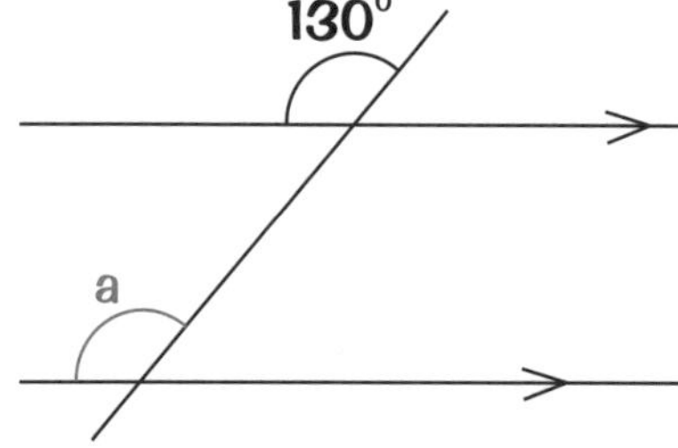

a = ...

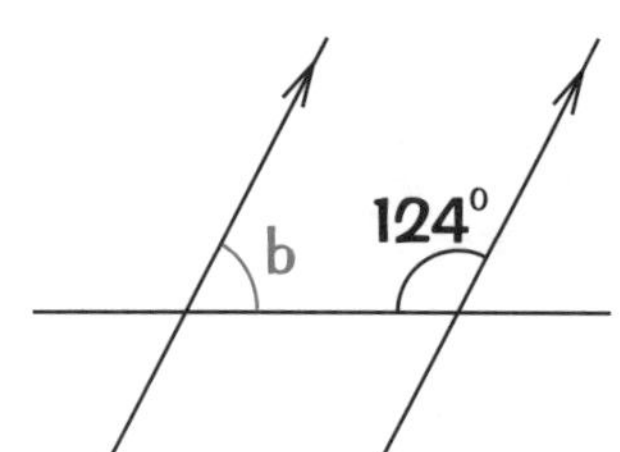

b = ...

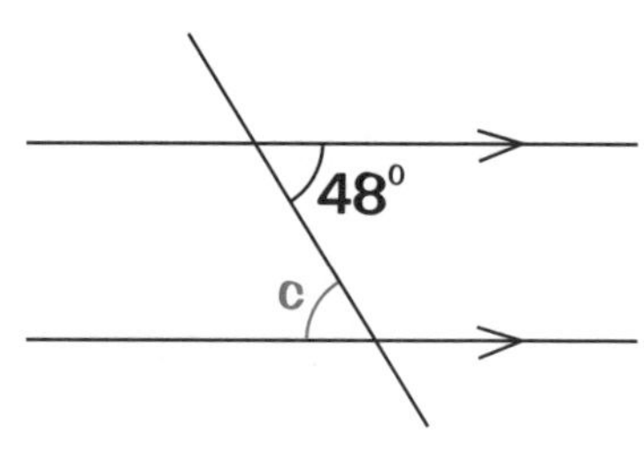

c = ...

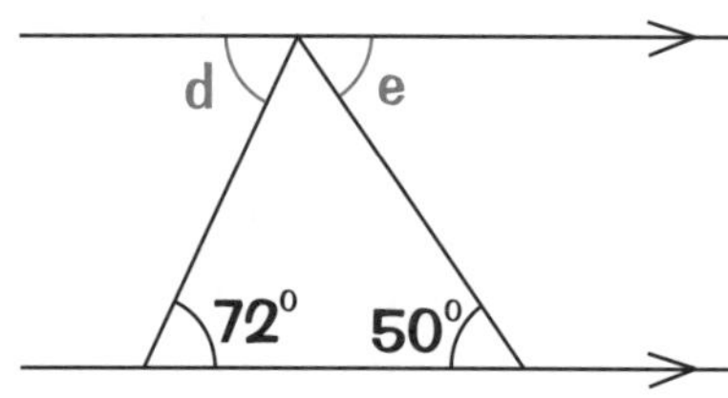

d = ...

e = ...

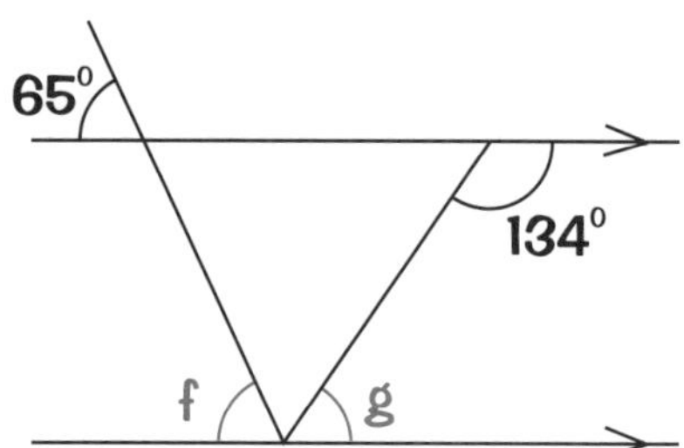

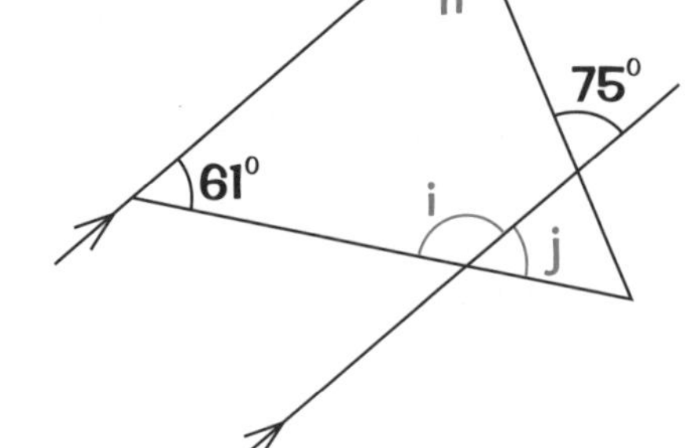

h = ...

f = ...

i = ...

g = ...

j = ...

Questions on Angles

Q6 Find the missing angles. The diagrams are not drawn to scale.

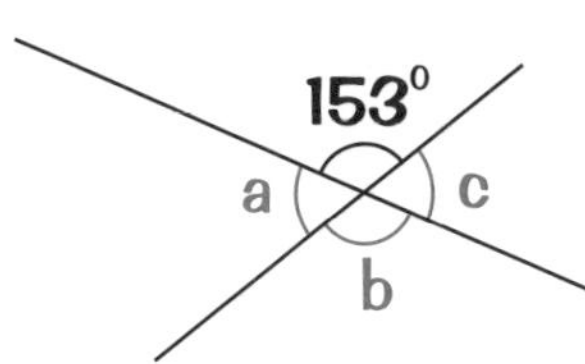

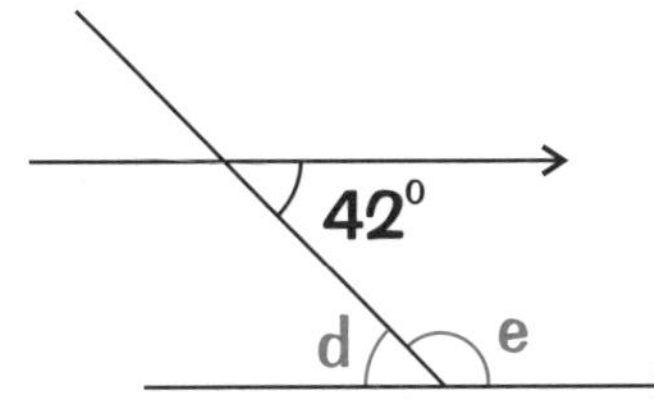

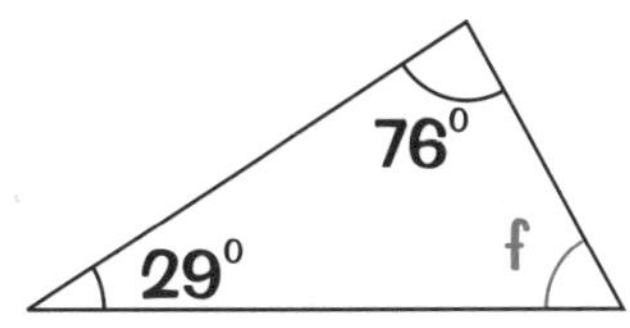

a =..........° b =..........° c =..........° d =..........° e =..........° f =..........°

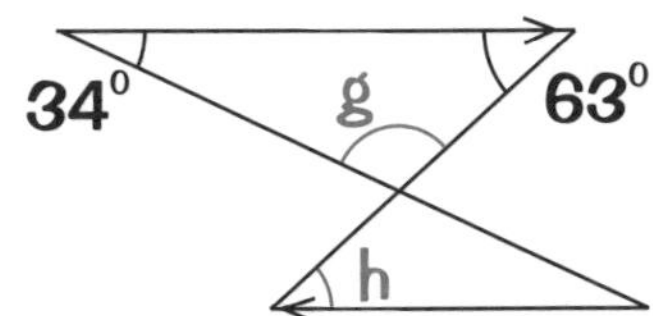

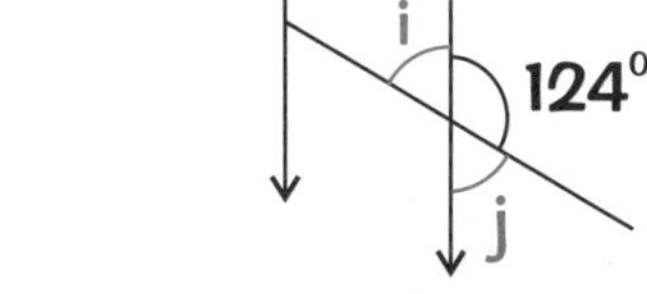

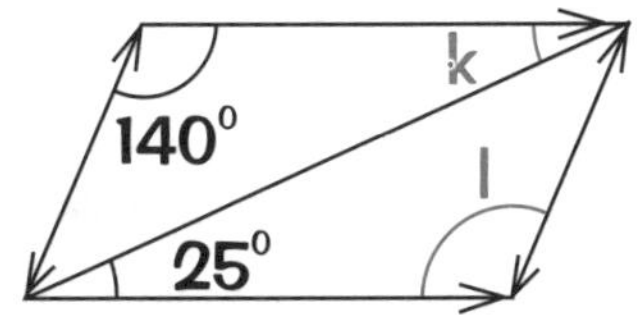

g=..........° h=..........° i=..........° j=..........° k=..........° l=..........°

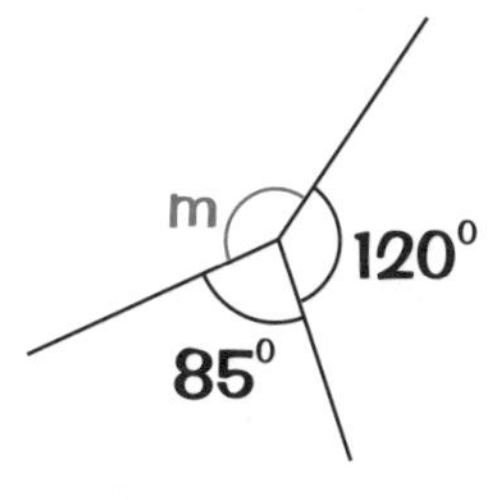

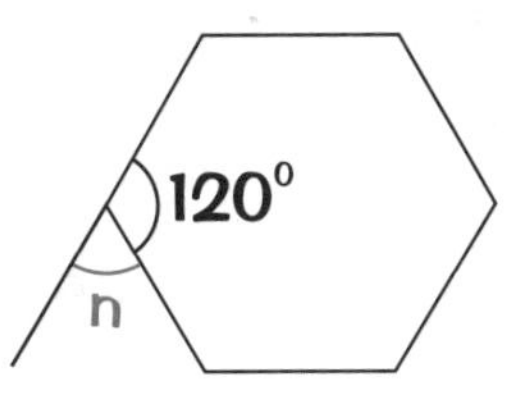

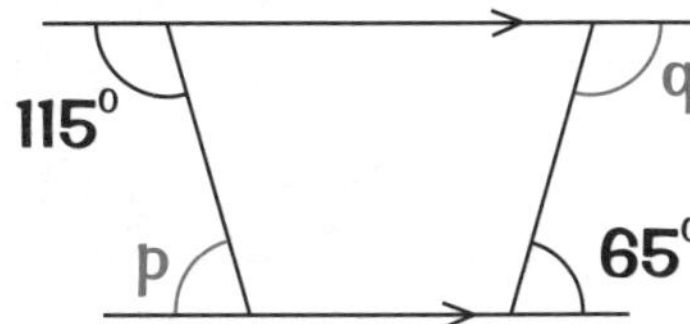

m=..........° n=..........° p=..........° q=..........°

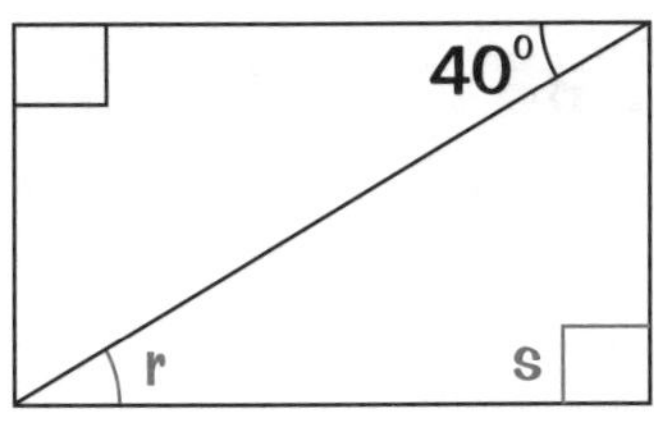

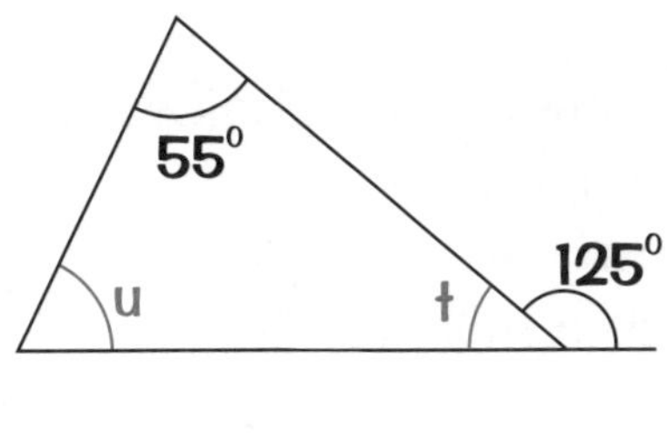

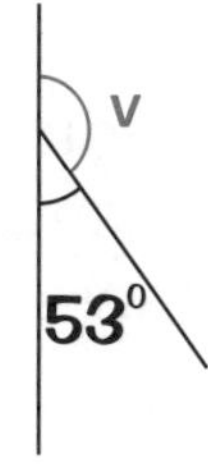

r=..........° s=..........° t=..........° u=..........° v=..........°

Q7 How many different types of angle are in this picture? ....

What are the names of the angles you have found?

....

Look for the shapes you know the rules for (triangles, quadrilaterals, parallel lines, etc.) — use them and you can fill in the gaps to your heart's content.

Questions on Constructions

You've gotta be ultra neat with these — you'll lose easy marks if your pictures are scruffy — and let's face it you'd rather have them, wouldn't you.

Constructions should always be done as accurately as possible using: sharp pencil, ruler, compasses, protractor (set-square).

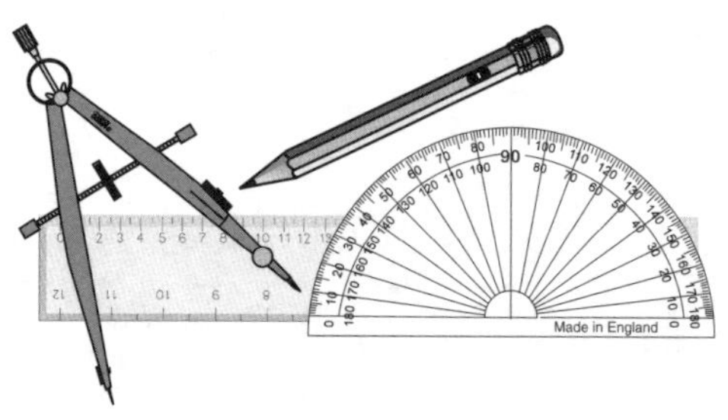

Q1 a) Draw a circle with radius 4 cm.

Draw in a diameter of the circle. Label one end of the diameter X and the other end Y.

Mark a point somewhere on the circumference – not too close to X or Y. Label your point T. Join X to T and T to Y.

Measure angle XTY. XTY = ...°

b) Construct an accurate drawing below of the triangle on the right. Measure side AB on your triangle giving your answer in millimetres.

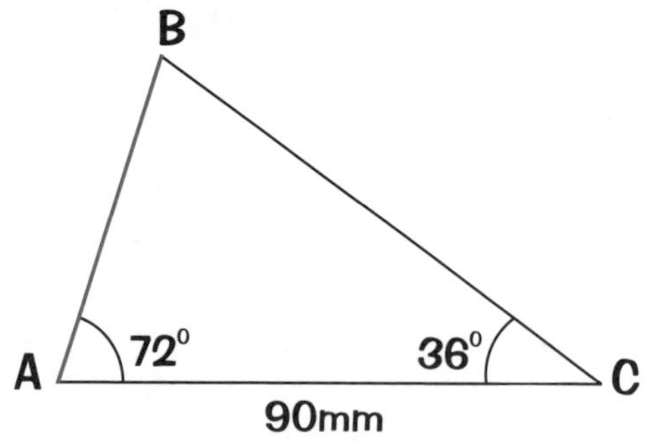

AB = ... mm

Questions on Family Triangles

Q1 Fill in the gaps in these sentences.

a) An isosceles triangle has .... equal sides and .... equal angles.

b) A triangle with all its sides equal and all its angles equal is called an .... triangle.

c) A scalene triangle has .... equal sides and .... equal angles.

d) A triangle with one right-angle is called a .... triangle.

Q2 By joining dots draw four different isosceles triangles, one in each box.

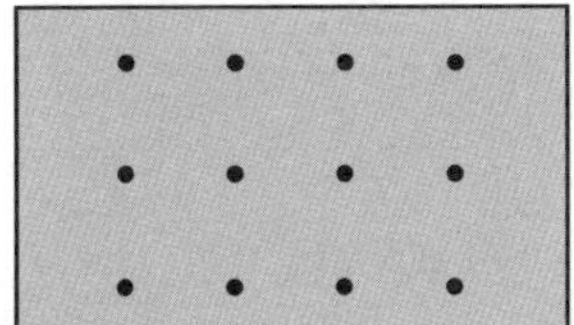
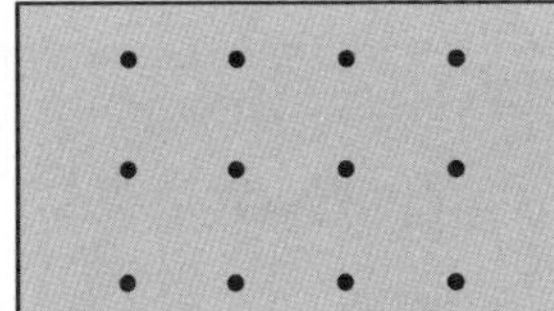
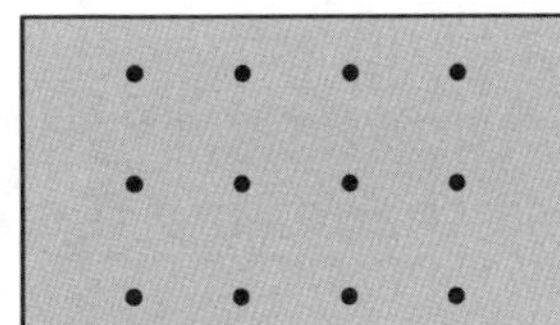
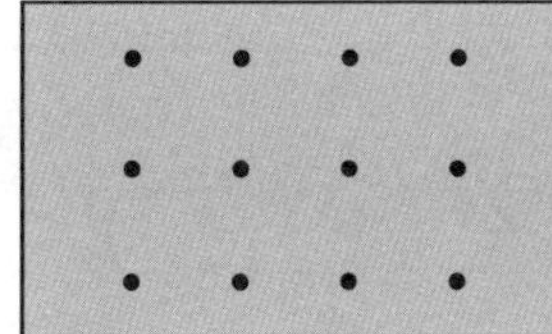

Q3 Using three different coloured pencils:
Find an equilateral triangle and shade it in.
Using a different colour, shade in two different right angled triangles.
With your last colour shade in two different scalene triangles.

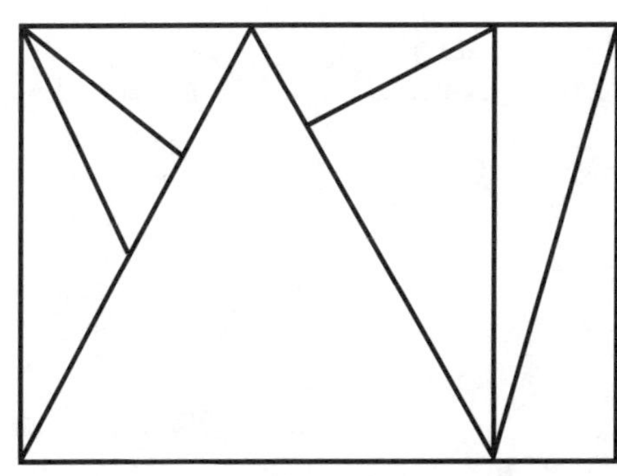

Q4 How many triangles are there in this diagram?

....

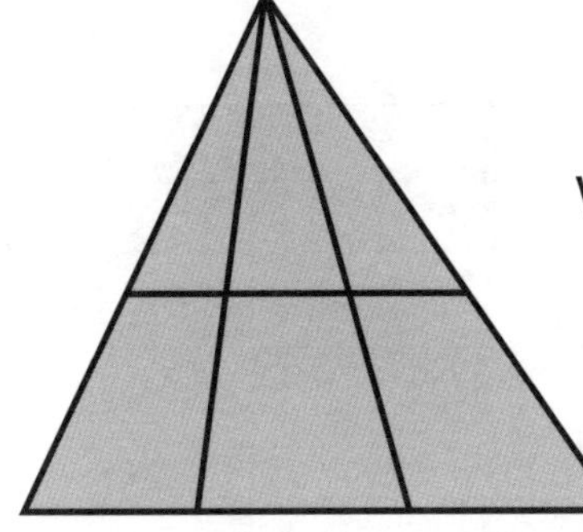

What sort of triangles are they?

....

There are only 4 types of triangle, so make sure you know them all — think of all those nice fat juicy marks...

Questions on Regular Polygons

A polygon is a shape with lots of sides. Regular just means all the sides are the same length and all the angles are the same. So a regular polygon is...

Q1 Can you name these regular shapes?

a)

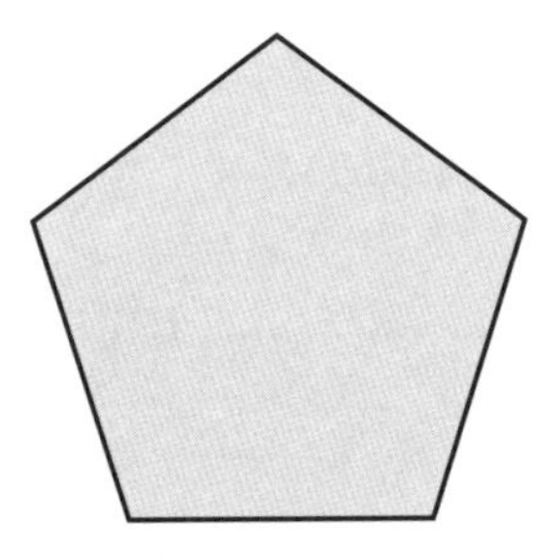

....

b)

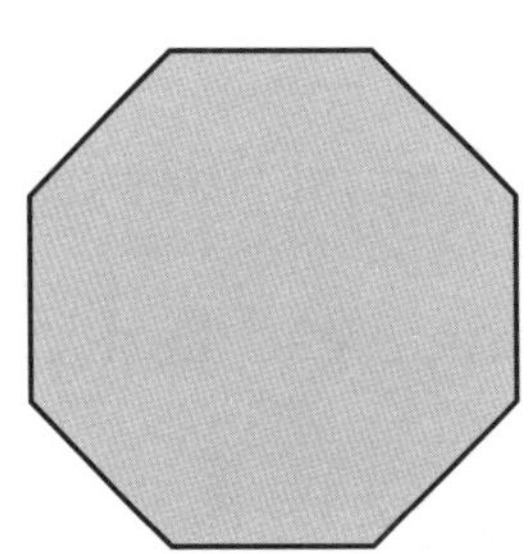

....

c)

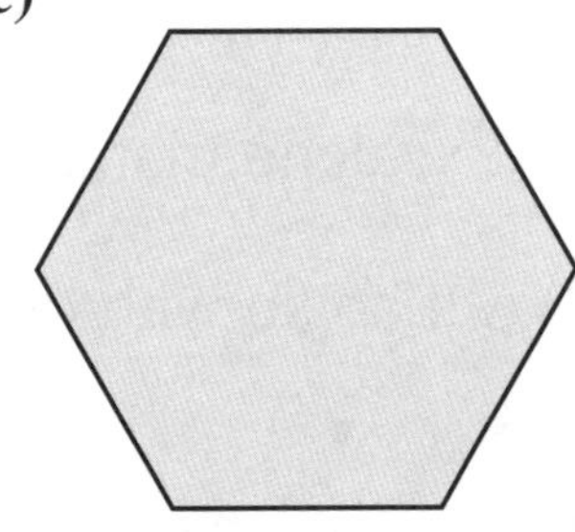

....

Q2 Which of these shapes are regular? (Yes/No?)

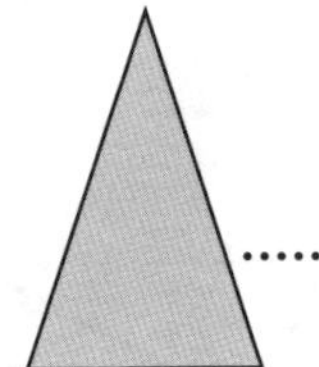

....

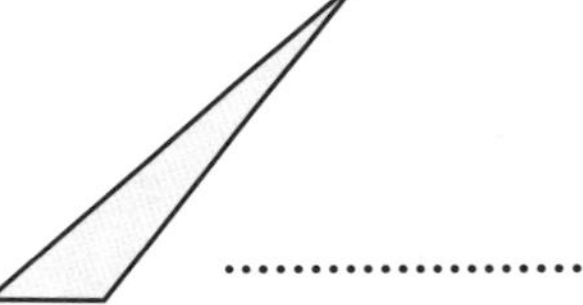

....

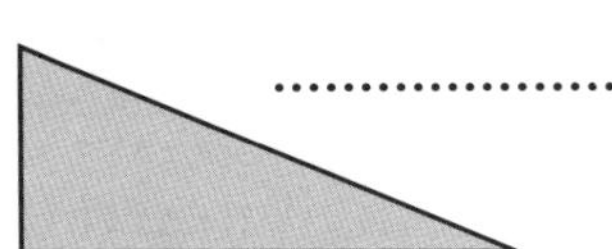

....

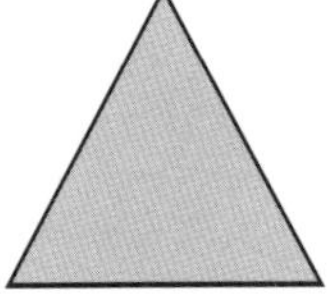

....

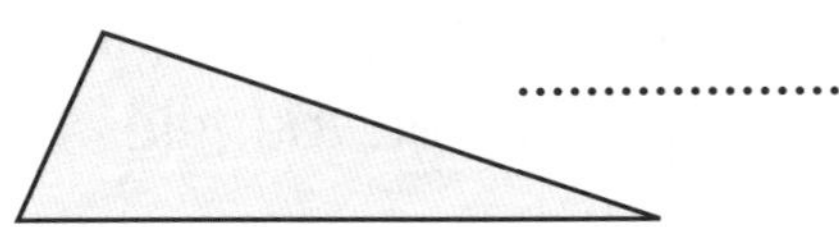

....

Q3 Which of these shapes are regular? (Yes/No?)

....

....

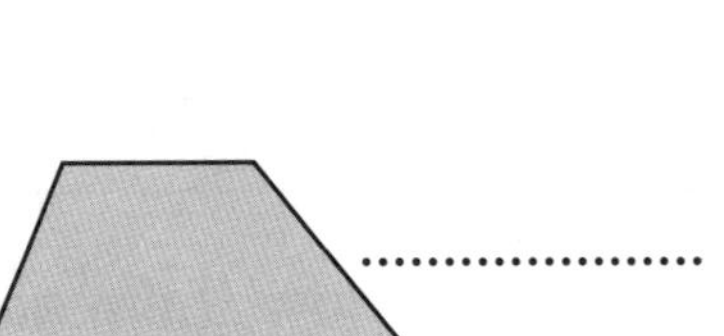

....

....

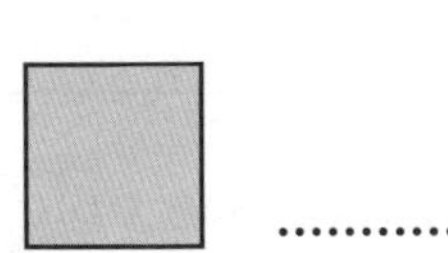

....

Questions on Polygons

Q1 Here is a regular octagon:

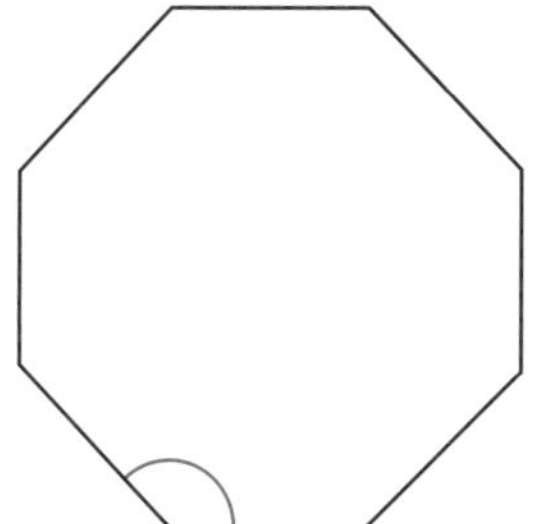

a) What is the total of its eight interior angles?

....

b) What is the size of the marked angle? ....

Here is an irregular hexagon:

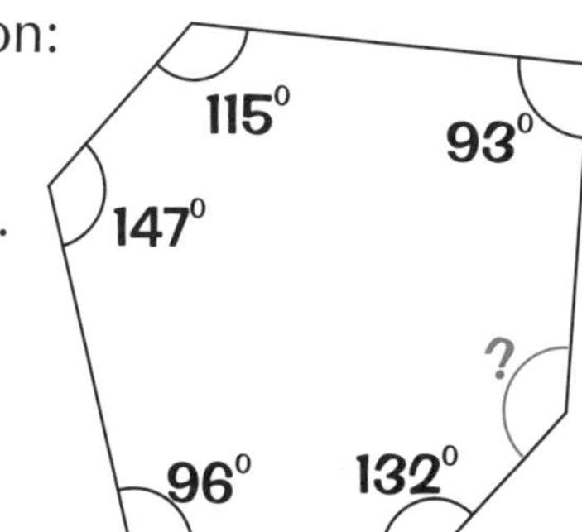

c) What is the total of its six interior angles? ....

d) What is the size of the missing angle? ....

Here is a regular pentagon:

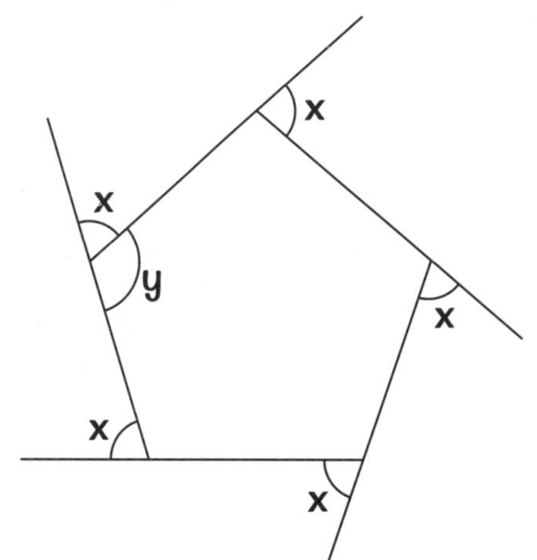

e) The five angles marked x are its exterior angles. What do they add up to?

....

f) Work out the value of x

....

g) Use your answer from part f to work out the value of angle y

....

Here is a diagram showing part of a regular polygon:

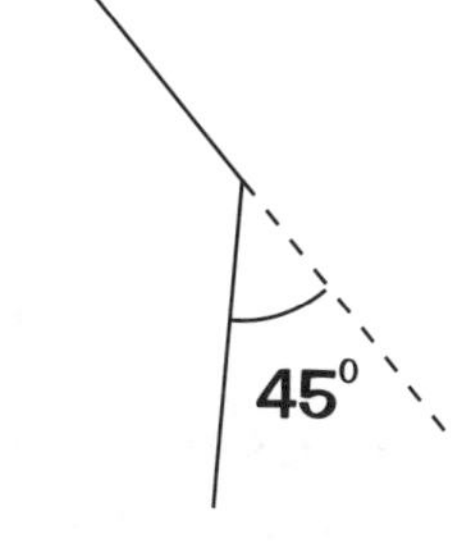

h) The angle shown is one of its exterior angles. From this, work out how many sides the polygon has.

....

A polygon can have <u>any</u> number of sides, but its <u>exterior</u> angles will always add up to 360° — ain't that just something...

Questions on Perimeters

What you've gotta do with these is add up all the sides to get the perimeter. If there's no drawing, do it yourself — then you won't forget any of the sides.

Q1 Work out the perimeters of the following shapes :

a)

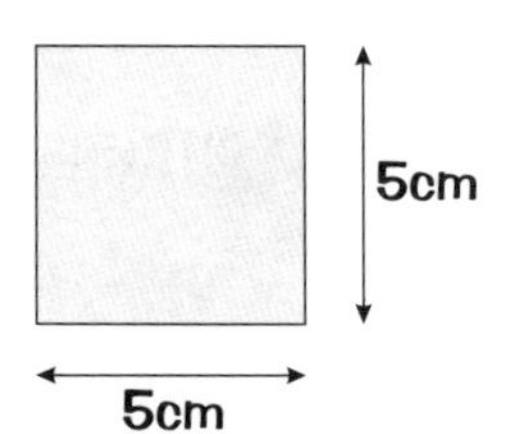

Square Perimeter = ... cm

b)

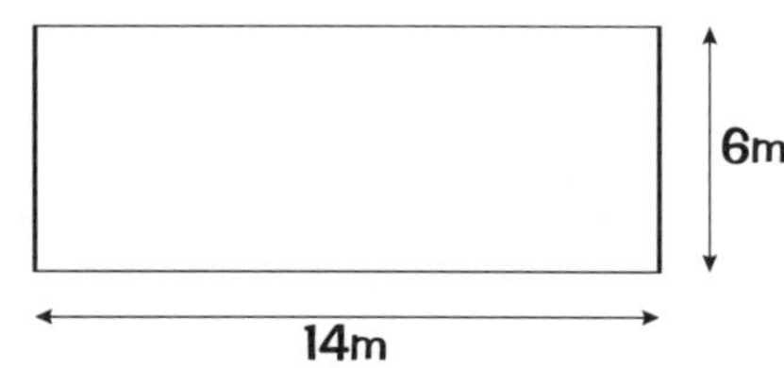

Rectangle Perimeter =
=(2 × ......) + (2 × ......) = ...m

c)

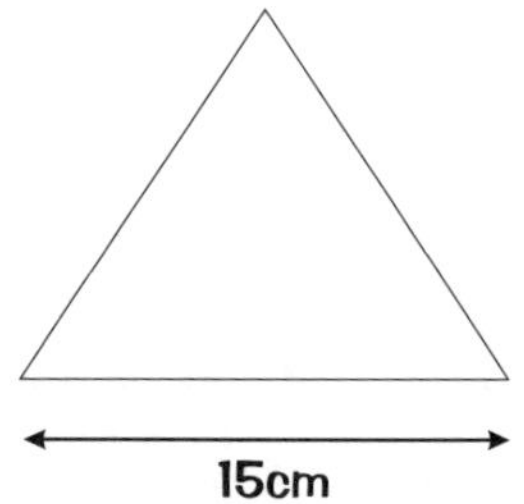

Equilateral Triangle
Perimeter = 3 × .... = ...cm

d)

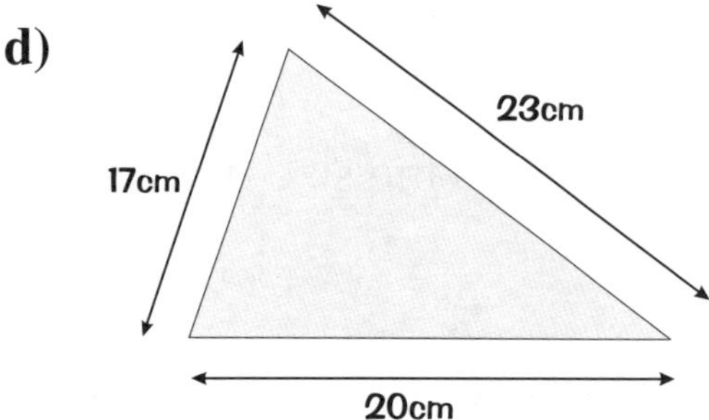

Triangle
Perimeter = ...+.......+.......=.......cm

e)

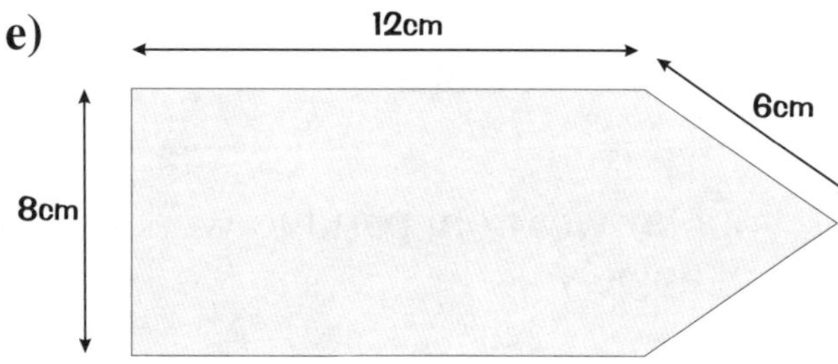

Five Sided Shape
Perimeter = ...+.......+.......+.......+.......
=.......cm

f)

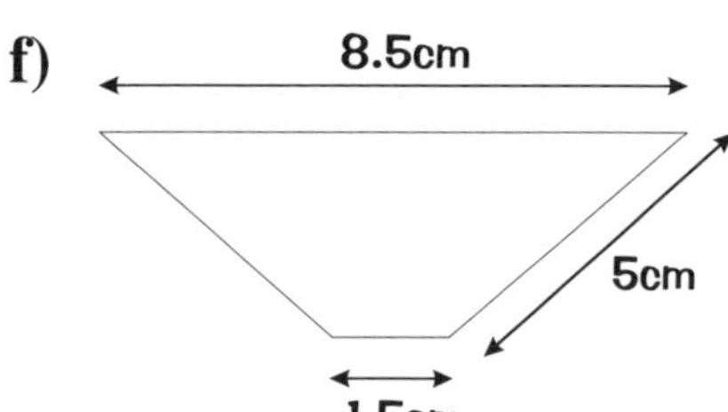

Four Sided Shape
Perimeter = ...+.......+.......+.......=.......cm

Q2 **a)** A square garden has sides of length 10m. How much fencing is needed to go around it? ....m.

b) A photo measures 17.5cm by 12.5 cm. What is the total length of the frame around it? ....cm.

Questions on Perimeters

Q3 Find the perimeter of these shapes (you may need to work out some of the lengths):

a)

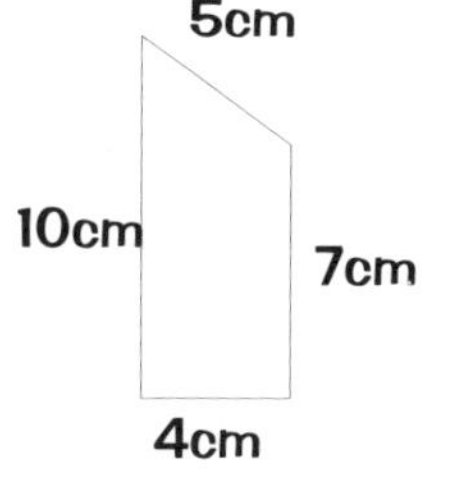

Perimeter ....

b)

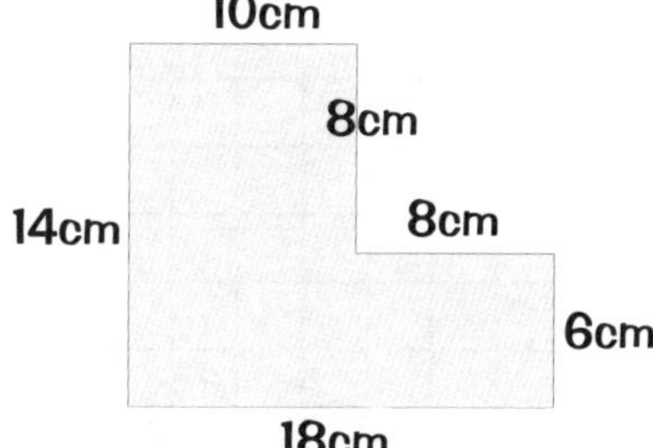

Perimeter ....

c)

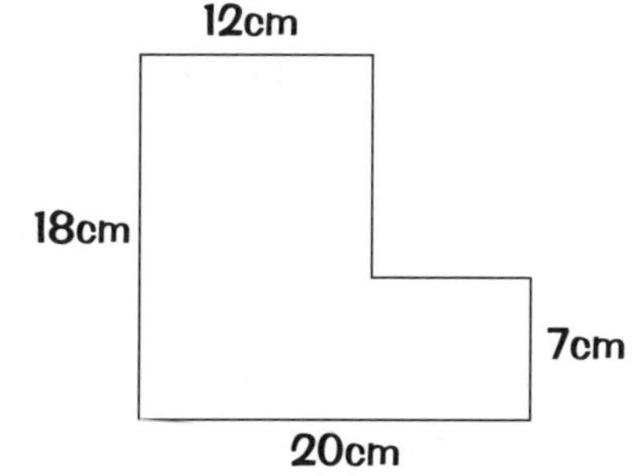

Perimeter ....

d)

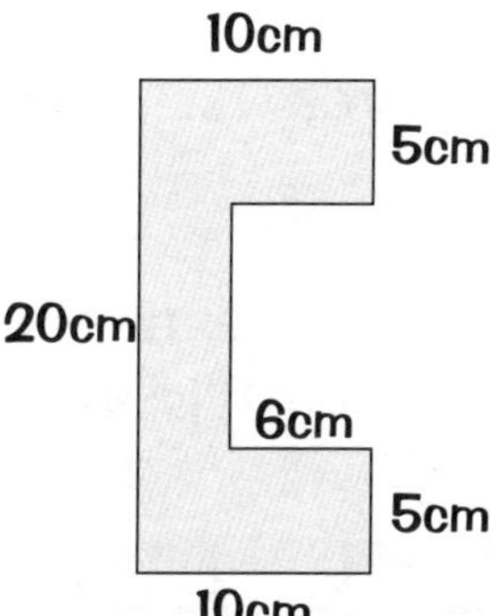

Perimeter ....

e)

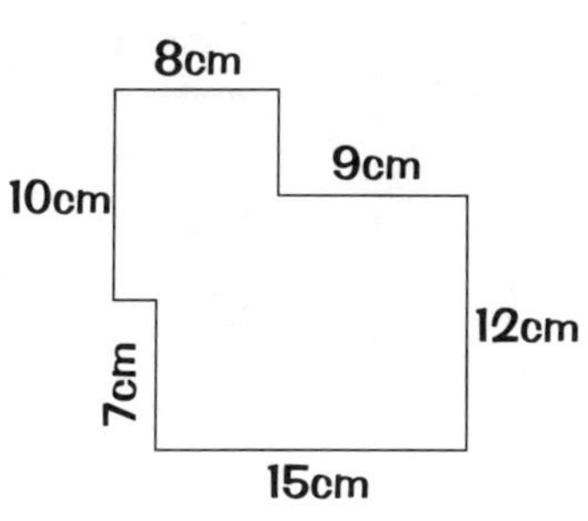

Perimeter ....

f)

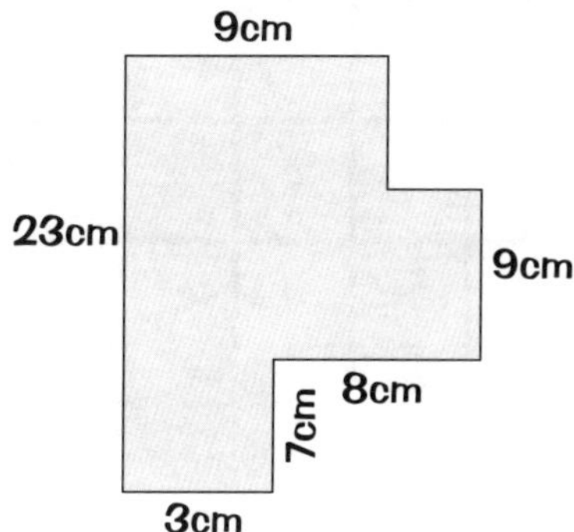

Perimeter ....

Questions on Areas

Q1 Here are the outlines of the footprints of some animals. Each square represents 1cm². Estimate the area of each footprint:

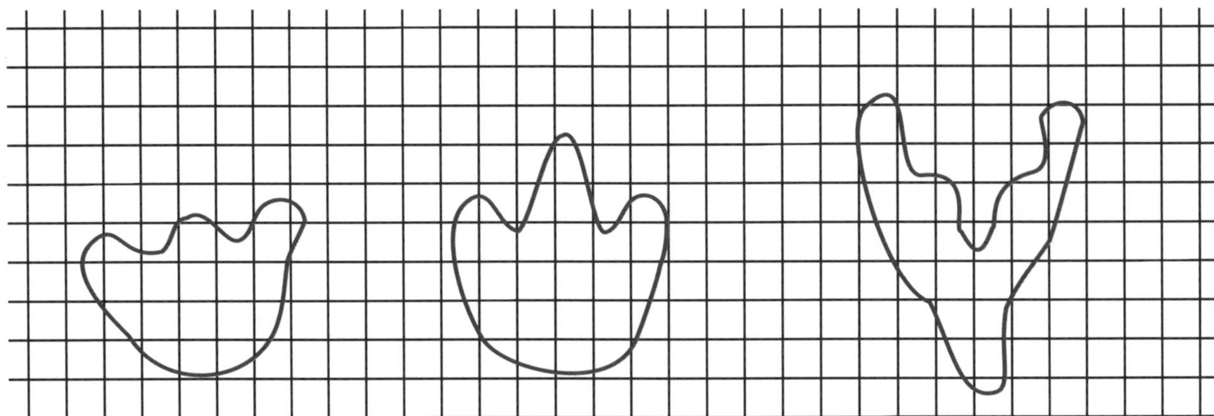

Area .... cm^2 Area .... cm^2 Area .... cm^2

Q2 Here are the maps of 2 islands. Each square represents 1km². Estimate the area of each island:

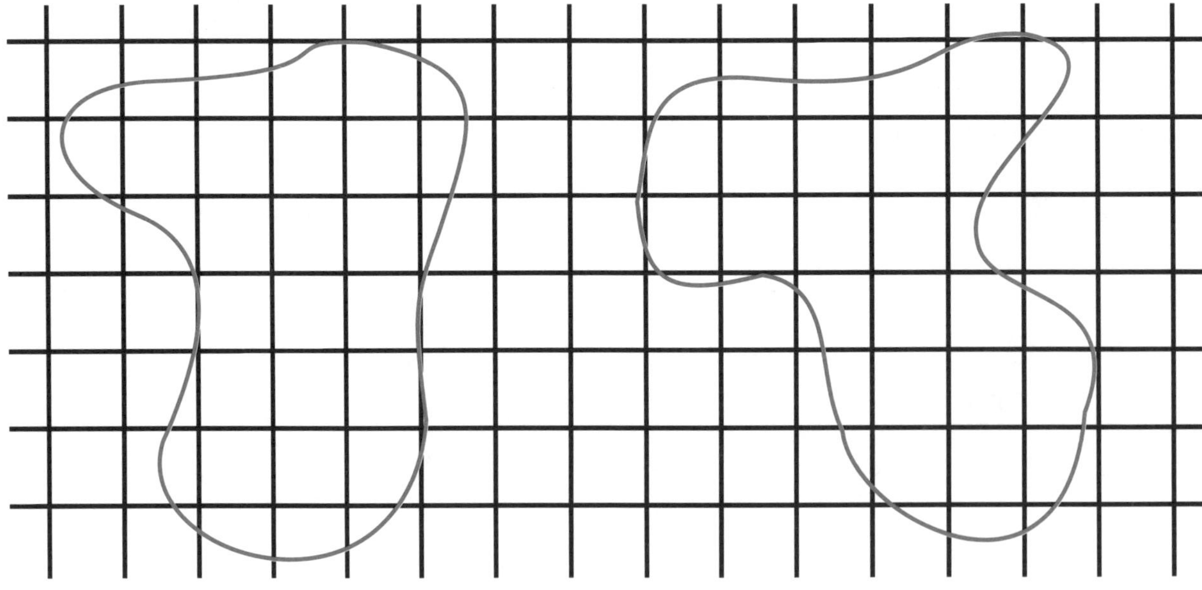

Area .... km^2 Area .... km^2

Add up all the whole squares first — then round off all the bits of squares to the nearest half, then add them all on afterwards.

Questions on Areas

For Rectangles,
AREA = LENGTH × WIDTH

Q3 Calculate the areas of the following :

a) Length = 10 cm, Width = 4 cm, Area = ... × ..... = ... cm^2.

b) Length = 55 cm, Width = 19 cm, Area = ... cm^2.

c) Length = 12 m, Width = 7 m, Area = ... m^2.

d) Length = 155 m, Width = 28 m, Area = ... m^2.

e) Length = 3.7 km, Width = 1.5 km, Area = ... km^2.

For Triangles,
Area = ½ (Height × Base)

Q4 Calculate the areas of the following :

a) Base = 12 cm, Height = 9 cm, Area = $\frac{1}{2}$ (...... × ......) = ... cm^2.

b) Base = 5 cm, Height = 3 cm, Area = ... cm^2.

c) Base = 25 m, Height = 7 m, Area = ... m^2.

d) Base = 1.6 m, Height = 6.4 m, Area = ... m^2.

e) Base = 700 cm, Height = 350 cm, Area = ... cm^2.

Q5 Measure each of these shapes, then calculate the area.

a)

Width = ... cm

Length = ... cm

Area = ...cm^2

b)

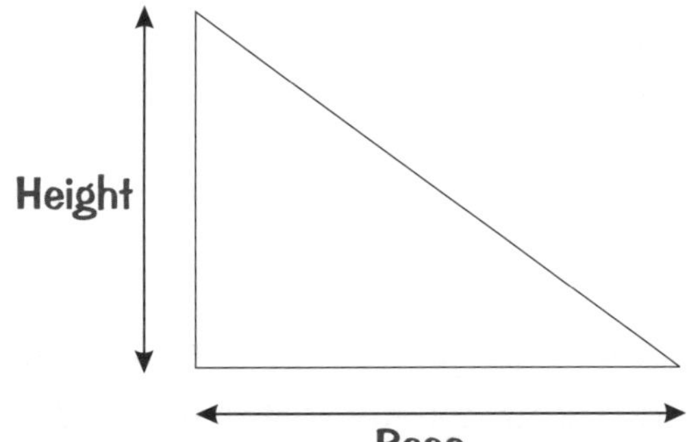

Height = ... cm

Base = ... cm

Area = ...cm^2

Questions on Composite Areas

Calculate the areas of these composite shapes...

Q1

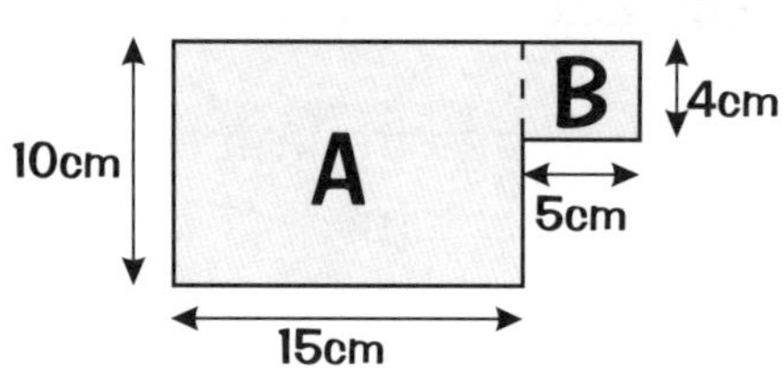

Shape A: length =........ width = ...
Area = ... × .... = ...cm²
Shape B: length = ... width = ...
Area = ... × .... = ...cm²
Total (area A + area B) = ... + ... = ...cm²

Q2 Shape A (rectangle): .... × .... = ...cm²
Shape B (triangle): ½ (base x height)
Base = ...cm , Height = ...cm
Area = ½ (........ × ....) = ...cm²
Total Area = ... + ... = ...cm²

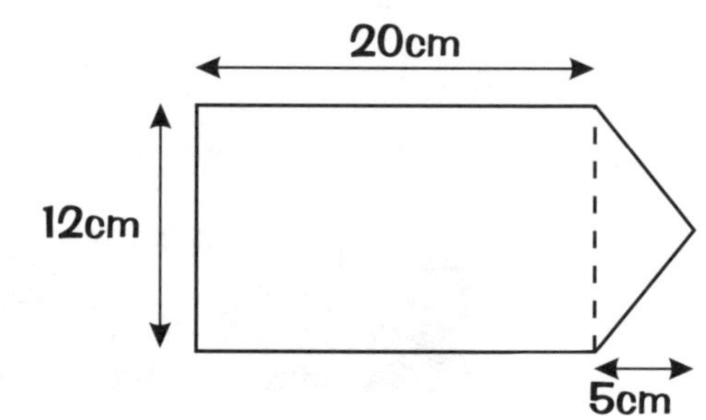

Q3

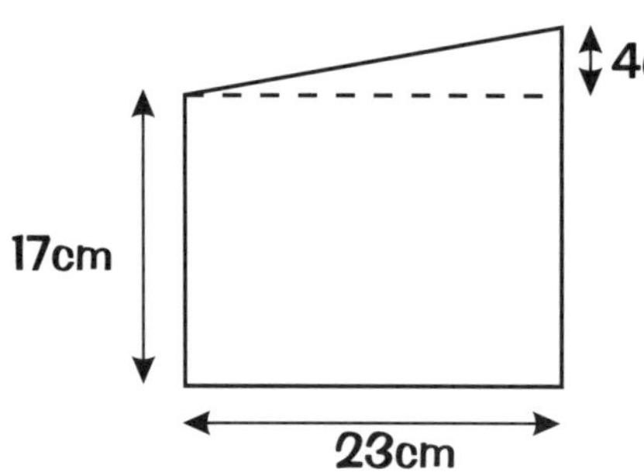

Shape A (rectangle): .... × .... = ...cm²
Shape B (triangle): ½ (....... × ....) = ...cm²

Total Area = ... + ... = ...cm²

Q4 Draw a dotted line to divide this shape.
Shape A (rectangle): .... × .... = ...m²
Shape B (triangle): ½(....... × ....)= ....m²
Total Area = ... + ... = ...m²

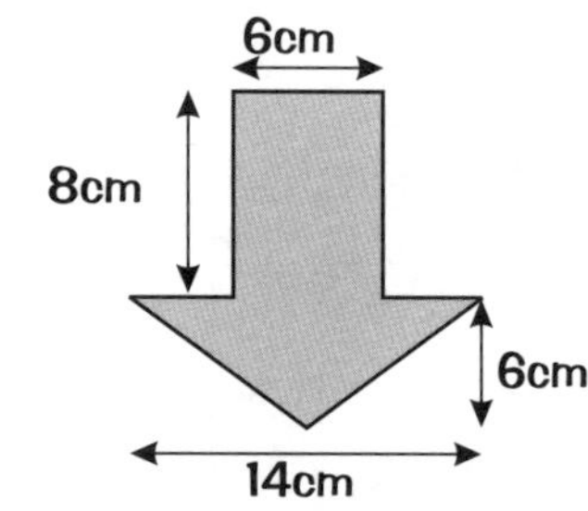

Q5

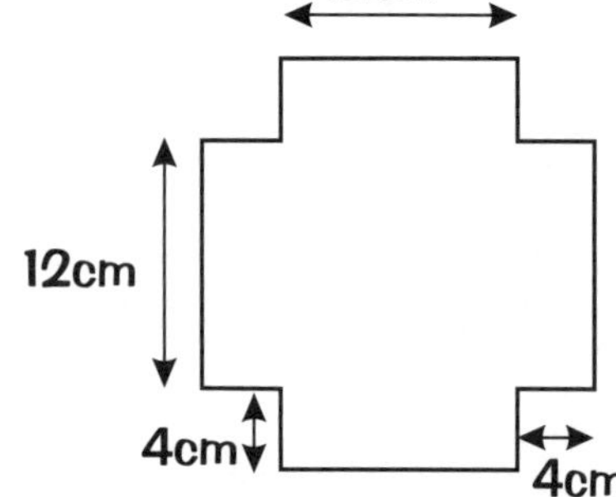

Draw dotted lines to divide this symmetrical shape.
Shape A (rectangle): .... × .... = ...m²
Shape B (square): .... × .... = ...m²
Total Area = (4 × Shape A) + Shape B =.........m²

Bit more tricky, these... but look — they're all just rectangles and triangles. Work out each bit separately, then add the areas together — easy.

Questions on The Circle

Don't worry about that π bit — it just stands for the number 3.14159... and then it's rounded off to 3 or 3.14, to make it a bit easier for you to use.

Q1 Draw a circle with radius 3cm. On your circle label the circumference, a radius and a diameter.

Q2 Calculate the circumference of these circles. Take π to be 3.14.

a) 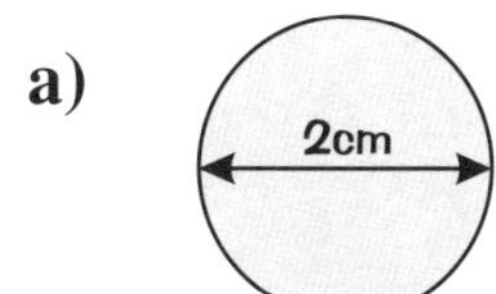

Circumference = π × diameter = ...

b) Circumference = π × diameter = ...

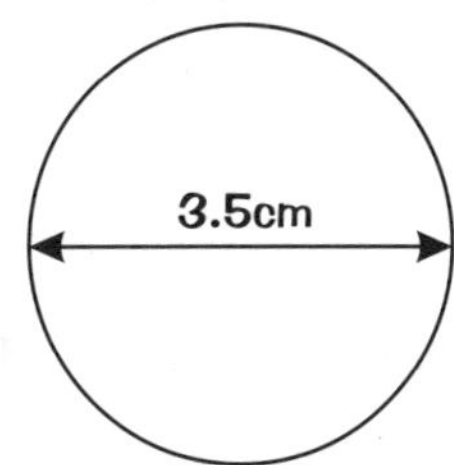

c)

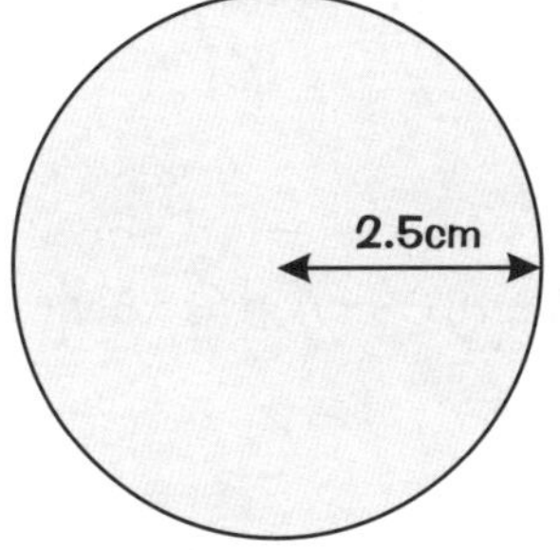

Remember to work out the diameter first.

Diameter = radius × 2 = ...

Circumference = ...

d) A circle radius 3.5 cm. ....

Q3 A coin has a diameter of 1.7cm. What is its circumference?

....

Q4 A plant is in a pot. The radius of the top of the pot is 4.5cm. Calculate the circumference of the pot.

....

Q5 The diameter of the wheels on Joe's bike is 0.6m. On the way to school the front wheel rotates 600 times. How far does Joe live from school?

....

Questions on The Circle

Q6 Calculate the area of each circle.

a)

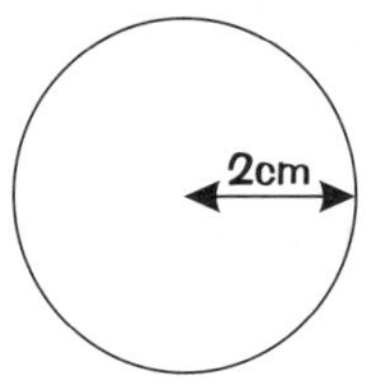

Area = $\pi \times \text{radius}^2$ = ...

b) A circle of radius 9cm.

Area = $\pi \times \text{radius}^2$ = ...

c)

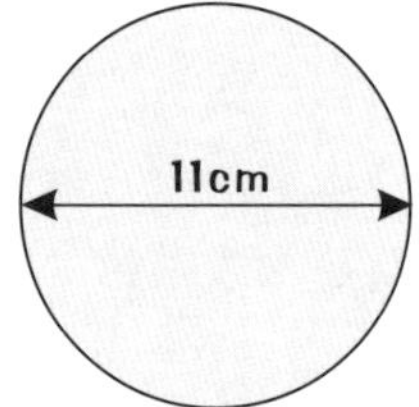

You must find the radius first.

Radius = diameter / 2 = ...

Area = ...

d) A circle of diameter 28cm. Radius = ...

Area = ...

Q7 Find the area of one face of a 10p coin, radius 1.2cm.

Area = ...

Q8 A circular table has a diameter of 50cm. Find the area of the table.

Area = ...

Q9 This circular pond has a circular path around it. The radius of the pond is 72m and the path is 2m wide.

path

pond

What is the area of the pond? ....

What is the area of the path? ....

....

Q10 What is the area of this semicircular rug?

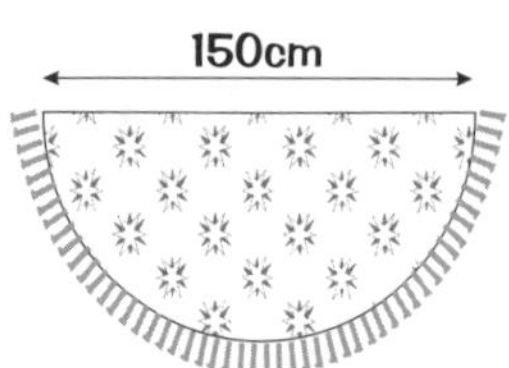

Area = ...

Q11 The circumference of a circle is 195cm.
Calculate its diameter.

Diameter = ...

Questions on Solids and Nets

There's usually more than one possible net for each shape, so don't worry if you get a couple of answers — as long as yours works, you'll get the marks.

Q1 Which of the following nets would make a cube?

a) **b)** **c)**

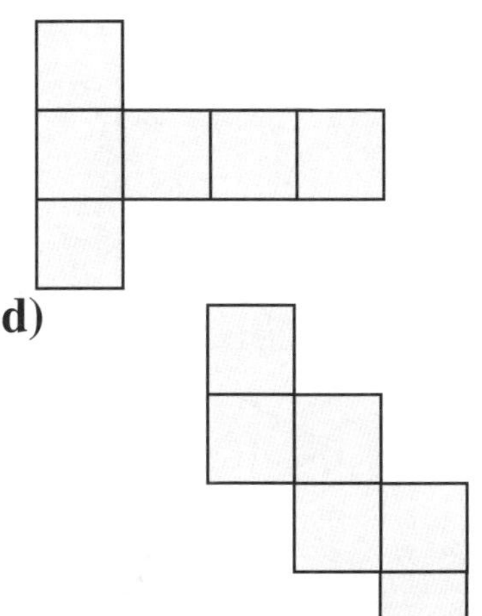

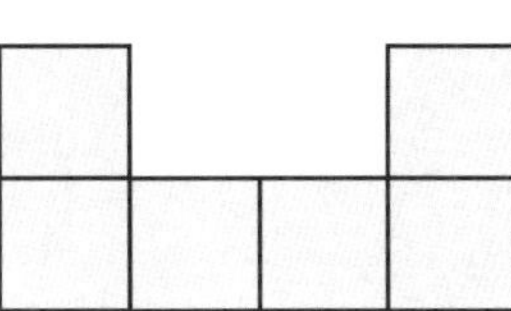

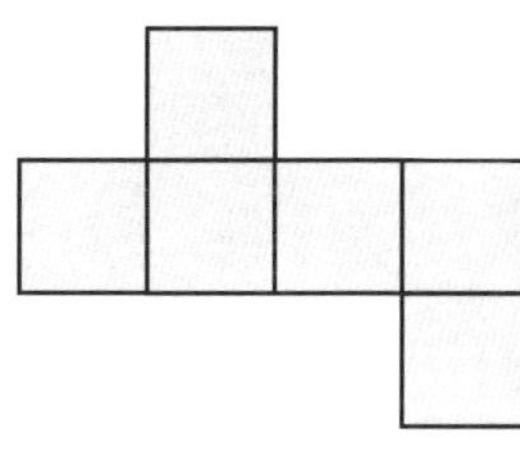

d) **e)** **f)**

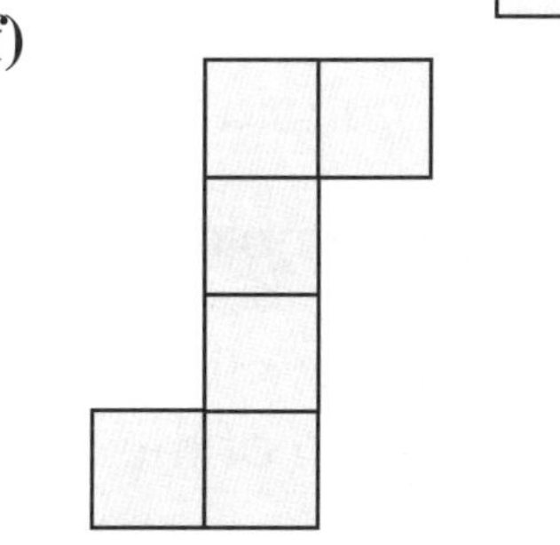

Q2 Below is a sketch of a cuboid and its net. The net is drawn to scale but not finished: it needs two more faces. Draw them in the correct position.

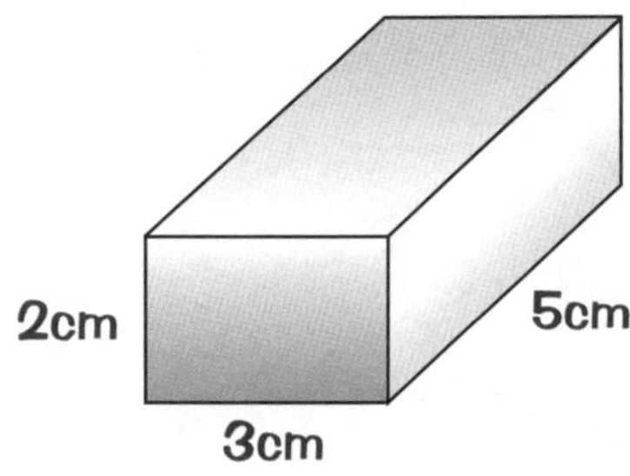

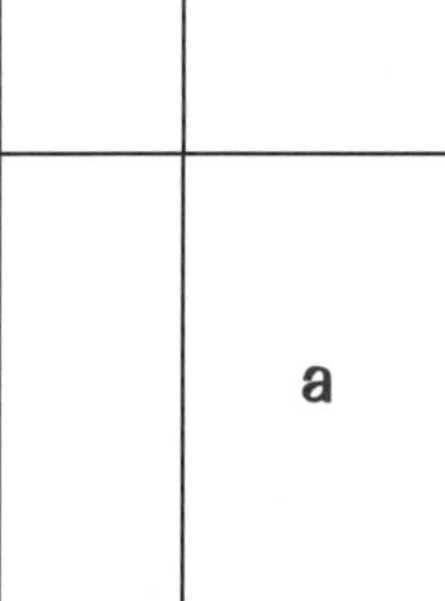

Q3 What is the total surface area of the cuboid in **Q2**?

Area = ...

Questions on Solids and Nets

Q4 On a 6-sided dice, opposite numbers should add up to 7. Fill in the rest of the dots on this net:

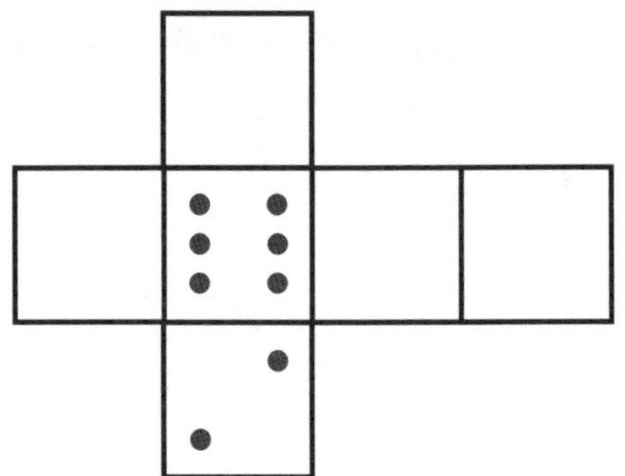

Q5 This unfinished isometric drawing shows a cuboid with dimensions 1 cm by 4 cm by 2 cm.

a) Complete the isometric drawing of the cuboid.

b) Draw the front elevation, side elevation and plan of the cuboid in the space below. Make sure your drawings are to scale.

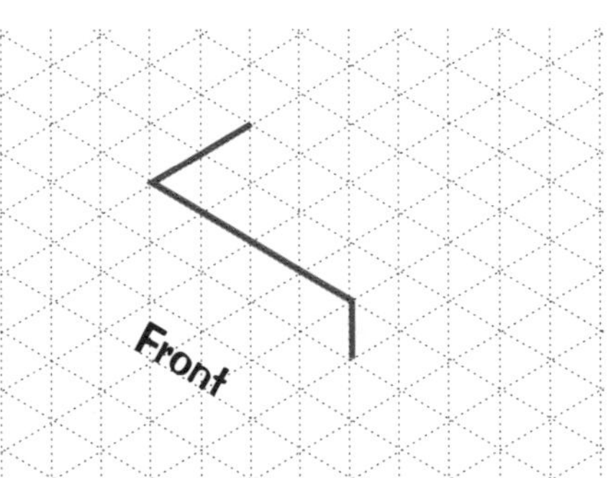

Q6 Draw an accurate net for each of the following solid shapes. (Use a spare page in this workbook or a separate piece of paper.)

a)

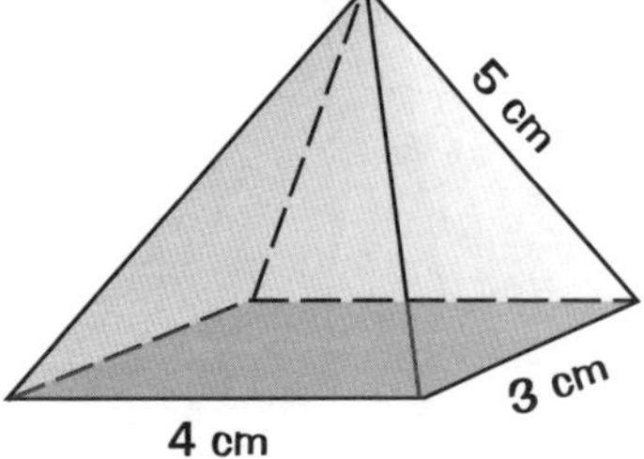

b)

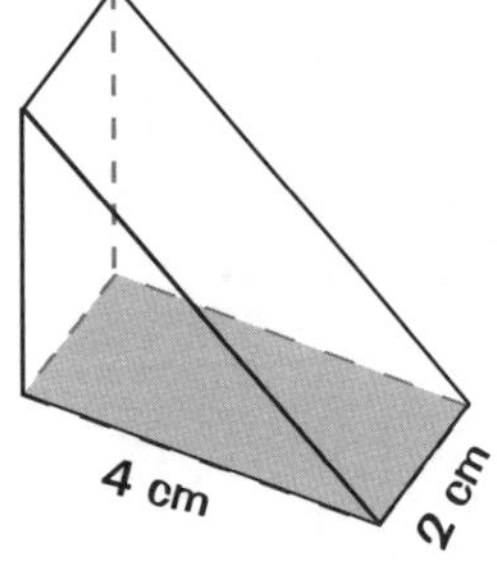

Q7 This net will make a common, mathematical solid. Name the solid:

....

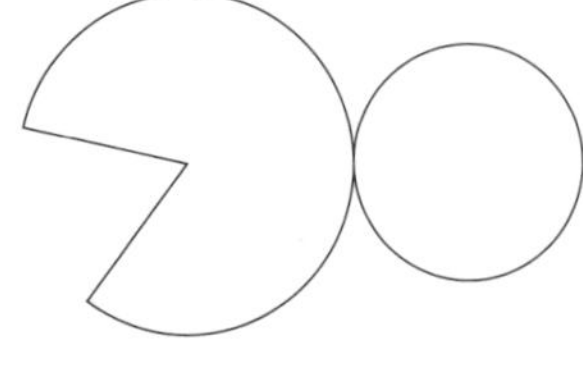

You've got to think about folding the net up to make the shape — if you're struggling, the best thing to do is practise your origami skills...

Questions on Volume

Q1 Each shape has been made from centimetre cubes. The volume of a centimetre cube is 1 cubic cm. How many cubes are there in each shape? What is the volume of each shape in cubic cm?

a)

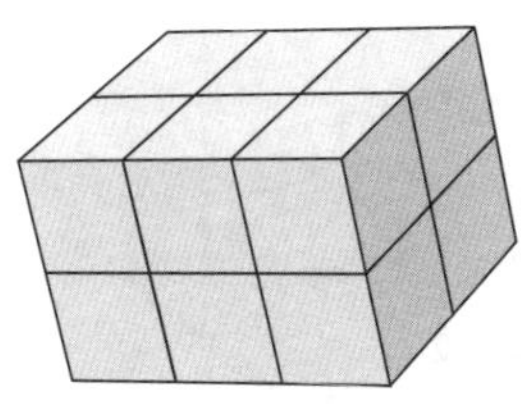

There are ...... cubes.
The volume is
...... cubic cm.

b)

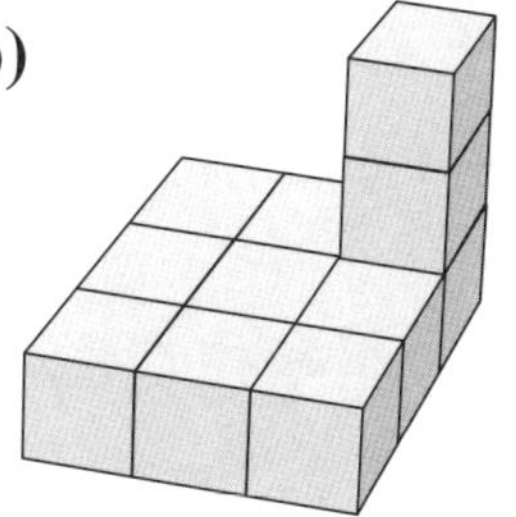

There are ...... cubes.
The volume is
...... cubic cm.

c)

There are ...... cubes.
The volume is
...... cubic cm.

d)

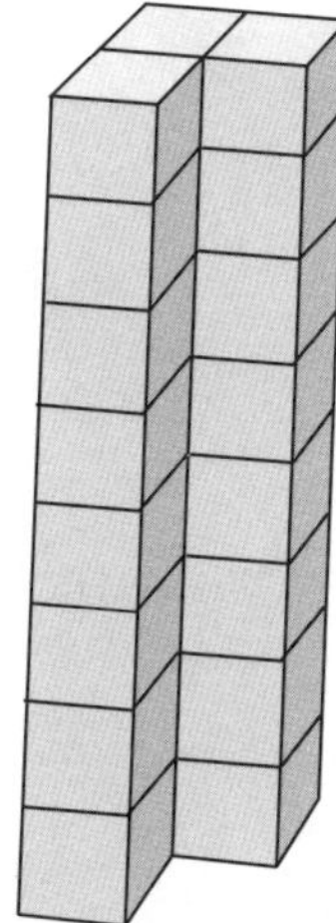

There are ...... cubes.
The volume is
...... cubic cm.

e)

There are ...... cubes.
The volume is
...... cubic cm.

f)

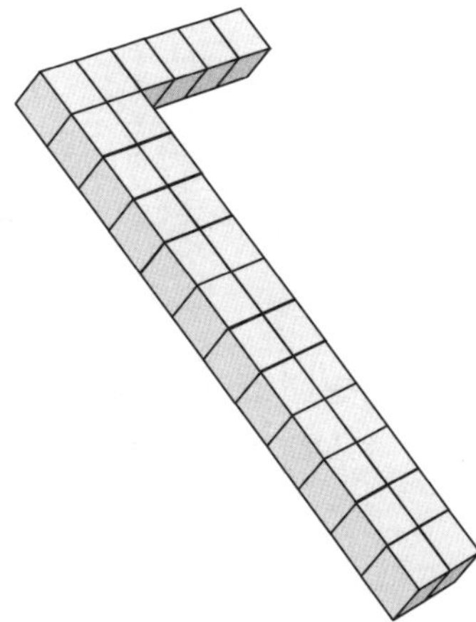

There are ...... cubes.
The volume is
...... cubic cm.

g)

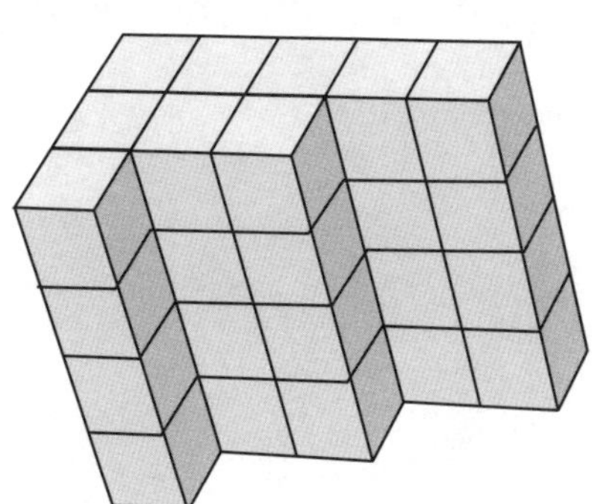

There are .... cubes.
The volume is .... cubic cm.

h)

There are .... cubes.
The volume is .... cubic cm.

You simply add up the cubes... but make sure you don't miss any — remember that there are some rows at the back too.

Questions on Volume

Volumes of cubes and cuboids are nearly as easy as areas of squares and rectangles — you've only got an extra side to multiply by.

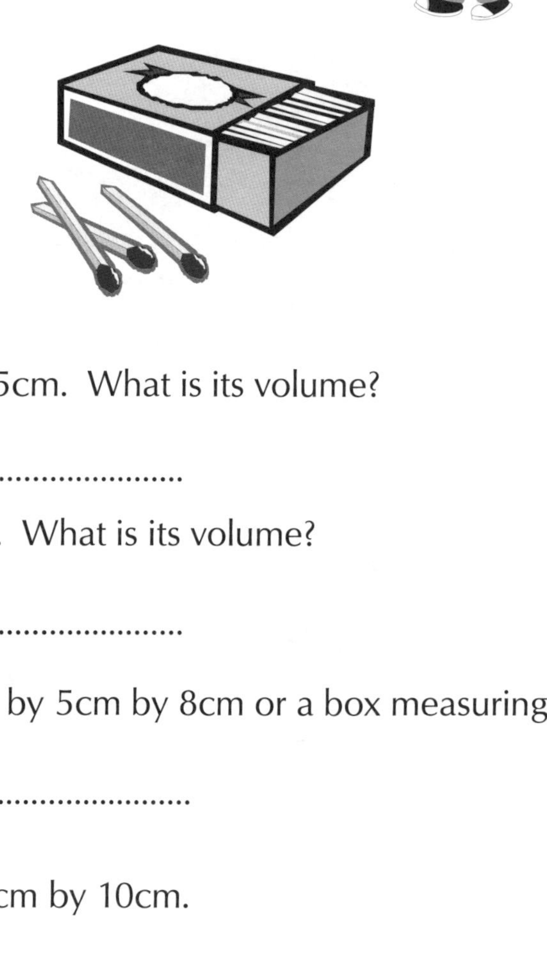

Q2 A match box measures 7cm by 4cm by 5cm. What is its volume?

....

Q3 A cereal box measures 30cm by 6cm by 15cm. What is its volume?

....

Q4 A room is 2.5m tall, 8m long and 5m wide. What is its volume?

....

Q5 Which holds more, a box measuring 12cm by 5cm by 8cm or a box measuring 10cm by 6cm by 9cm?

....

Q6 A video casette case measures 20cm by 3cm by 10cm. What is its volume?

....

Q7 An ice cube measures 2cm by 2cm by 2cm. What is its volume? ....
Is there enough room in a container measuring 8cm by 12cm by 10cm for 100 ice cubes?

....

Q8 What is the volume of a cube which measures:

a) 5cm ....

b) 9cm ....

c) 15cm .... ?

Q9 A box measures 9cm by 5cm by 8cm. What is its volume? ....
What is the volume of a box twice as long, twice as wide, and twice as tall?

....

Questions on Volume

This looks a bit familiar... one tricky shape made up of a few easier shapes. (You know what to do with this — individual volumes first, then add together)

Q10 Calculate the volume of these podiums...

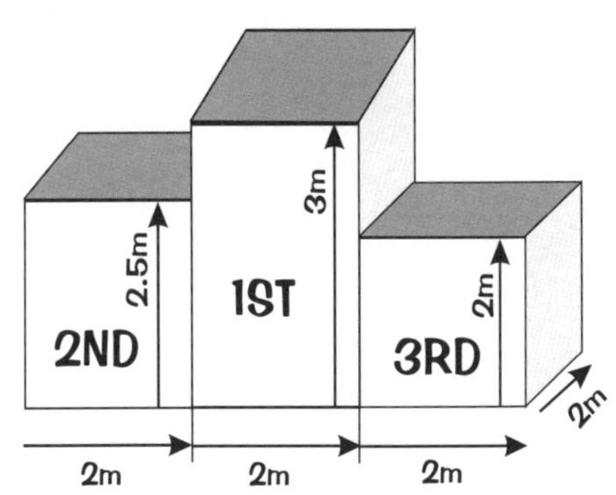

1st Place = length × width × height
= ..... × ...... × ...... = ...m^3

2nd Place = ... × ..... × ..... = ...m^3

3rd Place = ... × ..... × ..... = ...m^3

Total = ... + ... + ... = ...m^3

Q11 a) Which of these blocks of flats has the biggest volume?

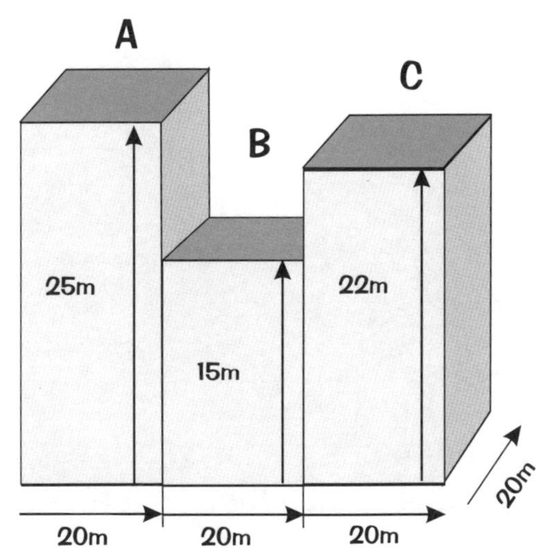

Block A = ... × ...... × ...... = ...m^3

Block B = ... × ...... × ...... = ...m^3

Block C = ... × ...... × ...... = ...m^3

Biggest Volume = ...

b) Total Volume = ... m^3

Q12 How much water would this tank hold when full to the brim?

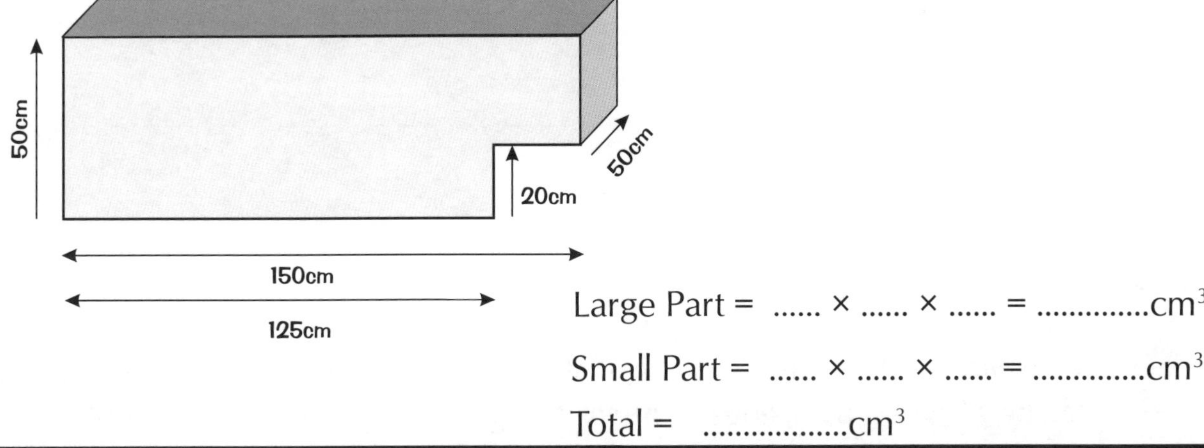

Large Part = ... × ...... × ...... = ...cm^3

Small Part = ... × ...... × ...... = ...cm^3

Total = ...cm^3

Questions on Translation

Translation is the movement along a straight line in a particular direction. The shape slides across from one position to another.

Q1 The arrow is to be translated 10 squares right then 2 squares up. Draw the image.

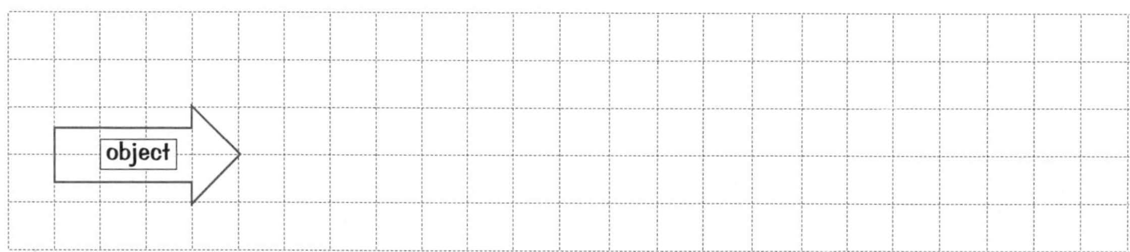

Q2 Translate the following shapes and draw the images. Label the images A′ B′ C′

A 4 left , 3 down B 5 right, 5 up C 4 right, 4 down

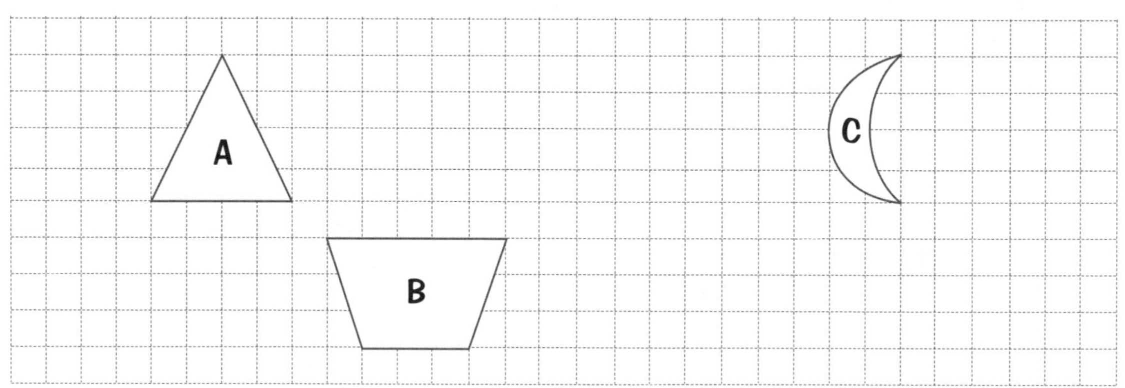

Q3 Translate this shape, drawing the image each time:
(3 right, 4 up) then (9 right, 2 up) then (3 right, 4 down) then (8 left, 4 down)
Label the images A′, A″ , A‴, A⁗.

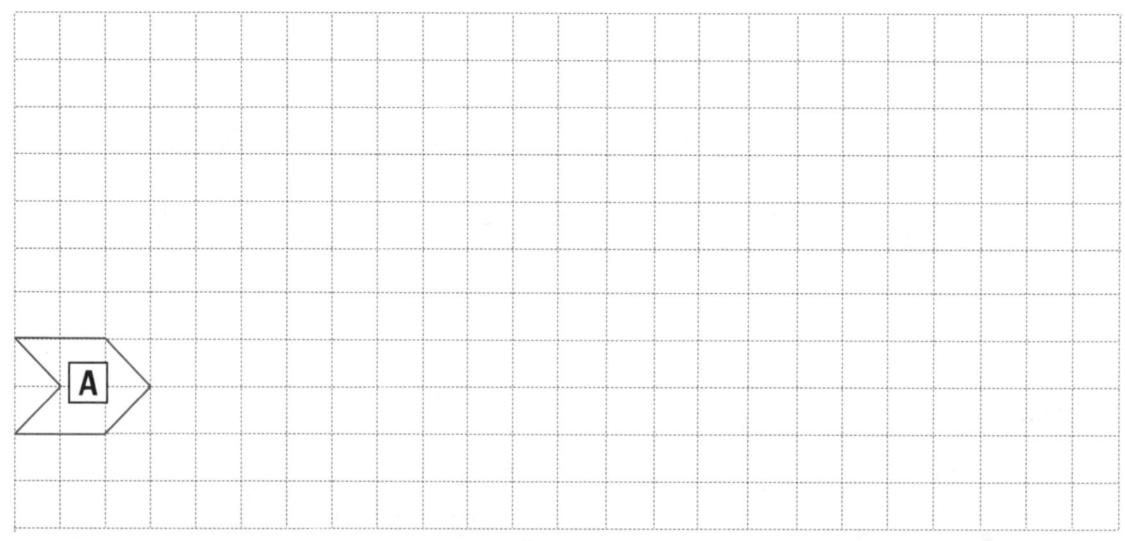

This has got to be the easiest of the lot — you don't have to change the shape at all — all it does is move along a bit, or up a bit... or both.

Questions on Rotation

Q1 The centre of rotation for each of these diagrams is *X*. Rotate (turn) each shape as asked then draw the new position of the shape onto each of the diagrams below.

a) 180°clockwise (or ½ turn).

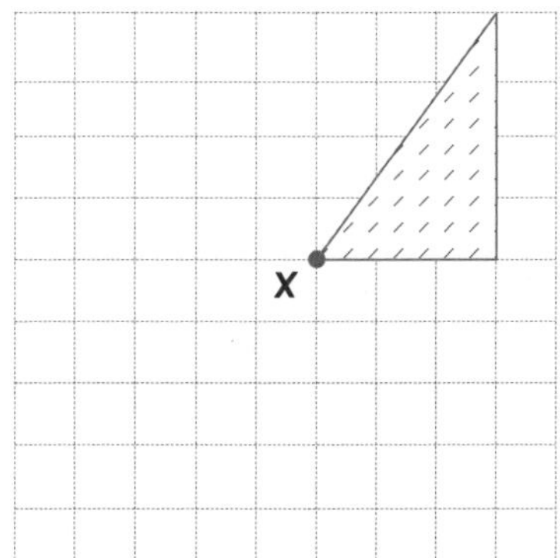

b) 270° anticlockwise (or ¾ turn anticlockwise).

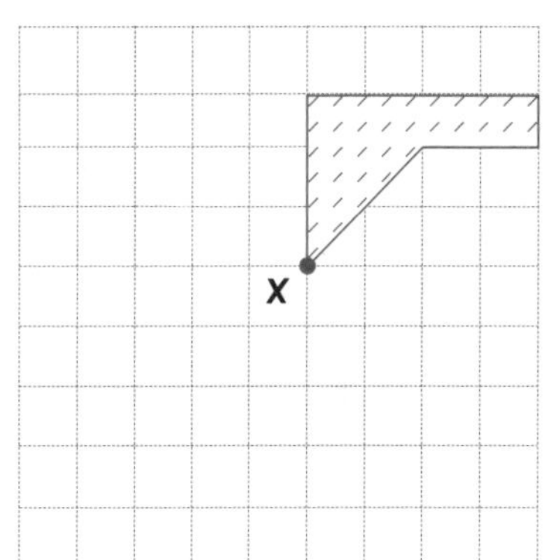

Q2 This is a scalene triangle PQR. The centre of rotation is the origin 0.

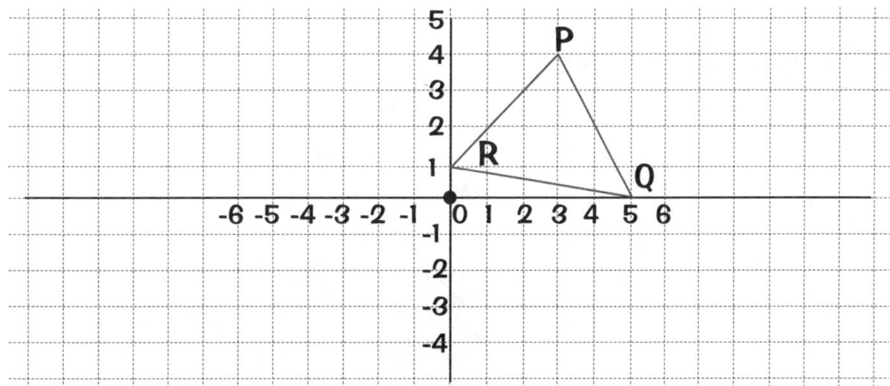

a) Write down the coordinates of...

P .... Q .... R ....

b) Rotate the triangle 90° anticlockwise about the origin 0. Label the new triangle P′ Q′ R′.

c) Write down the coordinates of ...

P′ .... Q′ .... R′ ....

A _½ turn clockwise_ is the same as a _½ turn anti-clockwise_ — and a _¼ turn clockwise_ is the same as a _¾ turn anti-clockwise_. Great fun, innit...

Questions on Reflection

Q1 Reflect each shape in the line x = 4.

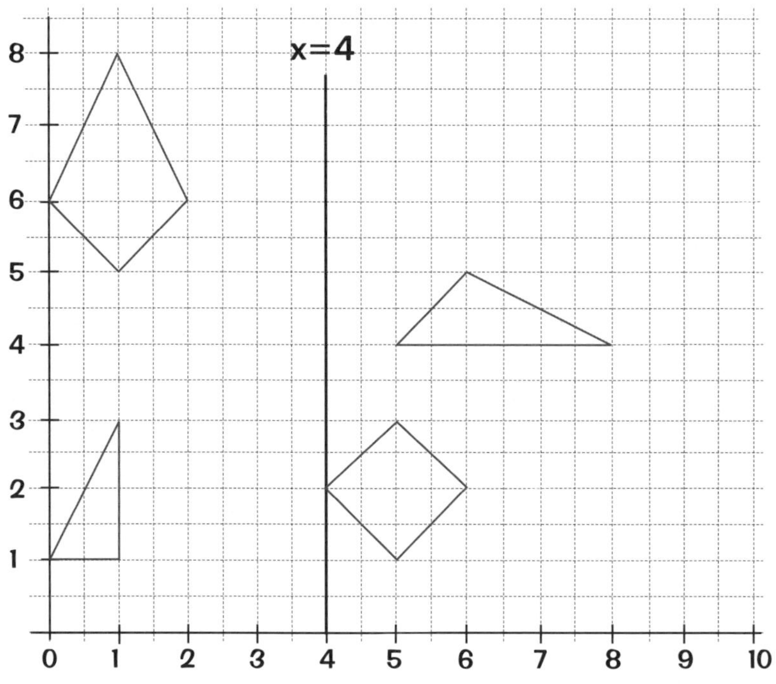

Q2 Reflect the shapes in the line y = x.

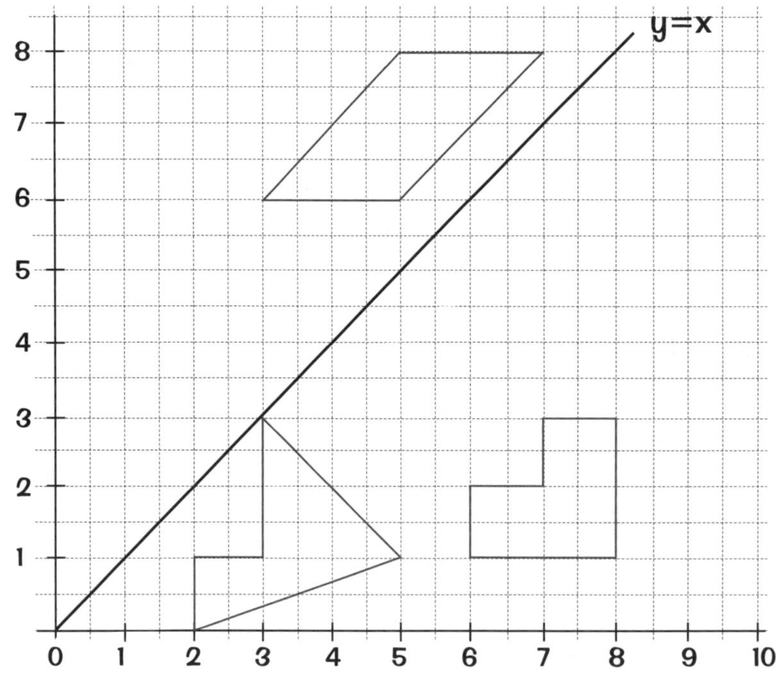

Nothing fancy here, is there — reflection's just mirror drawing really. And we've all done that before...

Questions on Enlargement

The scale factor is a fancy way of saying HOW MUCH BIGGER the enlargement is than the original.

Q1 Enlarge these figures with scale factor 2.

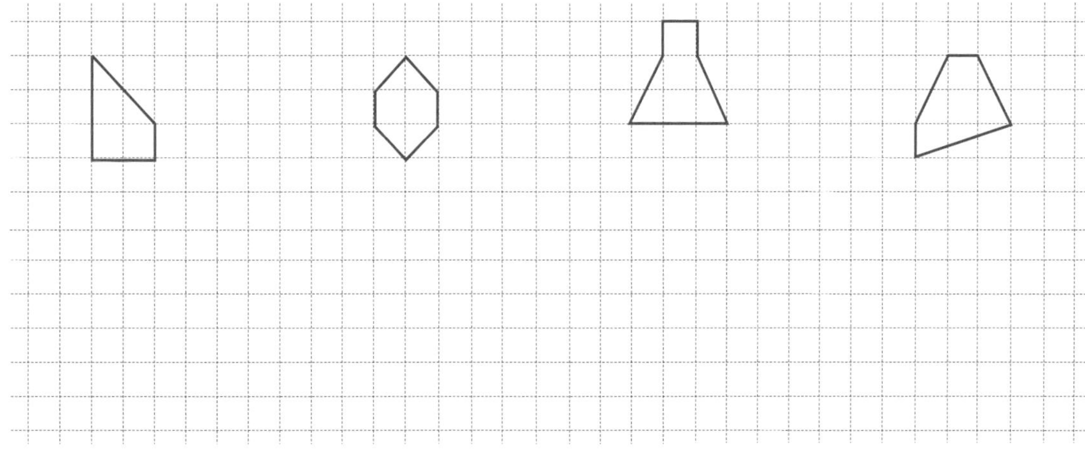

Q2 Enlarge this triangle by scale factor 3 with O as the centre of enlargement.

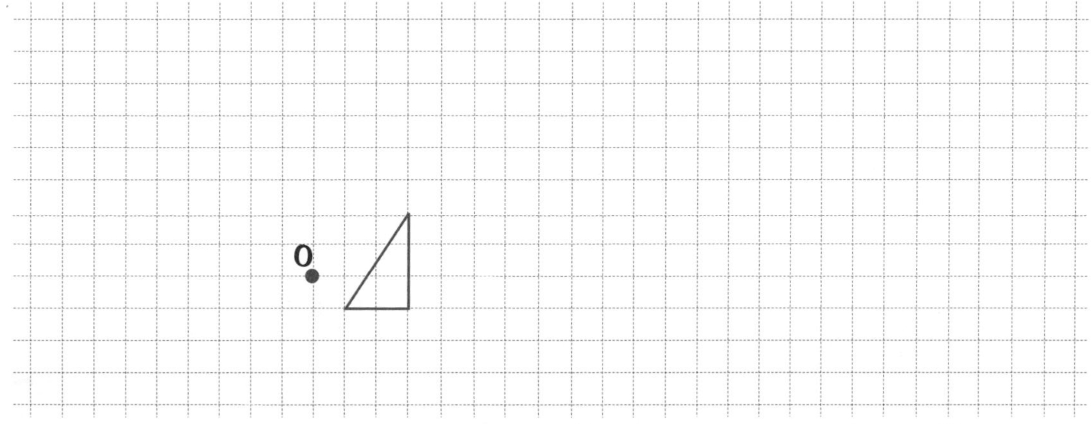

Q3 Enlarge each of these diagrams by scale factor 2, using the point (0,0) as the centre of enlargement.

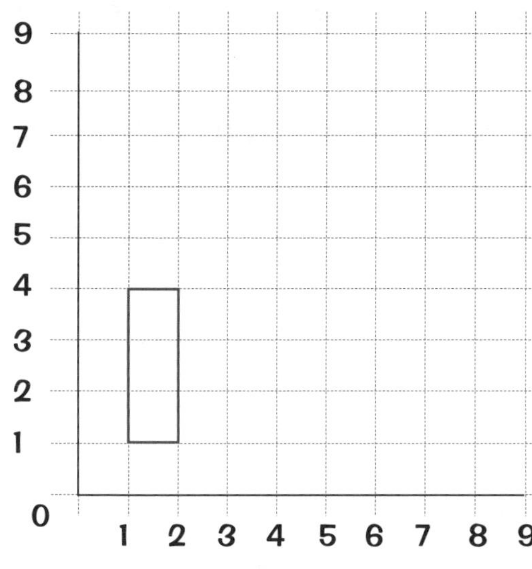

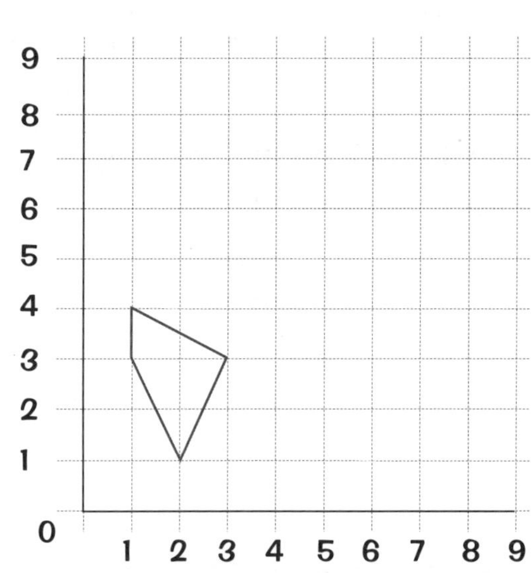

Questions on Symmetry

You've got a line of symmetry if you can draw a line across the picture so both sides fold exactly together. Have a go yourself — it'll be lots of fun...

Q1 These shapes have only one line of symmetry. Draw the line of symmetry using a dotted line.

a)

b)

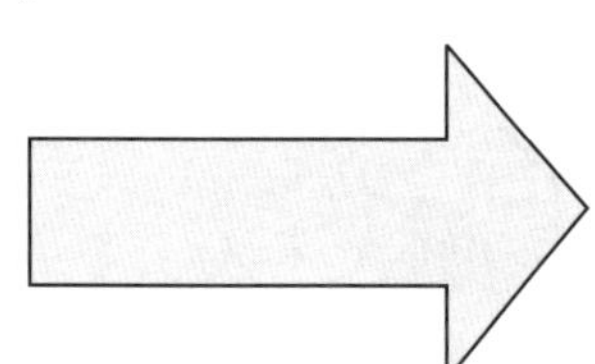

c)

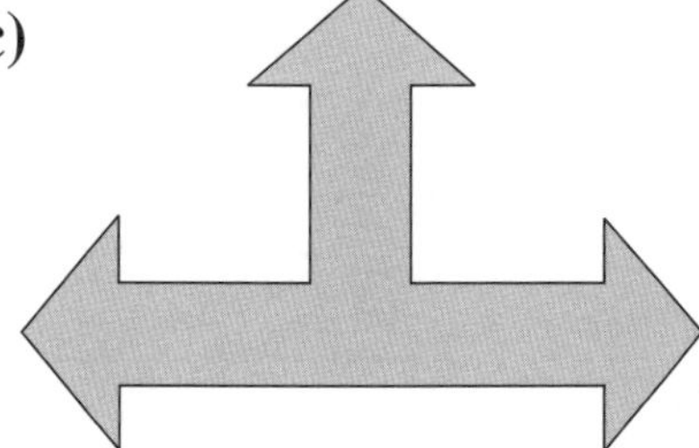

Q2 These shapes have more than one line of symmetry. Draw all the lines of symmetry using dotted lines.

a)

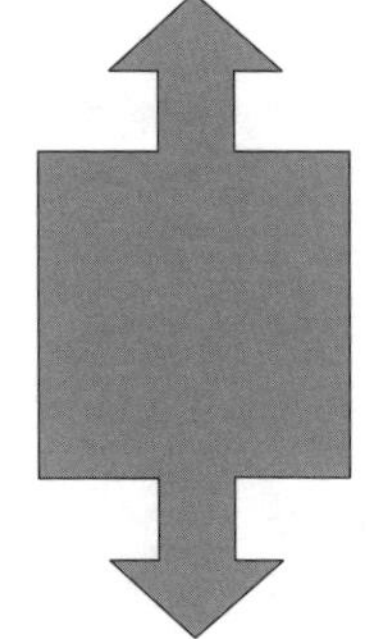

b)

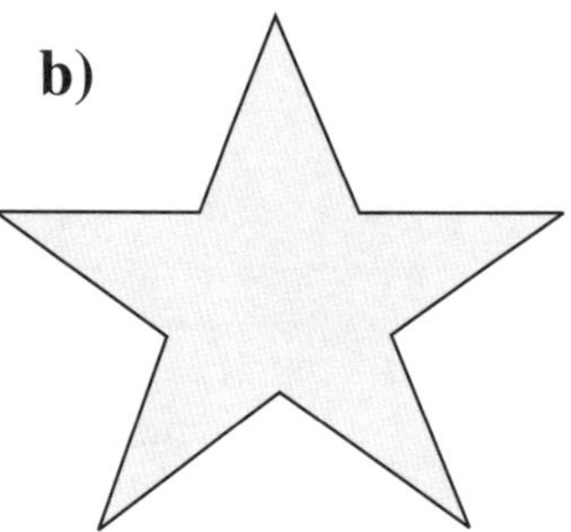

c)

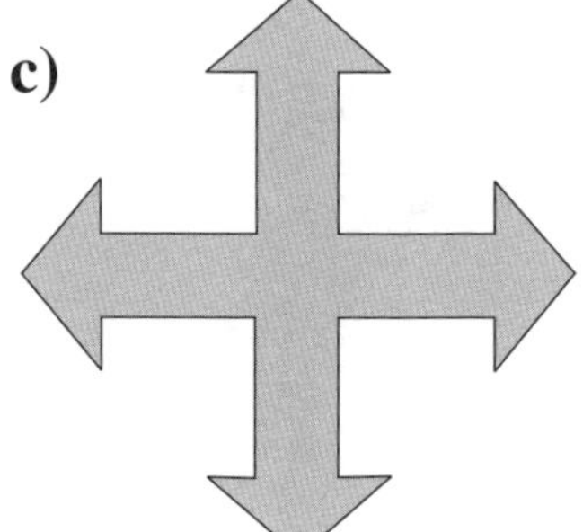

Q3 Some of the letters of the alphabet have lines of symmetry. Draw the lines of symmetry using dotted lines.

A B C D E F G H I J K L M

N O P Q R S T U V W X Y Z

Q4 Reflect the word in the X axis so that the X axis is the line of symmetry.
Reflect the word in the Y axis so that the Y axis is the line of symmetry.

a)

Y axis

COMPUTER

X axis

b)

Y axis

MOUSE

Questions on Symmetry

You can work out the rotational symmetry by sticking your pen in the middle of the shape and spinning your book round — how many times does the shape look the same before the book's back the right way up?

Q5 Write down the order of rotational symmetry of each of the following shapes:

a) 
square

b) 
rectangle

c) 
equilateral triangle

d) 
parallelogram

Q6 What is the order of rotational symmetry of the following capital letters?

a) 

b) T

c) S

d) C

Q7 Find the order of rotational symmetry for the following shapes:

a) 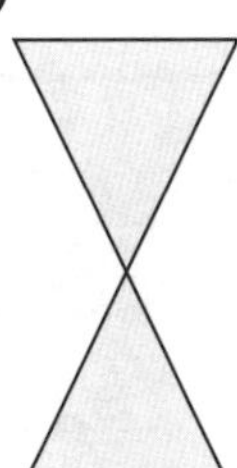

b) 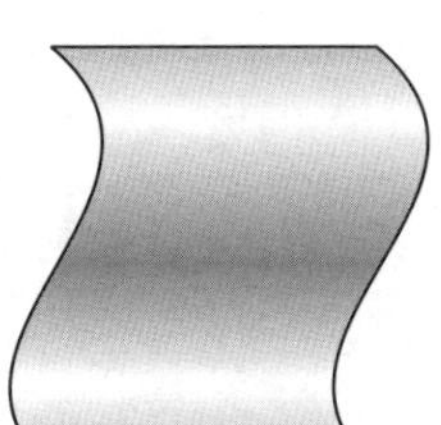

c) 

d) 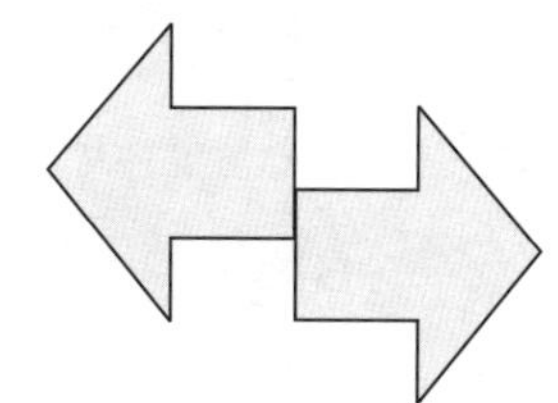

Q8 Which of the following shaded planes are planes of symmetry?

a) 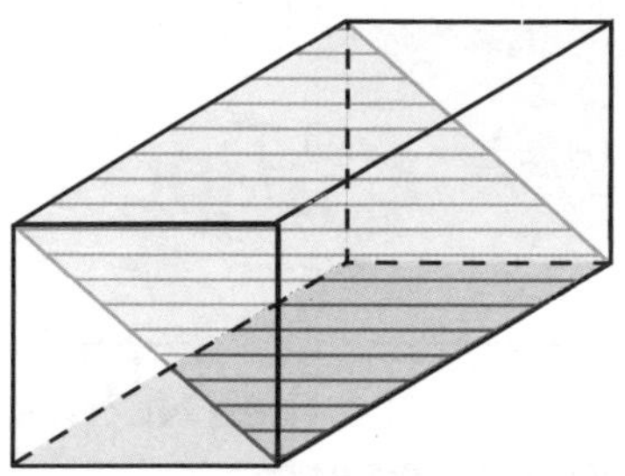

b) 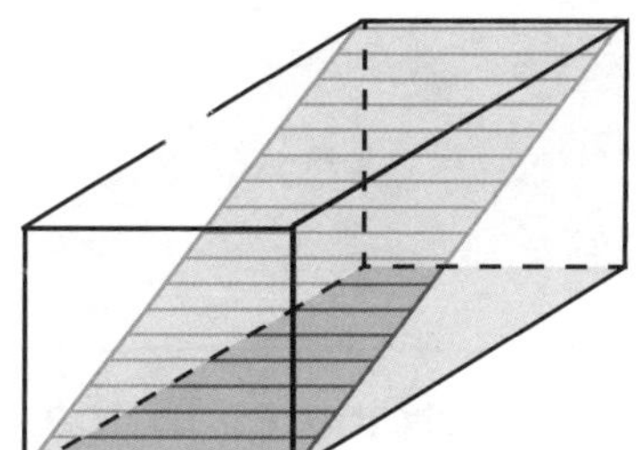

c) 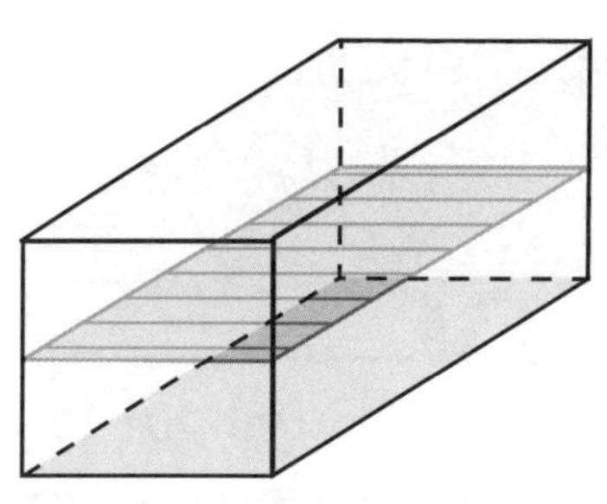

Questions on Coordinates

Q1 On the grid, plot the following points. Label the points A,B... Join the points with straight lines as you plot them.
A(0,8) B(4,6) C(4.5,6.5) D(5,6) E(9,8) F(8,5.5) G(5,5) H(8,4) I(7.5,2) J(6,2) K(5,4) L(4.5,3) M(4,4) N(3,2) O(1.5,2) P(1,4) Q(4,5) R(1,5.5) S(0,8).
You should see the outline of an insect. What is it?...............................

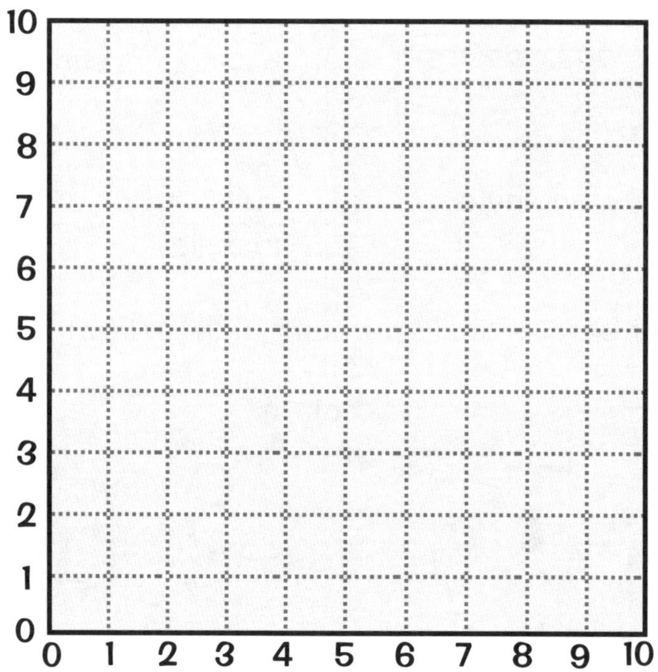

Q2 Write down the letter which is by each of the following points. The sentence it spells is the answer to question one.

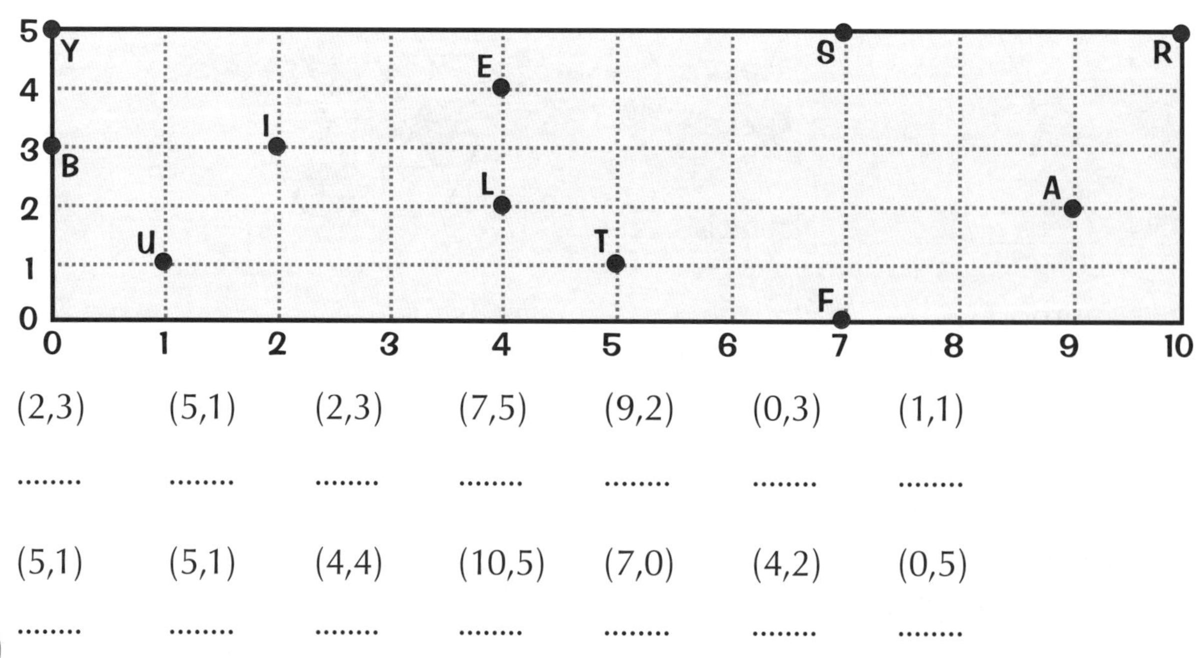

(2,3)	(5,1)	(2,3)	(7,5)	(9,2)	(0,3)	(1,1)
....	....	....	....	....	....	....
(5,1)	(5,1)	(4,4)	(10,5)	(7,0)	(4,2)	(0,5)
....	....	....	....	....	....	....

You've got to get your coordinates in the right order — or they're totally useless — you always go IN THE HOUSE then UP THE STAIRS.

Questions on Coordinates

Remember — 1) X comes before Y

2) X is a-cross (get it) the page. (Ah, the old ones are the best...)

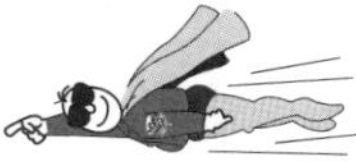

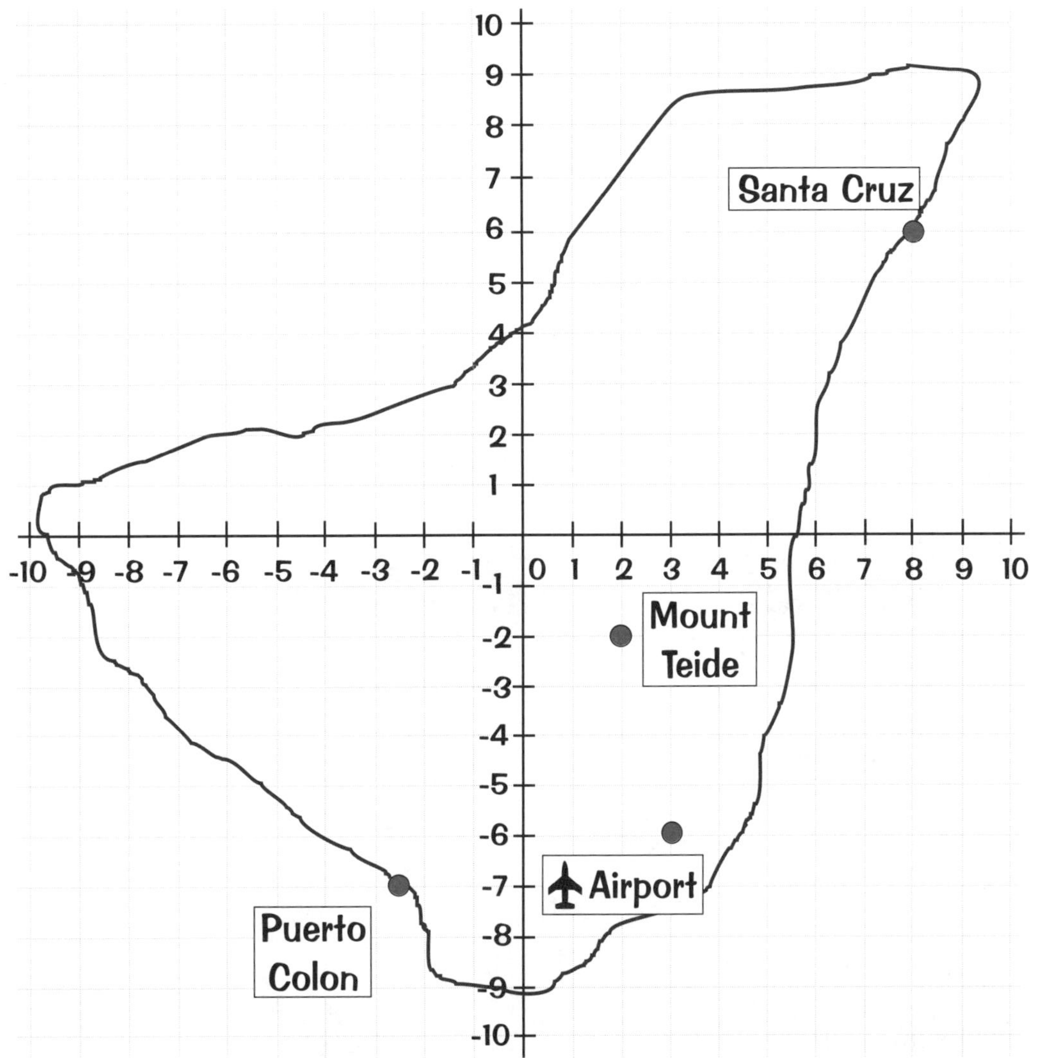

Q3 Here on the holiday island of Tenerife the sun always shines. Some important places are marked. What are their coordinates?
Airport (,) Mount Teide (,) Santa Cruz (,) Puerto Colon (,)

Q4 Use the following coordinates to locate these holiday spots. Put the place name on the map.
Las Americas (-4 , -6) El medano (5 , -4) Icod (-6 , 2) Laguna (3 , 7) Taganana (9 , 9)

Q5 A cable car takes you to the top of Mount Teide. It starts at (3 , 1) and ends at (2 , -2). Draw the cable car route on the map.

Questions on Graphs from Equations

With graphs from equations, you'll either get a straight line or a smooth curve — if you've got a point that looks wrong, it is wrong. So do it again.

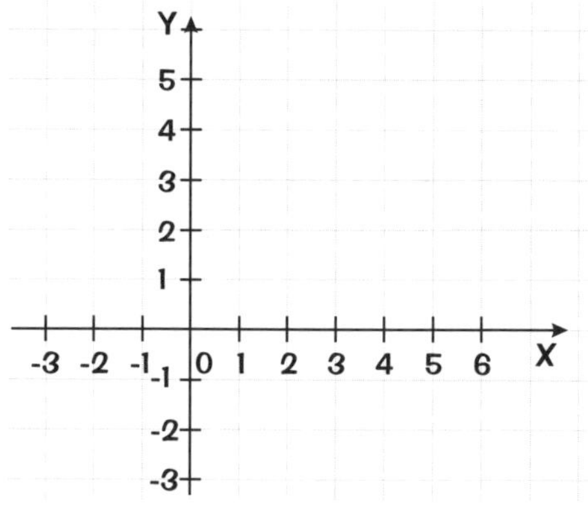

Q1 On the grid to the right draw the lines:

$y = 2$, $x = 5$, $y = 4$, $x = 0$, $y = -1$, $x = -2$.

Q2 a) To draw the line $y = x + 5$:

i) Complete this table

x	(y) x + 5
-3	2
-2	
-1	
0	
1	6
2	
3	

ii) Write the coordinates

Coordinates	
(-3,2)	....
	....
	....
	....
(1,6)	....
	....
	....

iii) Plot the points on the grid below and join them up.

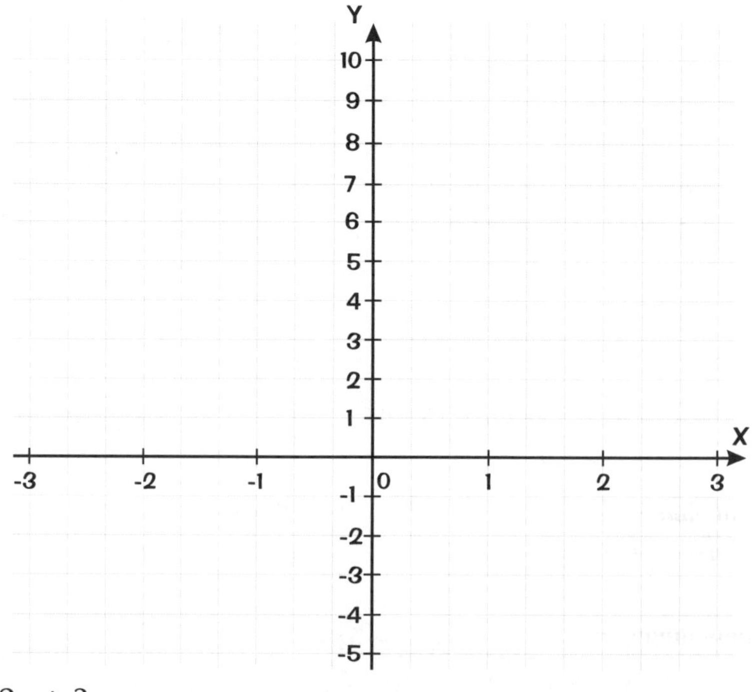

b) Repeat for the line $y = 2x + 3$.

Questions on Midpoints of Lines

Q1 Find the midpoint of the line AB, where A and B have coordinates:

a) A(2,3) B(4,5) ....

b) A(1,8) B(9,2) ....

c) A(0,11) B(12,11) ....

d) A(3,15) B(13,3) ....

e) A(6,6) B(0,0) ....

f) A(15,9) B(3,3) ....

ahh... nice'n'easy...

Q2 Find the midpoints of each of these lines:

a) Line PQ, where P has coordinates (1,5) and Q has coordinates (5,6). ....

b) Line AB, where A has coordinates (3,3) and B has coordinates (4,0). ....

c) Line RS, where R has coordinates (4,5) and S has coordinates (0,0). ....

d) Line PQ, where P has coordinates (1,3) and Q has coordinates (3,1). ....

e) Line GH, where G has coordinates (0,0) and H has coordinates (–6,–7). ....

Q3 Find the midpoint of each of the lines on this graph.

AB: ....

CD: ....

EF: ....

GH: ....

JK: ....

LM: ....

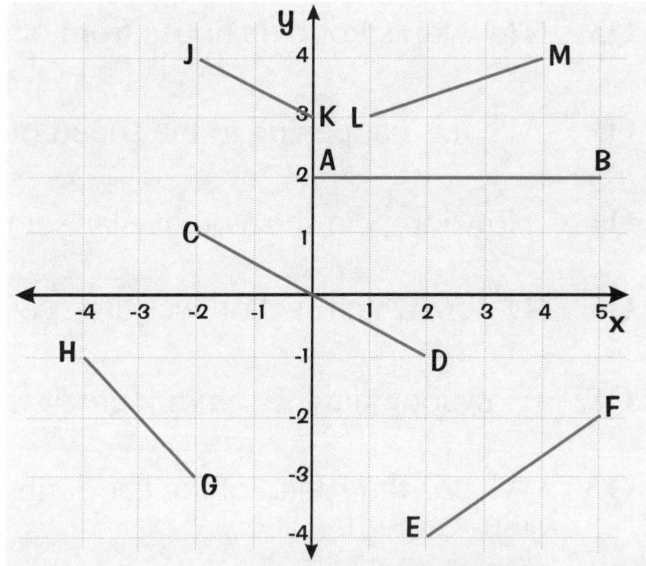

Questions on Travel Graphs

Say SOD IT every time you come to one of these questions... that'll help you remember the order of Speed, Distance and Time in the formula triangle.

The graph below shows Nicola's car journey from her house (0) to Alan's house (D) and back, picking up Robbie (B) on the way.

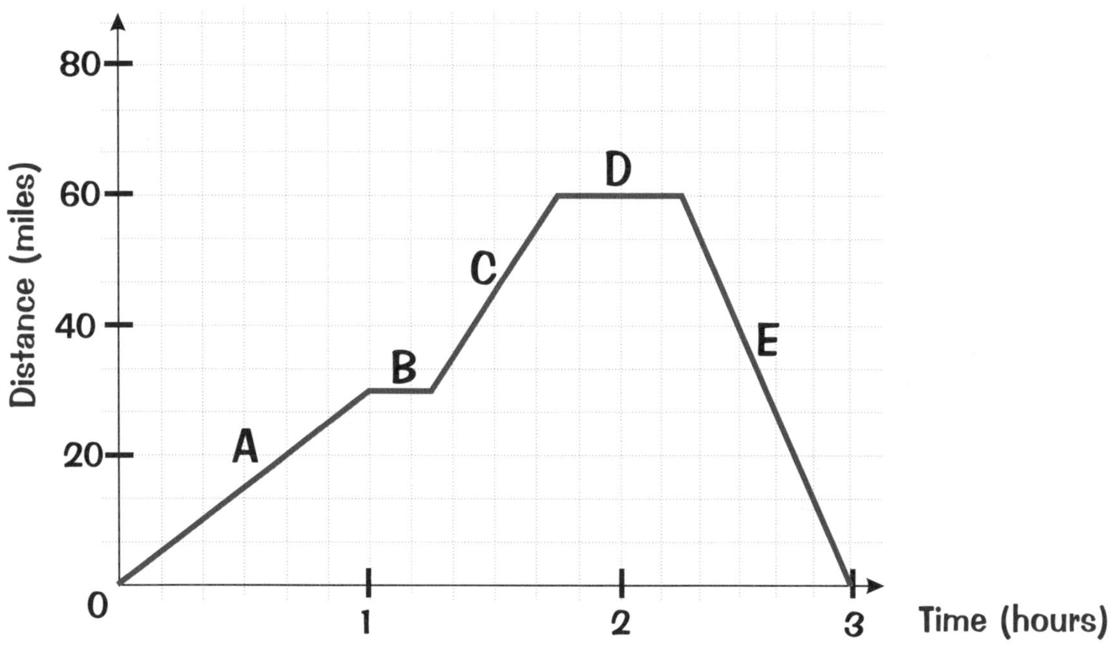

Q1 If Nicola started her trip at 10.00 am, at what time does she return home?

....

Q2 How far is Robbie's house from Nicola's? ....

Q3 What is happening to the speed of the car along section B? ....

Q4 How long did she stop at Alan's for? ....

Q5 During which section was the speed greatest? ....

Q6 How long did the return journey take? ....

Q7 What is the speed of the car during section E? ....

0904 - 1899

Serving suggestion only.

ISBN 1 84146 098 2

9 781841 460987

MAFW41

£4.50
(Retail Price)

Coordination Group Publications

www.cgpbooks.co.u

If you want the full picture on CGP and all
crazy books, then visit our groovy websi

Workbook

GCSE Mathematics Higher AQA

Letts

GCSE Success

Workbook

AQA Mathematics Higher

for the linear specification

Here are ten tips to help make your revision easier and the exams more stress free

1 Know your course

The ***Success*** series will help you to know your course as it covers the specifications for all exam boards. Each topic is covered in a double page spread with clearly labelled diagrams.

2 Make a revision timetable

Draw up a **plan** covering all topics and set a **realistic number of hours** for revision each week. Note the dates of your exams and leave a week or two before each exam for final revision.

3 Revise effectively

Short bursts of about **30 minutes** followed by a break work best. **Make your revision active** – summarise your notes, highlight key points, draw diagrams, use post-it notes, ask someone to test you.

4 Boost your memory

Find ways of learning that suit you best. Try using images, mnemonics, rhymes and colour-coding to trigger your memory. The ***Success Revision Guides*** break each topic into chunks and highlight key terms to aid recollection. The examiner's tips emphasise specific points you need to remember or give general advice for exam success.

5 Practice questions

To help you get used to the style of questions used in the exams, the ***Success Revision Guides*** feature a spread of practice questions at the end of each section. **Highlight the key words** in the question, **plan your response** and **ensure that your answer is relevant**. For further revision, an accompanying Workbook is available packed full of practice questions.

6 Think positive

Look back at your original plan from time to time, and **realise the progress you have made**. If there are areas that you find particularly difficult, ask your teacher for help.

7 Handling stress

Start preparing for the exams early. Take breaks from revising, exercise regularly, eat and sleep well. Remind yourself that it will all be over in a couple of months!

8 The week before

Allow time for **final revision** where you can go over essential or difficult points.

9 The night before

Look over a few points but **don't try to cram** lots of new information. Get all your equipment ready – pens, pencils, calculator, ruler, etc. Have an early night.

10 In the exam

Follow all instructions in the exam paper. **Read each question carefully** and ensure you **answer the question**. **Check the number of marks available** for each question and answer accordingly. Keep an eye on the time – make sure you answer the **correct number** of questions and **leave time** to read through your answers.

Shape, Space and Measures

Handling Data

Homework diary

TOPIC	SCORE
Fractions	/33
Percentages 1	/32
Percentages 2	/36
Fractions, decimals and percentages	/32
Approximations and using a calculator	/33
Ratio	/26
Indices	/46
Standard index form	/34
Recurring decimals and surds	/46
Direct and inverse proportion	/36
Upper and lower bounds of measurement	/29
Algebra	/38
Equations	/43
Equations and inequalities	/35
Further algebra and equations	/37
Straight line graphs	/20
Curved graphs	/24
Harder work on graphs	/22
Interpreting graphs	/19
Bearings, scale drawings and quadrilaterals	/20
Transformations 1	/22
Transformations 2	/21
Similarity and congruency	/25
Loci and coordinates in 3D	/21
Angle properties of circles	/23
Pythagoras' theorem	/31
Trigonometry 1	/27
Trigonometry 2	/32
Further trigonometry	/37
Measures and measurement	/34
Area of 2D shapes	/32
Volume of 3D shapes	/30
Further length, area and volume	/26
Vectors	/26
Collecting data	/18
Scatter diagrams and correlation	/21
Averages 1	/31
Averages 2	/22
Cumulative frequency graphs	/25
Histograms	/14
Probability	/33

Exam Hints

Planning and revising

- Mathematics should be revised **actively**. You should be doing **more than just reading**.
- Find out the dates of your first mathematics examination. Make an examination and revision timetable.
- After completing a topic in school, go through the topic again in the **GCSE Success Guide**. Copy out the **main points**, **results** and **formulae** into a notebook or use a **highlighter** to emphasise them.
- Try and write out the **key points** from **memory**. Check what you have written and see if there are any differences.
- Revise in short bursts of about **30 minutes**, followed by a **short break**.
- Learn **facts** from your exercise books, notebooks and the **Success Guide**. **Memorise** any formula you need to learn.
- Learn with a friend to make it easier and more fun!
- Do the **multiple choice** and **quiz-style** questions in this book and check your solutions to see how much you know.
- Once you feel **confident** that you know the topic, do the **GCSE**-style questions in this book. **Highlight** the key words in the question, **plan** your answer and then go back and **check** that you have answered the question.
- **Make a note** of any topics that you do not understand and **go back through** the notes again.

Different types of questions

- On the **GCSE Mathematics papers** you will have several types of questions:

  Calculate – In these questions you need to work out the answer. Remember that it is important to show full working out.

  Explain – These questions want you to explain, with a mathematical reason or calculation, what the answer is.

  Show – These questions usually require you to show, with mathematical justification, what the answer is.

  Write down or state – These questions require no explanation or working out.

  Prove – These questions want you to set out a concise logical argument, making the reasons clear.

  Deduce – These questions make use of an earlier answer to establish a result.

On the day

- **Follow the instructions** on the exam paper. Make sure that you understand what any **symbols** mean.
- Make sure that you **read the question** carefully so that you give the answer that an examiner wants.
- Always **show your working**; you may pick up some marks even if your final answer is wrong.
- Do **rough calculations** to check your answers and make sure that they are **reasonable**.
- When carrying out a calculation, **do not round the answer until the end**, otherwise your final answer will not be as accurate as is needed.
- Lay out your working **carefully** and **concisely**. Write down the calculations that you are going to make. You usually get marks for showing a **correct method**.
- Make your drawings and graphs **neat** and **accurate**.
- Know what is on the **formula sheet** and make sure that you **learn** those formulae that are not on it.
- If you cannot do a question, **leave it out** and **go back** to it at the end.
- Keep an eye on the time. Allow enough time to check through your answers.
- If you finish early, check through everything very carefully and try and fill in any gaps.
- Try and write something even if you are not sure about it. Leaving an empty space will score you no marks.

In this book, questions which may be answered with a calculator are marked with (C). All the other questions are intended to be answered without the use of a calculator.

Good luck!

Fractions

A Choose just one answer, a, b, c or d.

1 **Which one of these fractions is equivalent to $\frac{5}{9}$?** (1 mark)

a) $\frac{16}{27}$ b) $\frac{9}{18}$
c) $\frac{25}{45}$ d) $\frac{21}{36}$

2 **In a class of 24 students, $\frac{3}{8}$ wear glasses. How many students wear glasses?** (1 mark)

a) 9
b) 6
c) 3
d) 12

3 **Work out the answer to $1\frac{5}{9} - \frac{1}{3}$** (1 mark)

a) $\frac{1}{3}$ b) $1\frac{2}{9}$
c) $1\frac{4}{6}$ d) $\frac{4}{12}$

4 **Work out the answer to $\frac{2}{11} \times \frac{7}{9}$** (1 mark)

a) $\frac{14}{11}$ b) $\frac{14}{9}$
c) $\frac{14}{99}$ d) $\frac{2}{99}$

5 **Work out the answer to $\frac{3}{10} \div \frac{2}{3}$** (1 mark)

a) $\frac{9}{20}$ b) $\frac{6}{50}$
c) $\frac{6}{15}$ d) $\frac{4}{3}$

Score / 5

B Answer all parts of the questions.

1 **Work out the answers to the following.** (8 marks)

a) $\frac{2}{9} + \frac{1}{3}$ .... b) $\frac{7}{11} - \frac{1}{4}$ .... c) $\frac{4}{7} \times \frac{3}{8}$ ....

d) $\frac{9}{12} \div \frac{1}{4}$ .... e) $2\frac{5}{7} - 1\frac{1}{21}$ .... f) $\frac{4}{9} + \frac{3}{27}$ ....

g) $\frac{7}{12} \times 1\frac{1}{2}$ .... h) $1\frac{4}{7} \div \frac{7}{12}$ ....

2 **Arrange these fractions in order of size, smallest first.** (2 marks)

a) $\frac{2}{3}$ $\frac{4}{5}$ $\frac{1}{7}$ $\frac{3}{4}$ $\frac{1}{2}$ $\frac{3}{10}$

....

b) $\frac{5}{8}$ $\frac{1}{3}$ $\frac{2}{7}$ $\frac{1}{9}$ $\frac{3}{4}$ $\frac{2}{5}$ (2 marks)

....

3 **Decide whether these statements are true or false.**

a) $\frac{4}{5}$ of 20 is bigger than $\frac{6}{7}$ of 14. .... (1 mark)

b) $\frac{2}{9}$ of 27 is smaller than $\frac{1}{3}$ of 15. .... (1 mark)

4 **In a class of 32 pupils, $\frac{1}{8}$ are left-handed. How many students are not left-handed?** (1 mark)

....

Score / 15

Number FRACTIONS

C These are GCSE-style questions. Answer all parts of the questions. Show your workings (on separate paper if necessary) and include the correct units in your answers.

1 Gill says 'I've got three-fifths of a bottle of orange juice.'

Jonathan says 'I've got two-thirds of a bottle of orange juice and my bottle of orange juice is the same size as yours.'

Who has the most orange juice, Gill or Jonathan? Explain your answer. (2 marks)

....

....

2 Work out these.

a) $\frac{2}{3} + \frac{4}{5}$ .... (1 mark)

b) $3\frac{9}{11} - 2\frac{1}{3}$ .... (1 mark)

c) $\frac{2}{7} \times \frac{4}{9}$ .... (1 mark)

d) $\frac{3}{10} \div \frac{2}{5}$ .... (1 mark)

3 Charlotte's take home pay is £930. She gives her mother $\frac{1}{3}$ of this and spends $\frac{1}{5}$ of the £930 on going out.

What fraction of the £930 is left? Give your answer as a fraction in its lowest terms. (3 marks)

....

....

4 Reece works 15 hours per week. He earns £6 per hour. Reece saves $\frac{1}{5}$ of his earnings each week. He needs to save £120 for a holiday. How many weeks does it take Reece to save £120? (4 marks)

....

....

Score / 13

How well did you do? ✗ 1–12 Try again 13–19 Getting there 20–26 Good work 27–33 Excellent! ✓

For more information on this topic, see pages 8–9 of your Success Guide.

Percentages 1

A

Choose just one answer, a, b, c or d.

1 **Work out 10% of £850.** (1 mark)

a) £8.50
b) £0.85
c) £85
d) £42.50

2 **Work out 17.5% of £60.** (1 mark)

a) £9
b) £15
c) £10.50
d) £12.50

3 **In a survey, 17 people out of 25 said they preferred type A cola. What percentage of people preferred type A cola?** (1 mark)

a) 68% b) 60%
c) 72% d) 75%

4 **A CD player costs £60 in a sale after a reduction of 20%. What was the original price of the CD player?** (C) (1 mark)

a) £48
b) £70
c) £72
d) £75

5 **A new car was bought for £15 000. Two years later it was sold for £12 000. What is the percentage loss?** (C) (1 mark)

a) 25%
b) 20%
c) 80%
d) 70%

Score /5

B

Answer all parts of the questions.

1 **Work out the answers to the following.** (4 marks)

a) 20% of £60 .... b) 30% of £150 ....
c) 5% of £80 .... d) 12.5% of 40 g ....

2 **Colin earns £25 500 a year. This year he has a 3% pay rise. How much does Colin now earn?** (C)

£ .... (2 marks)

3 **A coat costs £140. In a sale it is reduced to £85. What is the percentage reduction?** (C) (2 marks)

.... %

4 **Lucinda scored 58 out of 75 in a test. What percentage did she get?** (C) (2 marks)

.... %

5 **The cost for a ticket for a pop concert has risen by 15% to £23. What was the original price of the ticket?** (C) (2 marks)

£ ....

6 **The price of a CD player has been reduced by 20% in a sale. It now costs £180. What was the original price?** (C) (2 marks)

£ ....

7 **12 out of 30 people wear glasses. What percentage wear glasses?** (C) (2 marks)

.... %

Score /16

(C) *Indicates that a calculator may be used*

C

These are GCSE-style questions. Answer all parts of the questions. Show your workings (on separate paper if necessary) and include the correct units in your answers.

1 The price of a television set is £175 plus VAT. VAT is charged at a rate of 17.5%. (C)

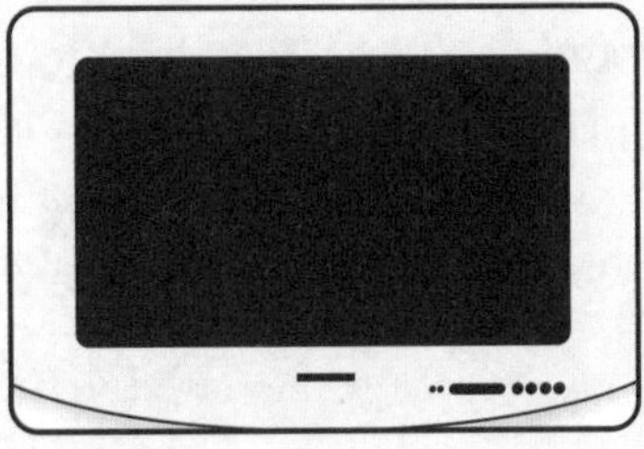

a) Work out the amount of VAT charged. (2 marks)

....

b) In a sale, normal prices are reduced by 15%. The normal price of a washing machine is £399.

Work out the sale price of the washing machine. (3 marks)

....

2 A car is bought for £17 900. Two years later it is sold for £14 320. Work out the percentage loss. (C) (3 marks)

....

3 In a sale, all normal prices are reduced by 18%. In the sale, Suki pays £57.40 for a jacket.

Calculate the normal price of the jacket. (C) (3 marks)

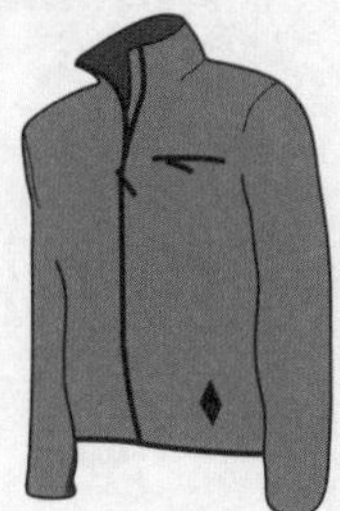

....

Score /11

How well did you do? 1–7 Try again 8–17 Getting there 18–26 Good work 27–32 Excellent!

For more information on this topic, see pages 12–13 of your Success Guide.

Percentages 2

A

Choose just one answer, a, b, c or d.

1 **£2000 is invested in a savings account. Compound interest is paid at 2.1%. How much interest is paid after 2 years?** (C) (1 mark)

a) £4
b) £5.20
c) £2.44
d) £84.88

2 **A bike was bought for £120. Each year it depreciated by 10%. What was the bike worth 2 years later?** (C) (1 mark)

a) £97.20
b) £98
c) £216
d) £110

3 **Roberto has £5000 in his savings account. Simple interest is paid at 3%. How much does he have in his savings account at the end of the year?** (C) (1 mark)

a) £4850
b) £5010
c) £5150
d) £5140.50

4 **Lily earns £23 500. National Insurance (NI) is deducted at 9%. How much NI must she pay?** (C) (1 mark)

a) £2250
b) £2115
c) £2200
d) £21 385

Score /4

B

Answer all parts of the questions.

1 **A meal costs £143. VAT at 17.5% is added to the price of the meal. What is the final price of the meal?** (C) (2 marks)

£ ....

2 **VAT of 5% is added to a gas bill of £72. Find the total amount to be paid.** (C) (2 marks)

£ ....

3 **A motorbike is bought for £9000. Each year it depreciates in value by 12%. Work out the value of the motorbike after 2 years.** (C) (2 marks)

£ ....

4 **Scarlett has £6200 in her savings account. If compound interest is paid at 2.7% p.a., how much interest will she earn after 3 years?** (C) (2 marks)

£ ....

5 **A house was bought for £112 000. After the first year the price had increased by 8%, during the second year it increased in price by a further 12%. What is the house now worth?** (C) (2 marks)

£ ....

6 **Petrol cost 113.7 pence per litre. The price increased by 2%. Six months later it increased again, by 5%. How much does a litre of petrol now cost?** (C) (2 marks)

.... pence

Score /12

(C) *Indicates that a calculator may be used*

C

These are GCSE-style questions. Answer all parts of the questions. Show your workings (on separate paper if necessary) and include the correct units in your answers.

1 a) Work out 40% of £2500. (2 marks)

....

b) Find the simple interest on £2000 invested for 2 years at 4% per year. (3 marks)

....

2 £7000 is invested for 3 years at 6% compound interest. Work out the total interest earned over the three years. (C) (3 marks)

....

3 Nigel opened an account with £450 at his local bank. After one year, the bank paid him interest. He then had £465.75 in his account.

a) Work out, as a percentage, his local bank's interest rate. (C) (3 marks)

....

b) Sarah opened an account at the same bank as Nigel. She invested £700 for 2 years at 4% compound interest. How much money did she have in her account after 2 years? (3 marks)

....

4 Sara buys a car for £14 000. Each year the value of the car depreciates by 12%. Work out the value of the car three years after she bought it. (3 marks)

....

5 A vintage bottle of champagne was valued at £42 000 on 1 January 2005.
The value of the champagne is predicted to increase at a rate of R% per annum. (C)
The predicted value, £V, of the champagne after n years is given by the formula

$$V = 42000 \times (1.045)^n$$

a) Write down the value of R. (1 mark)

....

b) Use your calculator to find the predicted value of the champagne after 8 years. (2 marks)

Score / 20

How well did you do? ✗ 1–8 Try again 9–15 Getting there 16–27 Good work 28–36 Excellent! ✓

For more information on this topic, see pages 12–15 of your Success Guide.

Fractions, decimals and percentages

A

Choose just one answer, a, b, c or d.

1 What is $\frac{3}{5}$ as a percentage? (1 mark)

a) 30% b) 25%
c) 60% d) 75%

2 What is $\frac{2}{3}$ written as a decimal? (1 mark)

a) 0.77 b) $0.\dot{6}$
c) 0.665 d) 0.6

3 What is the smallest value in this list of numbers? 29% 0.4 $\frac{3}{4}$ $\frac{1}{8}$ (1 mark)

a) 29% b) 0.4 c) $\frac{3}{4}$ d) $\frac{1}{8}$

4 What is the largest value in this list of numbers? $\frac{4}{5}$ 80% $\frac{2}{3}$ 0.9 (1 mark)

a) $\frac{4}{5}$ b) 80%
c) $\frac{2}{3}$ d) 0.9

5 Change $\frac{5}{8}$ into a decimal. (1 mark)

a) 0.625 b) 0.425
c) 0.125 d) 0.725

Score / 5

B

Answer all parts of the questions.

1 The table shows equivalent fractions, decimals and percentages. Fill in the gaps. (2 marks)

Fraction	Decimal	Percentage
$\frac{2}{5}$		
		5%
	$0.\dot{3}$	
	0.04	
		25%
$\frac{1}{8}$		

2 Put these cards in order of size, smallest first. (6 marks)

0.37 | 30% | $\frac{3}{8}$ | $\frac{1}{3}$ | 92% | $\frac{1}{2}$ | 0.62

☐ ☐ ☐ ☐ ☐ ☐ ☐

3 Decide whether these calculations give the same answer for this question: Increase £40 by 20%

Jack says: Multiply 40 by 1.2

Hannah says: Work out 10%, double it and then add 40

Explain your reasoning.

.... (2 marks)

....

Score / 10

C **These are GCSE-style questions. Answer all parts of the questions. Show your workings (on separate paper if necessary) and include the correct units in your answers.**

1 **Write this list of seven numbers in order of size. Start with the smallest number.** (3 marks)

25% $\frac{1}{3}$ 0.27 $\frac{2}{5}$ 0.571 72% $\frac{1}{8}$

....

2 **Philippa is buying a new television. She sees three different advertisements for the same television set.** (C)

Ed's Electricals
TV normal price
£250
Sale 10% off

Sheila's Bargains
TV £185 plus
VAT at $17\frac{1}{2}$%

GITA's TV SHOP
Normal price
£290
Sale: $\frac{1}{5}$ off normal price

a) Find the maximum and minimum prices that Philippa could pay for a television set. (7 marks)

Maximum price = ...

Minimum price = ...

b) The price of the television in a fourth shop is £235. This includes VAT at 17.5%. Work out the cost of the television before VAT was added. (3 marks)

....

3 A sundial is being sold in two different garden centres. The cost of the sundial is £89.99 in both garden centres. Both garden centres have a promotion.

Gardens are Us — Sundial 22% off

Rosebushes — Sundial $\frac{1}{4}$ off

In which garden centre is the sundial cheaper? Explain your reasoning. (2 marks)

....

....

4 **Place these fractions in order of size, smallest first.** (2 marks)

$\frac{2}{3}$, $\frac{1}{10}$, $\frac{5}{8}$, $\frac{3}{5}$, $\frac{9}{10}$

.............., ..., ..., ..., ...

Score / 17

How well did you do? ✗ 1–8 Try again 9–14 Getting there 15–23 Good work 24–32 Excellent! ✓

For more information on this topic, see page 16 & 12–13 of your Success Guide.

Approximations & using a calculator

A

Choose just one answer, a, b, c or d.

1 Estimate the answer to the calculation 27×41 (1 mark)

a) 1107 b) 1200
c) 820 d) 1300

2 A carton of orange juice costs 79p. Estimate the cost of 402 cartons of orange juice. (1 mark)

a) £350
b) £250
c) £400
d) £320

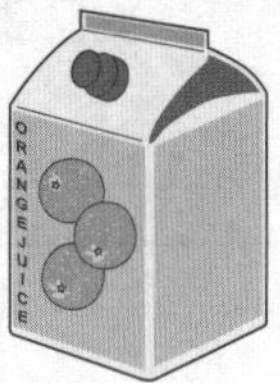

3 A school trip is organised. 396 pupils are going on the trip. Each coach seats 50 pupils. Approximately how many coaches are needed? (1 mark)

a) 12 b) 5
c) 8 d) 10

4 Estimate the answer to the calculation $\frac{(4.2)^2}{107}$ (1 mark)

a) 16 b) 1.6
c) 0.16 d) 160

5 Round 5379 to 3 significant figures. (1 mark)

a) 538 b) 5370
c) 537 d) 5380

Score / 5

B

Answer all parts of the questions.

1 Decide whether each statement is true or false. (4 marks)

a) 2.742 rounded to 3 significant figures is 2.74 ....

b) 2793 rounded to 2 significant figures is 27 ....

c) 32 046 rounded to 1 significant figure is 40 000 ....

d) 14.637 rounded to 3 significant figures is 14.6 ....

2 Round each of the numbers in the calculations to 1 significant figure then work out an approximate answer.

a) $\frac{(32.9)^2}{9.1}$ .... (1 mark)

b) $\frac{(906 \div 31.4)^2}{7.1 + 2.9}$ .... (1 mark)

3 Work these out on your calculator. Give your answers to 3 s.f.  (4 marks)

a) $\frac{4.2(3.6 + 5.1)}{2 - 1.9}$ ....

b) $6 \times \sqrt{\frac{12.1}{4.2}}$ ....

c) $\frac{12^5}{4.3 \times 9.15}$ ....

d) $\frac{4\cos 30° + 2\sin 60°}{4^3}$ ....

Score / 10

Ⓒ *Indicates that a calculator may be used*

C These are GCSE-style questions. Answer all parts of the questions. Show your workings (on separate paper if necessary) and include the correct units in your answers.

1 Use your calculator to work out the value of this. (C)

$$\frac{\sqrt{(4.9^2 + 6.3)}}{2.1 \times 0.37}$$

Give your answer correct to 3 significant figures. (3 marks)

....

2 a) Use your calculator to work out the value of this. (C)

$$\frac{27.1 \times 6.2}{38.2 - 9.9}$$

Write down all the figures on your calculator display. (2 marks)

....

b) Round each of the numbers in the above calculation to 1 significant figure and obtain an approximate answer. (3 marks)

....

3 Circle the best estimate for each of these calculations. (4 marks)

	A	B	C
a) 52×204	700	10000	1000
b) $904 \div 31$	320	30	300
c) 1.279×4.9	4	6	8
d) $2795 \div 19.1$	150	195	102

4 Estimate the answer to the following. (3 marks)

$$\frac{4.9\,(6.1^2 + 2.8^2)}{10.02 \times 5}$$

....

5 Use your calculator to work out the value of the following.

a) Write down all the figures on your calculator display. (2 marks)

$$\frac{(12.6 + 9.41)^2}{2.7 - 1.06}$$

....

b) Round your answer to 3 significant figures. (1 mark)

....

Score / 18

How well did you do? ✗ 1–11 Try again 12–19 Getting there 20–27 Good work 28–33 Excellent! ✓

For more information on this topic, see pages 17–19 of your Success Guide.

Ratio

A Choose just one answer, a, b, c or d.

1 **What is the ratio 6 : 18 written in its simplest form?** (1 mark)

a) 3 : 1 b) 3 : 9
c) 1 : 3 d) 9 : 3

2 **Write the ratio 200 : 500 in the form 1 : *n*.** (1 mark)

a) 1 : 50 b) 1 : 5
c) 1 : 25 d) 1 : 2.5

3 **If £140 is divided in the ratio 3 : 4, what is the size of the larger share?** (1 mark)

a) £45 b) £60
c) £80 d) £90

4 **A recipe for 4 people needs 800 g of flour. How much flour is needed for 6 people?** (1 mark)

a) 12 g b) 120 g
c) 12 kg d) 1200 g

5 **If 9 oranges cost £1.08, how much would 14 similar oranges cost?** (1 mark)

a) £1.50 b) £1.68
c) £1.20 d) £1.84

Score /5

B Answer all parts of the questions.

1 **Write down each of the following ratios in the form 1 : *n*.**

a) 10 : 15 .... (1 mark)
b) 6 : 10 .... (1 mark)
c) 9 : 27 .... (1 mark)

2 **Seven bottles of lemonade have a total capacity of 1680 ml. Work out the total capacity for five similar bottles.**

.... ml (1 mark)

3 **a) Increase £4.10 in the ratio 2 : 5** .... (1 mark)

b) Decrease 120 g in the ratio 5 : 2 .... (1 mark)

4 **Mrs London inherited £55 000. She divided the money between her children in the ratio 3 : 3 : 5. How much did the child with the largest share receive?** (2 marks)

£ ....

5 **It takes 6 people 3 days to dig and lay a cable. How long would it take 4 people? (All people work at the same rate.)** (2 marks)

.... days

Score /10

C These are GCSE-style questions. Answer all parts of the questions. Show your workings (on separate paper if necessary) and include the correct units in your answers.

1 13 metres of fabric costs £107.12. Work out the cost of 25 metres of the same fabric. (2 marks)

£ ....

2 Vicky and Tracy share £14 400 in the ratio 4 : 5. Work out how much each of them receives.

Vicky: £ .... Tracy: £ .... (3 marks)

3 James uses these ingredients to make 12 buns.

50 g butter
40 g sugar
2 eggs
45 g flour
15 ml milk

James wants to make 18 similar buns. Write down how much of each ingredient he needs for 18 buns. (3 marks)

butter .... g sugar .... g

eggs .... flour .... g

milk .... ml

4 It takes 3 builders 16 days to build a wall. All the builders work at the same rate. How long would it take 8 builders to build a wall the same size? (3 marks)

.... days

Score /11

How well did you do? ✗ 1–6 Try again 7–12 Getting there 13–18 Good work 19–26 Excellent! ✓

For more information on this topic, see pages 20–21 of your Success Guide.

Indices

A

Choose just one answer, a, b, c or d.

1 **In index form, what is the value of $8^3 \times 8^{11}$?** (1 mark)

a) 8^{14} b) 8^{33}
c) 64^{14} d) 64^{33}

2 **In index form, what is the value of $(4^2)^3$?** (1 mark)

a) 12^2 b) 4^5
c) 4^6 d) 16^6

3 **What is the value of 5^0?** (1 mark)

a) 5 b) 0
c) 25 d) 1

4 **What is the value of 5^{-2}?** (1 mark)

a) $\frac{1}{25}$ b) -5
c) 25 d) -25

5 **What is the value of $7^{-12} \div 7^2$ written in index form?** (1 mark)

a) 7^{10} b) 7^{-14}
c) 7^{14} d) 7^{-10}

Score / 5

B

Answer all parts of the questions.

1 **Decide whether each of these expressions is true or false.**

	True	False	
a) $a^4 \times a^5 = a^{20}$	☐	☐	(1 mark)
b) $2a^4 \times 3a^2 = 5a^8$	☐	☐	(1 mark)
c) $10a^6 \div 2a^4 = 5a^2$	☐	☐	(1 mark)
d) $20a^4b^2 \div 10a^5b = 2a^{-1}b$	☐	☐	(1 mark)
e) $(2a^3)^3 = 6a^9$	☐	☐	(1 mark)
f) $4^0 = 1$	☐	☐	(1 mark)

2 **Simplify the following expressions.** (4 marks)

a) $(5a)^0 =$ .... b) $(2a^2)^4 =$ ....

c) $12a^4 \div 16a^7 =$ .... d) $(3a^2b^3)^3 =$ ....

3 **Write these using negative indices.** (3 marks)

a) $\frac{4}{x^2} =$ .... b) $\frac{a^2}{b^3} =$ .... c) $\frac{3}{y^5} =$ ....

4 **Evaluate these expressions.** (4 marks)

a) $25^{-\frac{1}{2}}$ b) $49^{\frac{3}{2}}$ c) $(\frac{4}{5})^{-2}$ d) $81^{\frac{-3}{4}}$

....

Score / 17

INDICES

Number

C These are GCSE-style questions. Answer all parts of the questions. Show your workings (on separate paper if necessary) and include the correct units in your answers.

1 Simplify these.

a) $p^3 \times p^4$ .... (1 mark)

b) $\frac{n^3}{n^7}$ .... (1 mark)

c) $\frac{a^3 \times a^4}{a}$ .... (1 mark)

d) $\frac{12a^2b}{3a}$ .... (1 mark)

2 Work out these. (5 marks)

a) 3^0 .... b) 9^{-2} .... c) $3^4 \times 2^3$ ....

d) $64^{\frac{2}{3}}$ .... e) $125^{-\frac{1}{3}}$ ....

3 a) Evaluate the following.

i) 8^0 .... (1 mark)

ii) 4^{-2} .... (1 mark)

iii) $\left(\frac{4}{9}\right)^{-\frac{1}{2}}$ .... (1 mark)

b) Write this as a single power of 5.

$\frac{5^7 \times 5^3}{(5^2)^3}$ .... (2 marks)

4 Evaluate the following, giving your answers as fractions.

a) 5^{-3} .... (1 mark)

b) $(\frac{2}{3})^{-2}$ .... (1 mark)

c) $(8)^{-\frac{2}{3}}$ .... (1 mark)

5 Simplify these, leaving your answer in the form 2^n.

a) $4^{-\frac{1}{2}}$ .... (1 mark)

b) $\frac{2^7 \times 2^9}{2^{-4}}$ .... (1 mark)

c) $(\sqrt{2})^5$ .... (1 mark)

6 Simplify these expressions. (4 marks)

a) $(5x)^{-3}$ b) $(y^5)^4$ c) $(3y)^{-3}$ d) $(2xy^3)^5$

....

Score /24

How well did you do? ✗ 1–12 Try again 13–23 Getting there 24–36 Good work 37–46 Excellent! ✓

For more information on this topic, see pages 22–23 of your Success Guide.

Standard index form

A

Choose just one answer, a, b, c or d.

1 **What is this number written in standard form?**
42 710 (1 mark)

a) 42.71×10^3 b) 4.271×10^4
c) 4271.0×10 d) 427.1×10^2

2 **What is 6.4×10^{-3} written as an ordinary number?** (1 mark)

a) 6400 b) 0.0064
c) 64 d) 0.064

3 **What is 2.7×10^4 written as an ordinary number?** (1 mark)

a) 27 000 b) 0.27
c) 270 d) 0.000 27

4 **What would $(4 \times 10^9) \times (2 \times 10^6)$ worked out and written in standard form be?** (1 mark)

a) 8×10^{54} b) 8×10^{15}
c) 8×10^3 d) 6×10^{15}

5 **What would $(3 \times 10^4)^2$ worked out and written in standard form be?** (1 mark)

a) 9×10^6 b) 9×10^8
c) 9×10^9 d) 3×10^8

Score /5

B

Answer all parts of the questions.

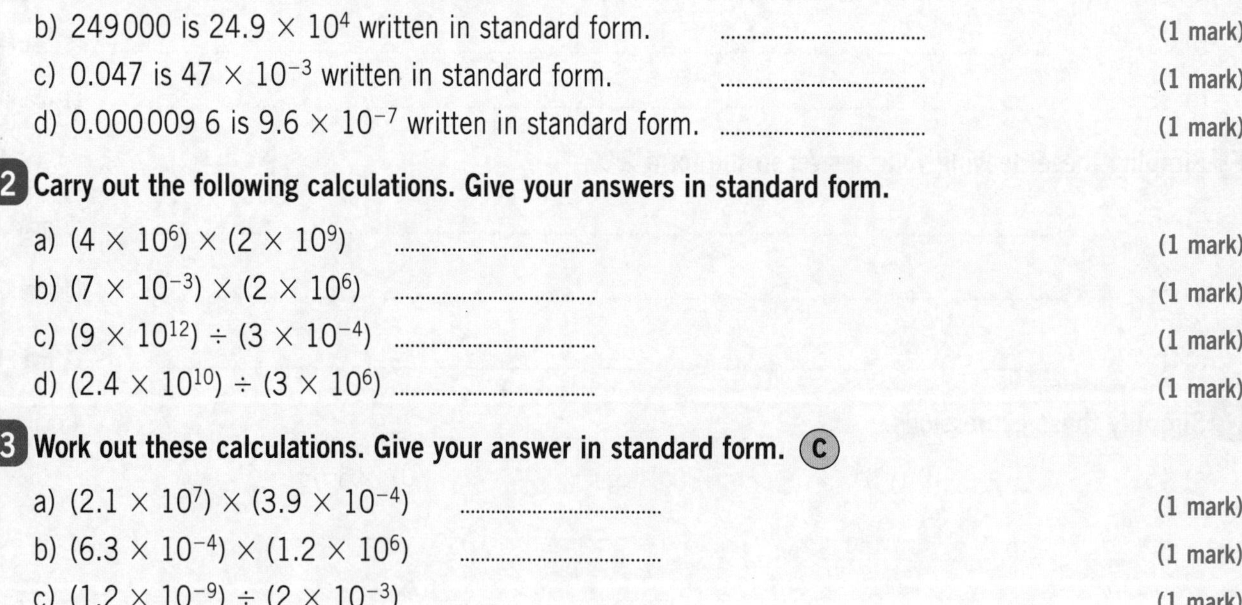

1 **Decide whether each of the statements is true or false.**

a) 4710 is 4.71×10^3 written in standard form. .... (1 mark)
b) 249 000 is 24.9×10^4 written in standard form. .... (1 mark)
c) 0.047 is 47×10^{-3} written in standard form. .... (1 mark)
d) 0.000 009 6 is 9.6×10^{-7} written in standard form. .... (1 mark)

2 **Carry out the following calculations. Give your answers in standard form.**

a) $(4 \times 10^6) \times (2 \times 10^9)$ .... (1 mark)
b) $(7 \times 10^{-3}) \times (2 \times 10^6)$ .... (1 mark)
c) $(9 \times 10^{12}) \div (3 \times 10^{-4})$ .... (1 mark)
d) $(2.4 \times 10^{10}) \div (3 \times 10^6)$ .... (1 mark)

3 **Work out these calculations. Give your answer in standard form.** (C)

a) $(2.1 \times 10^7) \times (3.9 \times 10^{-4})$ .... (1 mark)
b) $(6.3 \times 10^{-4}) \times (1.2 \times 10^6)$ .... (1 mark)
c) $(1.2 \times 10^{-9}) \div (2 \times 10^{-3})$ .... (1 mark)
d) $(8.9 \times 10^6) \div (4 \times 10^{-2})$ .... (1 mark)

4 **The mass of an atom is 2×10^{-23} grams.** (3 marks)

What is the total mass of 9×10^{15} of these atoms? .... (C)

Score /15

(C) *Indicates that a calculator may be used*

C **These are GCSE-style questions. Answer all parts of the questions. Show your workings (on separate paper if necessary) and include the correct units in your answers.**

1 **Write in standard form.**

a) 538 000 .... (1 mark)

b) 0.00 629 .... (1 mark)

c) 36 x 10^4 .... (1 mark)

2 **a) i) Write the number 2.07×10^5 as an ordinary number.** (2 marks)

....

ii) Write the number 0.000 046 in standard form.

....

b) Multiply 7×10^4 by 5×10^7

Give your answer in standard form. (2 marks)

....

3 **Calculate the value of** $\dfrac{4.68 \times 10^9 + 3.14 \times 10^7}{2.14 \times 10^{-3}}$

Give your answer in standard form, correct to 2 significant figures. (C) (3 marks)

....

4 3.8×10^8 seeds weigh 1 kilogram.

Each seed weighs the same. Calculate the mass in grams of one seed.
Give your answer in standard form, correct to 2 significant figures. (C) (2 marks)

.... g

5 **If $a = 3.2 \times 10^4$ and $b = 2 \times 10^{-3}$, calculate the answer to $\dfrac{b^2}{a + b}$**
giving your answer in standard form, correct to 3 significant figures. (C) (2 marks)

....

Score / 14

How well did you do? ✗ 1–9 Try again 10–19 Getting there 20–27 Good work 28–34 Excellent! ✓

For more information on this topic, see pages 24–25 of your Success Guide.

Recurring decimals & surds

A

Choose just one answer, a, b, c or d.

1 **Which fraction is the same as $0.\dot{5}$?** (1 mark)

a) $\frac{1}{2}$ b) $\frac{5}{10}$

c) $\frac{5}{9}$ d) $\frac{5}{8}$

2 **Which fraction is equivalent to $0.\dot{6}\dot{3}$...?** (1 mark)

a) $\frac{63}{100}$ b) $\frac{6}{99}$

c) $\frac{636}{999}$ d) $\frac{7}{11}$

3 **Which fraction is equivalent to $0.2\dot{1}$...?** (1 mark)

a) $\frac{19}{90}$ b) $\frac{21}{99}$

c) $\frac{211}{999}$ d) $\frac{2}{9}$

4 **Which expression is equivalent to $\sqrt{12}$?** (1 mark)

a) $2\sqrt{6}$ b) $2\sqrt{3}$

c) $6\sqrt{2}$ d) $3\sqrt{2}$

5 **Which expression is equivalent to $\frac{1}{\sqrt{3}}$?** (1 mark)

a) $\frac{\sqrt{3}}{3}$ b) $\frac{\sqrt{3}}{9}$

c) $\frac{9}{\sqrt{3}}$ d) $\frac{3}{\sqrt{3}}$

Score / 5

B

Answer all parts of the questions.

1 **Match each of the recurring decimals to the equivalent fraction.** (5 marks)

$0.\dot{3}$	$\frac{7}{9}$
$0.\dot{7}$	$\frac{244}{333}$
$0.\dot{2}\dot{4}$	$\frac{13}{30}$
$0.\dot{7}\dot{3}\dot{2}$	$\frac{1}{3}$
$0.4\dot{3}$	$\frac{8}{33}$

2 **Find the fraction which is equivalent to $0.1\dot{2}\dot{5}$. Express the fraction in its simplest form.** (2 marks)

....

....

3 **Express each of the following in the form, $a\sqrt{b}$ where a and b are integers and b is as small as possible.**

a) $\sqrt{24}$ .... (1 mark)

b) $\sqrt{75}$ .... (1 mark)

c) $\sqrt{48} + \sqrt{12}$ .... (2 marks)

d) $\sqrt{80} + \sqrt{20}$ .... (2 marks)

Score / 13

C **These are GCSE-style questions. Answer all parts of the questions. Show your workings (on separate paper if necessary) and include the correct units in your answers.**

1 a) Change the decimal $0.\dot{5}\dot{4}$ into a fraction in its lowest terms. (2 marks)

....

b) Write the recurring decimal $0.0\dot{2}\dot{6}$ as a fraction. (2 marks)

....

2 a) Find the value of $\sqrt{3} \times \sqrt{27}$ .... (1 mark)

b) $\sqrt{3} + \sqrt{27} = a\sqrt{3}$, where a is an integer.

Find the value of a. (1 mark)

....

c) Find the value of $\dfrac{\sqrt{3} + \sqrt{12}}{\sqrt{75}}$ (3 marks)

....

3 a) Show that $\sqrt{60} = 2\sqrt{15}$ .... (1 mark)

b) Expand and simplify $(\sqrt{3} + \sqrt{10})^2$ .... (2 marks)

4 Write down the recurring decimal $0.1\dot{2}\dot{3}$ in the form $\frac{a}{b}$ where a and b are integers. (2 marks)

....

5 Simplify $(4 - \sqrt{3})^2$ (2 marks)

....

6 Express $\dfrac{\sqrt{125} + \sqrt{50}}{\sqrt{5}}$ in the form $a + \sqrt{b}$ (4 marks)

7 Work out $\dfrac{(2 - \sqrt{2} + (4 + 3\sqrt{2})}{2}$ (3 marks)

Give your answer in the form $a + b\sqrt{c}$

....

8 Write down the recurring decimal $0.\dot{7}\dot{5}$ as a fraction in its simplest form. (2 marks)

....

9 Prove that the recurring decimal $0.\dot{4}\dot{5}$ is $\frac{5}{11}$. (3 marks)

....

Score / 28

How well did you do? ✗ 1–13 Try again 14–25 Getting there 26–38 Good work 39–46 Excellent! ✓

For more information on this topic, see page 27 of your Success Guide.

Direct and inverse proportion

A Choose just one answer, a, b, c or d.

1 If a is directly proportional to b and $a = 10$ when $b = 5$, what is the formula that connects a and b? (1 mark)

a) $a = 5b$ b) $a = 10b$
c) $a = \frac{1}{2}b$ d) $a = 2b$

2 If y is directly proportional to x and $y = 12$ when $x = 4$, what is the formula that connects x and y? (1 mark)

a) $y = 3x$ b) $x = 3y$
c) $y = 12x$ d) $y = \frac{1}{3x}$

3 If d is inversely proportional to c, so that $d = \frac{k}{c}$ and $d = 6$ when $c = 3$, what is the value of k? (1 mark)

a) 12 b) 18
c) 2 d) 9

4 If v is inversely proportional to w^2 and $v = 3$ when $w = 2$, what is the formula that connects v and w^2? (1 mark)

a) $v = \frac{18}{w^2}$ b) $v = \frac{2}{w^2}$
c) $v = \frac{12}{w^2}$ d) $v = \frac{3}{2w^2}$

Score /4

B Answer all parts of the questions.

1 Given that $a \propto b$, calculate the values missing from this table. (2 marks)

a		12	30
b	2		6

2 The variables x and y are related so that y is directly proportional to the square of x. Complete this table for values of x and y. (3 marks)

x	2	4		
y	12		27	75

3 z is inversely proportional to the square of v.

a) Express z in terms of v and a constant of proportionality k. (2 marks)

....

b) If $z = 10$ when $v = 5$, calculate

i) the value of z when $v = 2$ .... (2 marks)

ii) the value of v when $z = 1000$ .... (2 marks)

Score /11

C

These are GCSE-style questions. Answer all parts of the questions. Show your workings (on separate paper if necessary) and include the correct units in your answers.

1 a is directly proportional to b. (C)
$a = 40$ when $b = 5$
Calculate the value of a when $b = 12$ .... (2 marks)

2 P is directly proportional to the square root of q when
$P = 6$, $q = 25$
Calculate the value of P when $q = 64$ .... (3 marks)

3 The extension E of a spring is directly proportional to the force F pulling the spring.
The extension is 6 cm when a force of 15 N is pulling it.
Calculate the extension when the force is 80 N. (4 marks)

....

....

4 The volume (V) of a toy is proportional to the cube of its height (h).
When the toy's volume is 60 cm^3 the height is 2 cm.
Find the volume of a similar toy whose height is 5 cm. (C) (4 marks)

....

....

5 I is inversely proportional to the square of d.

When d equals 2, I equals 50.

a) Calculate the value of I when d is 3.5. (C) (3 marks)

....

....

b) Calculate the value of d when I equals 12.5. (3 marks)

....

....

6 c is inversely proportional to b and $b = 10$ when $c = 4$. (2 marks)

Daisy says that the formula connecting c and b is given by $c = \frac{40}{b}$.

Decide whether Daisy is correct, giving a reason for your answer.

....

....

Score /21

How well did you do? 1–6 Try again 7–14 Getting there 15–23 Good work 24–36 Excellent!

For more information on this topic, see page 26 of your Success Guide.

Upper & lower bounds of measurement

A

Choose just one answer, a, b, c or d.

1 **The length of an object is 5.6 cm, correct to the nearest millimetre. What is the lower bound of the length of the object?** (1 mark)

a) 5.56 cm b) 5.55 cm
c) 5.64 cm d) 5.65 cm

2 **The mass of an object is 2.23 grams, correct to two decimal places. What is the upper bound of the mass of the object?** (1 mark)

a) 2.225 g b) 2.234 g
c) 2.235 g d) 2.32 g

3 **A hall can hold 40 people to the nearest ten. What is the upper boundary for the number of people in the hall?** (1 mark)

a) 45 b) 35
c) 44 d) 36

4 **A square has a length of 3 cm to the nearest centimetre. What is the lower bound for the perimeter of the square?** (1 mark)

a) 12 cm b) 10 cm
c) 10.4 cm d) 14 cm

5 **Using the information given in the previous question, what is the upper bound for the area of the square?** (1 mark)

a) 6.25 cm^2 b) 9 cm^2
c) 12.5 cm^2 d) 12.25 cm^2

Score / 5

B

Answer all parts of the questions.

1 **Complete the inequalities in the questions below, which show the upper and lower bounds of some measurements.**

a) .... $\leqslant 5.24 < 5.245$ (1 mark)

b) $3.5 \leqslant 4 <$ .... (1 mark)

c) $0.3235 \leqslant 0.324 <$ .... (1 mark)

d) $8.435 \leqslant$ .... < 8.445 (1 mark)

2 $a = \dfrac{(3.4)^2 \times 12.68}{2.4}$

3.4 and 2.4 are correct to 1 decimal place.
12.68 is correct to 2 decimal places.
Which of the following calculations gives the lower bound for *a* and the upper bound for *a*? (Write down the letters.) (2 marks)

a) $\dfrac{(3.45)^2 \times 12.685}{2.35}$ b) $\dfrac{(3.35)^2 \times 12.675}{2.35}$ c) $\dfrac{(3.45)^2 \times 12.685}{2.45}$

d) $\dfrac{(3.45)^2 \times 12.675}{2.35}$ e) $\dfrac{(3.35)^2 \times 12.675}{2.45}$

Lower bound .... Upper bound ....

Score / 6

(C) *Indicates that a calculator may be used*

C

These are GCSE-style questions. Answer all parts of the questions. Show your workings (on separate paper if necessary) and include the correct units in your answers.

1 A book has a mass of 112 grams, correct to the nearest gram.
Write down the least possible mass of the book. .... (1 mark)

2 $p = 3.1$ cm and $q = 4.7$ cm, correct to one decimal place.

a) Calculate the upper bound for the value of $p + q$ (C) (2 marks)

....

....

b) Calculate the lower bound for the value of $\frac{p}{q}$ (3 marks)

Give your answer correct to 3 significant figures.

....

....

....

3 The volume of a cube is given as 62.7 cm^3, correct to 1 decimal place. Find the upper and lower bounds for the length of an edge of this cube. (C) (4 marks)

Lower bound = ...

Upper bound = ...

4 The mass of an object is measured as 120 g, and its volume as 630 cm^3. Both of these measurements are correct to 2 significant figures. Find the range of possible values for the density of the object. (C) (4 marks)

....

....

5 To the nearest centimetre, $a = 3$ cm, $b = 5$ cm.
Calculate the lower bound for ab. .... cm^2 (C) (2 marks)

6 The mass of a bag of flour is 2 kg, but it is found to have a mass of 2.21 kg.
Calculate the percentage error. (C) (2 marks)

....

....

Score / 18

How well did you do? 1–6 Try again 7–11 Getting there 12–19 Good work 20–29 Excellent!

For more information on this topic, see pages 28–29 of your Success Guide.

Algebra

A

Choose just one answer, a, b, c or d.

1 **What is the expression $7a - 4b + 6a - 3b$ when it is fully simplified?** (1 mark)

a) $7b - a$ b) $13a + 7b$
c) $a - 7b$ d) $13a - 7b$

2 **If $m = \sqrt{\frac{r^2p}{4}}$ and $r = 3$ and $p = 6$, what is the value of m to 1 decimal place?** (C) (1 mark)

a) 13.5 b) 182.3
c) 3.7 d) 3

3 **What is $(n - 3)^2$ when it is multiplied out and simplified?** (1 mark)

a) $n^2 + 9$ b) $n^2 + 6n - 9$
c) $n^2 - 6n - 9$ d) $n^2 - 6n + 9$

4 **$P = a^2 + b$. Rearrange this formula to make a the subject.** (1 mark)

a) $a = \pm\sqrt{(P - b)}$

b) $a = \pm\sqrt{(P + b)}$

c) $a = \frac{P - b}{2}$

d) $a = \frac{P + b}{2}$

5 **Factorising $n^2 + 7n - 8$ gives:** (1 mark)

a) $(n - 2)(n - 6)$
b) $(n - 2)(n + 4)$
c) $(n - 1)(n + 8)$
d) $(n + 1)(n - 8)$

Score /5

B

Answer all parts of the questions.

1 **John buys b books costing £6 each and p magazines costing 67 pence each. Write down a formula for the total cost (T) of the books and magazines.** (2 marks)

$T =$ ....

2 $a = \frac{b^2 + 2c}{4}$

a) Calculate a if $b = 2$ and $c = 6$. (C) .... (1 mark)

b) Calculate a if $b = 3$ and $c = 5.5$. .... (1 mark)

c) Calculate b if $a = 25$ and $c = 18$. .... (1 mark)

3 **Factorise the following expressions.**

a) $10n + 15$ .... (1 mark) b) $24 - 36n$ .... (1 mark)

c) $n^2 + 6n + 5$ .... (1 mark) d) $n^2 - 64$ .... (1 mark)

e) $n^2 - 3n - 4$ .... (1 mark)

4 **Rearrange each of the formulae below to make b the subject.**

a) $p = 3b - 4$ .... (1 mark)

b) $y = \frac{b^2 - 6}{4}$ .... (1 mark)

c) $5(n + b) = 2b + 2$ .... (1 mark)

Score /13

(C) *Indicates that a calculator may be used*

C

These are GCSE-style questions. Answer all parts of the questions. Show your workings (on separate paper if necessary) and include the correct units in your answers.

1 Peter uses this formula to calculate the value of V. (C) (3 marks)

$$V = \frac{\pi x(2R^2 + t^2)}{500}$$

$\pi = 3.14, \quad x = 20, \quad R = 5.2, \quad t = -4.1$

Calculate the value of V, giving your answer to 2 significant figures. (C)

$\frac{3.14 \cdot 20\,(2(5.2)^2 + (-4.1)^2}{500}$

$V =$ ....

2 a) Expand and simplify $3(2x + 1) - 2(x - 2)$ (2 marks)

b) (i) Factorise $6a + 12$ (1 mark)

(ii) Factorise completely $10a^2 - 15ab$ (2 marks)

c) (i) Factorise $n^2 + 5n + 6$ (2 marks)

(ii) Hence simplify fully $\frac{2(n + 3)}{n^2 + 5n + 6}$ $\quad \frac{2(n+3)}{(n+3)(n+2)} = \frac{2}{n+2}$ (2 marks)

d) Factorise $(x + y)^2 - 2(x + y)$ (2 marks)

3 Show that $(n - 1)^2 + n + (n - 1)$ simplifies to n^2 (3 marks)

4 Simplify fully $\frac{x^2 - 8x}{x^2 - 9x + 8}$ (3 marks)

Score / 20

How well did you do? 1–13 Try again 14–18 Getting there 19–30 Good work 31–38 Excellent!

For more information on this topic, see pages 32–35 of your Success Guide.

Equations

A Choose just one answer, a, b, c or d.

1 Solve the equation $4n - 2 = 10$ (1 mark)

a) $n = 4$ b) $n = 2$
c) $n = 3$ d) $n = 3.5$

2 Solve the equation $4(x + 3) = 16$ (1 mark)

a) $x = 9$ b) $x = 7$
c) $x = 4$ d) $x = 1$

3 Solve the equation $4(n + 2) = 8(n - 3)$ (1 mark)

a) $n = 16$ b) $n = 8$
c) $n = 4$ d) $n = 12$

4 Solve the equation $10 - 6n = 4n - 5$ (1 mark)

a) $n = 2$
b) $n = -2$
c) $n = 1.5$
d) $n = -1.5$

5 What is the value of k in $y^k = y^{\frac{3}{2}} \div y^{-\frac{1}{2}}$ (1 mark)

a) 2
b) $\frac{1}{2}$
c) 1
d) -2

Score /5

B Answer all parts of the questions.

1 Solve the following equations. (6 marks)

a) $5n = 25$ .... b) $\frac{n}{3} = 12$ ....
c) $2n - 4 = 10$ .... d) $3 - 2n = 14$ ....
e) $\frac{n}{5} + 2 = 7$ .... f) $4 - \frac{n}{2} = 2$ ....

2 Solve the following equations. (4 marks)

a) $12n + 5 = 3n + 32$ .... b) $5n - 4 = 3n + 6$ ....
c) $5(n + 1) = 25$ .... d) $4(n - 2) = 3(n + 2)$ ....

3 Solve the following equations. (4 marks)

a) $n^2 - 4n = 0$ .... b) $n^2 + 6n + 5 = 0$ ....
c) $n^2 - 5n + 6 = 0$ .... d) $n^2 - 3n - 28 = 0$ ....

4 The angles in a triangle add up to 180°. Form an equation in n and solve it. (2 marks)

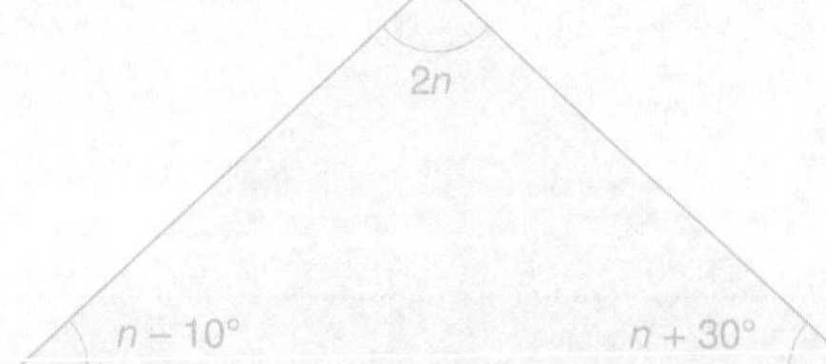

$n =$ ....

Score /16

Algebra EQUATIONS

C

These are GCSE-style questions. Answer all parts of the questions. Show your workings (on separate paper if necessary) and include the correct units in your answers.

1 **Solve these equations.**

a) $5m - 3 = 12$ (2 marks)

$m =$ ....

b) $8p + 3 = 9 - 2p$ (2 marks)

$p =$ ....

c) $5(x - 1) = 3x + 7$ (2 marks)

$x =$ ....

d) $\frac{w}{2} + \frac{(3w + 2)}{3} = \frac{1}{3}$ (2 marks)

$w =$ ....

2 **a) Solve** $7y - 2 = 3y + 6$ .... (2 marks)

b) $5y + 2 = 2(y - 4)$ .... (2 marks)

3 **The width of a rectangle is y centimetres.**

The length of a rectangle is $(y + 2)$ centimetres.

a) Find an expression, in terms of y, for the perimeter of the rectangle. .... (2 marks)

b) The perimeter of the rectangle is 64 centimetres.

Work out the length of the rectangle. .... (2 marks)

4 **a) Factorise $x^2 - 4x + 3$** (2 marks)

....

b) Hence solve the equation $x^2 - 4x + 3 = 0$ (1 mark)

$x =$ ....

and $x =$ ....

5 **Solve the following equations.** (1 mark)

a) $3^y = 27$

....

b) $2^{k-3} = 64$ (2 marks)

....

Score / 22

How well did you do? 1–10 Try again 11–23 Getting there 24–33 Good work 34–43 Excellent!

For more information on this topic, see pages 36–41 of your Success Guide.

Equations & inequalities

A

Choose just one answer, a, b, c or d.

1 **Solve these simultaneous equations to find the values of a and b.** (1 mark)

$a + b = 10$

$2a - b = 2$

a) $a = 4, b = 6$ b) $a = 4, b = -2$
c) $a = 5, b = 5$ d) $a = 3, b = 7$

2 **Solve these simultaneous equations to find the values of x and y.** (1 mark)

$3x - y = 7$

$2x + y = 3$

a) $x = 3, y = 2$ b) $x = 2, y = 1$
c) $x = -3, y = 2$ d) $x = 2, y = -1$

3 **The equation $y^3 + 2y = 82$ has a solution between 4 and 5. By using a method of trial and improvement, find the solution to one decimal place.** (C) (1 mark)

a) 3.9 b) 4.1 c) 4.2 d) 4.3

4 **Solve the inequality $3x + 1 < 19$** (1 mark)

a) $x < 3$ b) $x < 7$ c) $x < 5$ d) $x < 6$

5 **Solve the inequality $2x - 7 < 9$** (1 mark)

a) $x < 9$ b) $x < 10$
c) $x < 8$ d) $x < 6.5$

Score / 5

B

Answer all parts of the questions.

1 **Solve these simultaneous equations to find the values of *a* and *b*.**

a) $2a + b = 8$ 5a = 10
$3a - b = 2$ (2 marks)

$a =$ 2

$b =$ 4

b) $5a + b = 24$
$2a + 2b = 24$ (2 marks)

$a =$ ....

$b =$ ....

c) $a - b = 7$
$3a + 2b = 11$ (2 marks)

$a =$ ....

$b =$ ....

d) $4a + 3b = 6$
$2a - 3b = 12$ (2 marks)

$a =$ ....

$b =$ ....

2 **Use a trial and improvement method to solve the following equation. Give your answer to one decimal place.** (C) (2 marks)

$t^2 - 2t = 20$ $t =$ ....

3 **Solve the following inequalities.**

a) $5x + 2 < 12$ (1 mark)

....

b) $\frac{x}{3} + 1 \geq 3$ (1 mark)

....

c) $3 \leq 2x + 1 \leq 9$ (1 mark)

....

d) $3 \leq 3x + 2 \leq 8$ (1 mark)

....

Score / 14

(C) Indicates that a calculator may be used

C These are GCSE-style questions. Answer all parts of the questions. Show your workings (on separate paper if necessary) and include the correct units in your answers.

1 n is an integer.

a) Write down the values of n which satisfy the inequality $-4 < n \leqslant 2$ (2 marks)

....

b) Solve the inequality $5p - 2 \leqslant 8$ (2 marks)

....

2 Use the method of trial and improvement to solve the equation $x^3 + 3x = 28$
Give your answer correct to one decimal place.
You must show all your working. (C) (4 marks)

....

....

....

$x =$ ....

3 Solve these simultaneous equations. (4 marks)

$3x - 2y = -12$
$2x + 6y = 3$

$x =$ ....

$y =$ ....

4 Solve these simultaneous equations.

a) $2a - b = 14$
$a + 3b = 14$ (2 marks)

$a =$ ....

$b =$ ....

b) $5a + 4b = 23$
$3a - 5b = -1$ (2 marks)

$a =$ ....

$b =$ ....

Score / 16

How well did you do? 1–9 Try again 10–19 Getting there 20–27 Good work 28–35 Excellent!

For more information on this topic, see pages 38–42 of your Success Guide.

Further algebra & equations

A

Choose just one answer, a, b, c or d.

1 The quadratic equation $x^2 + 4x + 7$ is written in the form $(x + a)^2 + b$. What are the values of a and b? (1 mark)

a) $a = 3, b = 6$ b) $a = 4, b = -3$
c) $a = 2, b = 3$ d) $a = 4, b = 2$

2 What are the solutions of the quadratic equation $2x^2 + 5x + 2 = 0$? (1 mark)

a) $x = -\frac{1}{2}, x = -2$ b) $x = \frac{1}{2}, x = -2$
c) $x = -\frac{1}{2}, x = 2$ d) $x = 2, x = -2$

3 What are the solutions of the quadratic equation $x^2 - 4 = 0$? (1 mark)

a) $x = 2, x = 2$ b) $x = -2, x = -2$
c) $x = 0, x = 4$ d) $x = 2, x = -2$

4 What are the solutions of the quadratic equation $6x^2 + 2x = 8$? (1 mark)

a) $x = 1, x = \frac{3}{4}$ b) $x = 1, x = -\frac{4}{3}$
c) $x = -1, x = \frac{4}{3}$ d) $x = -1, x = -\frac{3}{4}$

5 The quadratic equation $x^2 - 2x + 3$ is written in the form $(x + a)^2 + b$. What are the values of a and b? (1 mark)

a) $a = 1, b = 2$ b) $a = -1, b = -2$
c) $a = -1, b = 2$ d) $a = 1, b = -2$

Score / 5

B

Answer all parts of the questions.

1 a) Factorise $x^2 + 11x + 30$ .... (2 marks)

b) Write the following as a single fraction in its simplest form: (4 marks)

$$\frac{4}{x + 6} + \frac{4}{x^2 + 11x + 30}$$ ....

....

2 $(x + 4)(x - 3) = 2$ (C)

a) Show that $x^2 + x - 14 = 0$ (2 marks)

....

b) Solve the equation $x^2 + x - 14 = 0$
Give your answers correct to 3 significant figures. (3 marks)

....

3 The formula $a = \frac{3(b + c)}{bc}$ is rearranged to make c the subject. Greg says the answer is $c = \frac{3b}{ab - 3}$
Decide whether Greg is right. You must justify your answer. (3 marks)

....

....

Score / 14

(C) *Indicates that a calculator may be used*

C These are GCSE-style questions. Answer all parts of the questions. Show your workings (on separate paper if necessary) and include the correct units in your answers.

1 The diagram shows a right-angled triangle with base $(x - 3)$ and height $(x + 4)$. All measurements are given in centimetres.

The area of the triangle is 12 square centimetres.

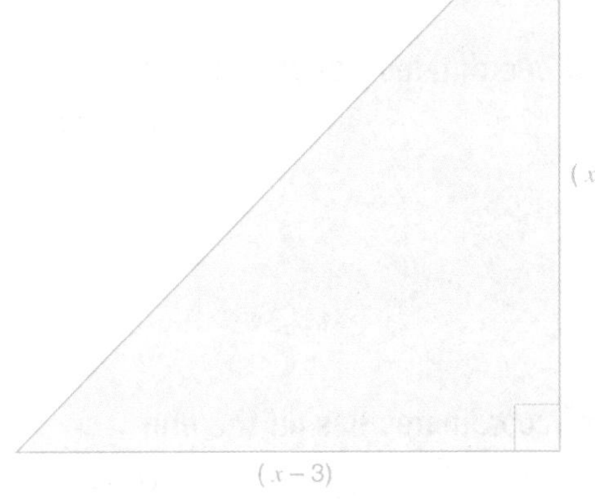

a) Show that $x^2 + x - 36 = 0$ (C) (3 marks)

....

....

b) Find the length of the base of the triangle. Give your answer correct to 2 d.p. (C) (4 marks)

....

....

.... cm

2 Make b the subject of the formula $a = \dfrac{8b+5}{4 - 3b}$ (4 marks)

....

....

3 The expression $x^2 + 6x + 3$ can be written in the form $(x + a)^2 + b$ for all values of x. (3 marks)

a) Find a and b.

$a =$ ....

$b =$ ....

b) The expression $x^2 + 6x + 3$ has a minimum value. Find this minimum value. (1 mark)

....

....

4 Make y the subject of the formula $a(y - b) = a^3 + by$ (3 marks)

....

....

Score / 18

How well did you do? ✗ 1–7 Try again 8–18 Getting there 19–28 Good work 29–37 Excellent! ✓

For more information on this topic, see pages 35–41 of your Success Guide.

Straight line graphs

A

Choose just one answer, a, b, c or d.

1 Which pair of coordinates lies on the line $x = 2$? (1 mark)

a) (1, 3)
b) (2, 3)
c) (3, 2)
d) (0, 2)

2 Which pair of coordinates lies on the line $y = -3$? (1 mark)

a) (−3, 5)
b) (5, −2)
c) (−2, 5)
d) (5, −3)

3 What is the gradient of the line $y = 2 - 5x$? (1 mark)

a) −2 b) −5 c) 2 d) 5

4 These graphs have been drawn: $y = 3x - 1$, $y = 5 - 2x$, $y = 6x + 1$, $y = 2x - 3$
Which graph is the steepest? (1 mark)

a) $y = 3x - 1$
b) $y = 5 - 2x$
c) $y = 6x + 1$
d) $y = 2x - 3$

5 At what point does the graph $y = 3x - 4$ intercept the y axis? (1 mark)

a) (0, −4)
b) (0, 3)
c) (−4, 0)
d) (3, 0)

Score / 5

B

Answer all parts of the questions.

1 a) On the grid, draw the graph of $y = 6 - x$.
Join your points with a straight line. (2 marks)

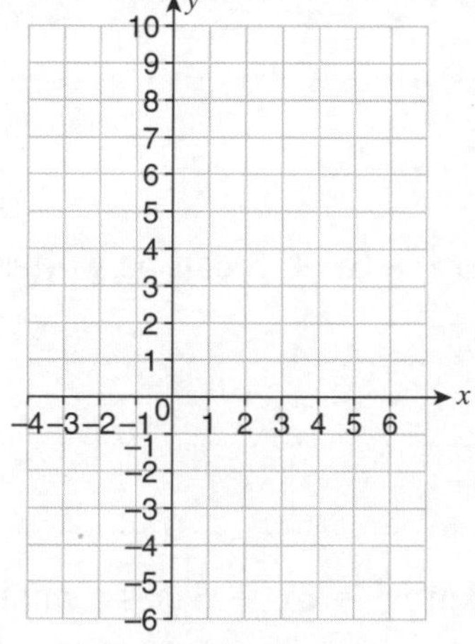

b) A second line goes through the coordinates (1, 5), (−2, −4) and (2, 8).

i) Draw this line on the grid. (1 mark)
ii) Write down the equation of the line you have just drawn. (2 marks)

....

c) What are the coordinates of the point where the two lines meet? (1 mark)

....

2 The equations of five straight lines are: $y = 2x - 4$, $y = 3 - 2x$, $y = 4 - 2x$, $y = 5x - 4$, $y = 3x - 5$
Two of the lines are parallel. Write down the equations of these two lines.

.... and .... (2 marks)

Score / 8

C

These are GCSE-style questions. Answer all parts of the questions. Show your workings (on separate paper if necessary) and include the correct units in your answers.

1 **The diagram shows a scale drawing of one side AB of a triangular playground, ABC.**

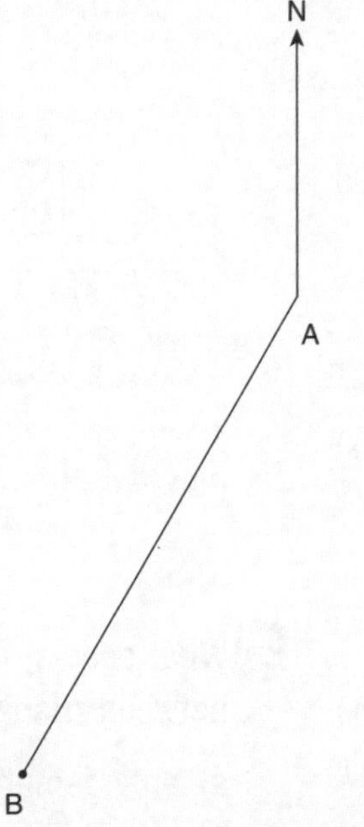

a) Use the diagram to calculate the actual distance from A to B. (2 marks)

....

b) Measure and write down the three figure bearing of B from A. (1 mark)

....

c) The bearing of C from A is 160°.
The actual distance from A to C is 135 metres.
Plan the point C on the diagram. (2 marks)

2 **Here is a sketch of a triangle. Using compasses and a ruler and a scale of 1 cm to 2 m, make an accurate scale drawing of the triangle.** (3 marks)

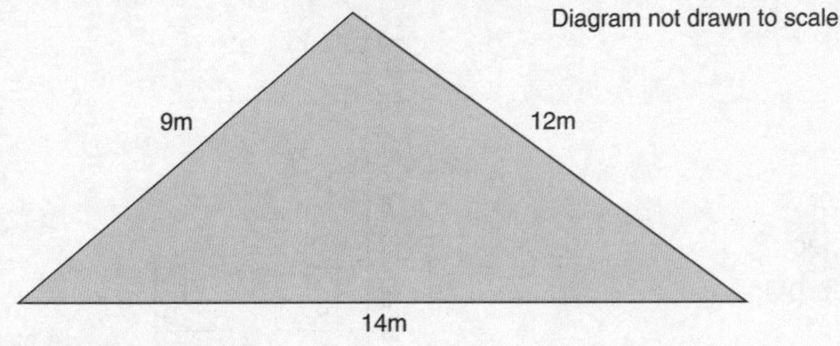

Score /8

How well did you do? 1–4 Try again 5–10 Getting there 11–15 Good work 16–20 Excellent!

For more information on this topic, see pages 58–59 of your Success Guide.

Transformations 1

A Choose just one answer, a, b, c or d.

Questions 1–4 refer to the diagram opposite.

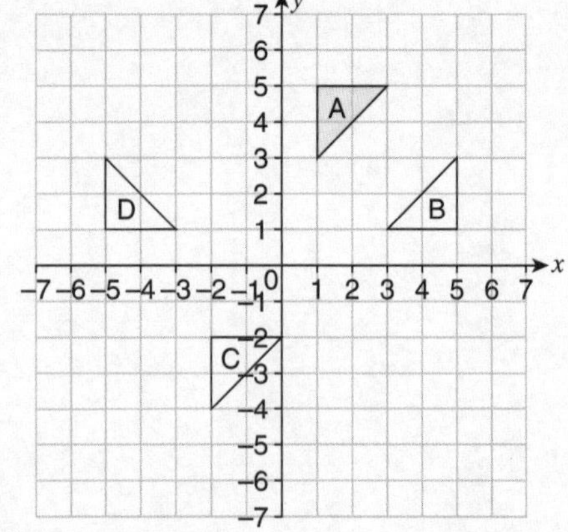

1 **What is the transformation that would map shape A onto shape B?** **(1 mark)**

a) reflection b) rotation
c) translation d) enlargement

2 **What is the transformation that would map shape A onto shape C?** **(1 mark)**

a) reflection b) rotation
c) translation d) enlargement

3 **What is the transformation that would map shape A onto shape D?** **(1 mark)**

a) reflection b) rotation
c) translation d) enlargement

4 **What special name is given to the relationship between triangles A, B, C, and D?** **(1 mark)**

a) enlargement b) congruent
c) translation d) similar

Score /4

B Answer all parts of the questions.

1 **On the grid, carry out the following transformations.** **(3 marks)**

a) Reflect shape A in the y axis.
Call the new shape R.

b) Rotate shape A 90° clockwise, about (0, 0).
Call the new shape S.

c) Translate shape A by the vector $\begin{pmatrix} -3 \\ 4 \end{pmatrix}$.
Call the new shape T.

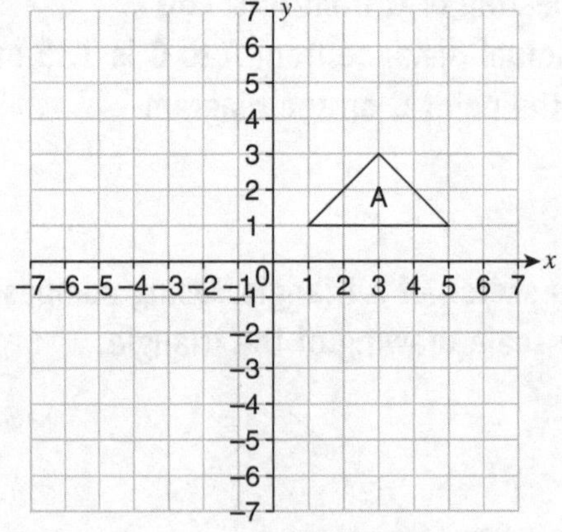

2 **All the shapes in the diagram are either a reflection, rotation or translation of object P. State the transformation that has taken place in each of the following.** **(4 marks)**

a) P is transformed to A ....

b) P is transformed to B ....

c) P is transformed to C ....

d) P is transformed to D ....

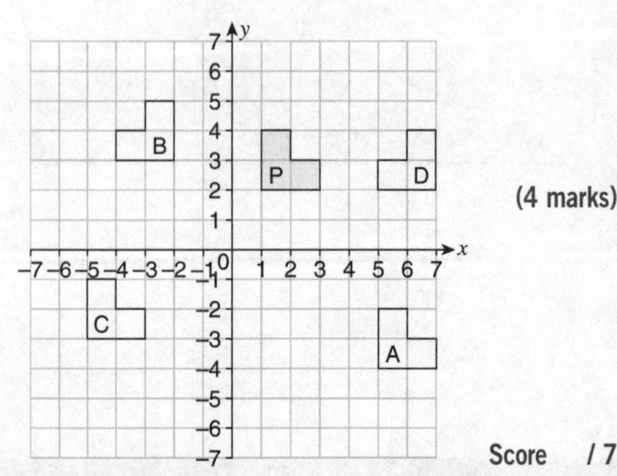

Score /7

Shape, Space and Measures TRANSFORMATIONS 1

These are GCSE-style questions. Answer all parts of the questions. Show your workings (on separate paper if necessary) and include the correct units in your answers.

1

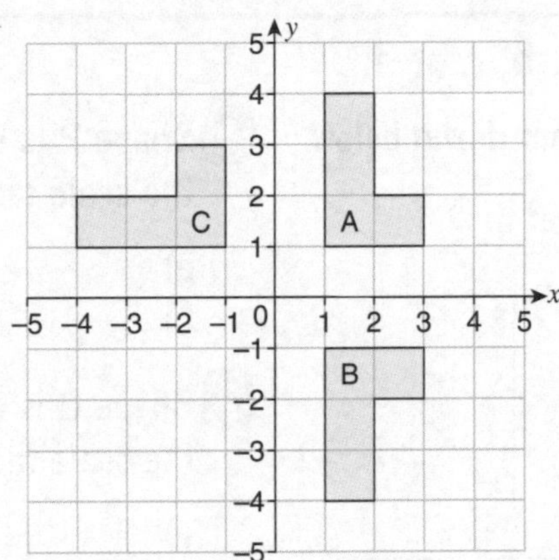

a) Describe fully the single transformation which takes shape A onto shape B. (2 marks)

....

....

b) Describe fully the single transformation which takes shape A onto shape C. (3 marks)

....

....

2

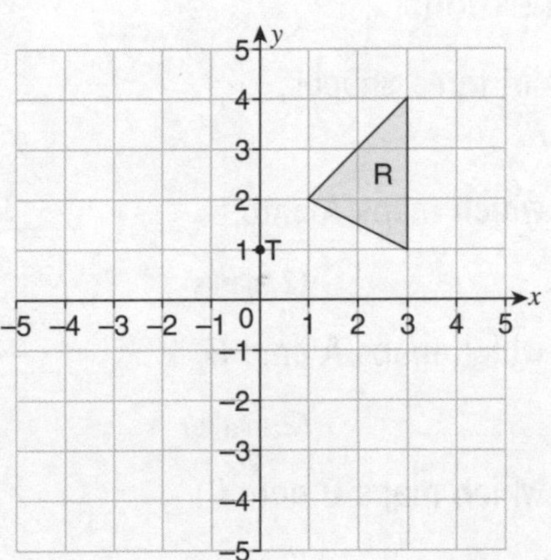

The triangle R has been drawn on the grid.

a) Rotate triangle R 90° clockwise about the point T (0, 1) and call the image P. (3 marks)

b) Translate triangle R by the vector $\begin{pmatrix} -4 \\ -3 \end{pmatrix}$ and call the image Q. (3 marks)

Score / 11

How well did you do? 1–6 Try again 7–10 Getting there 11–16 Good work 17–22 Excellent!

For more information on this topic, see pages 60–61 of your Success Guide.

Transformations 2

A

Choose just one answer, a, b, c or d.

Questions 1–3 refer to the diagram drawn below.

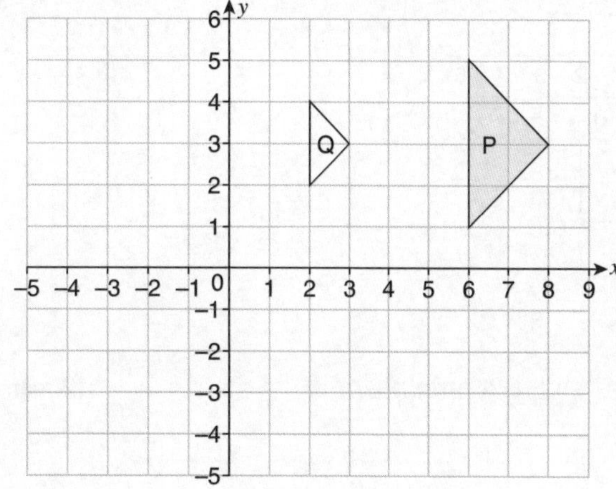

1 Shape P is enlarged to give shape Q. What is the scale factor of the enlargement? (1 mark)

a) $\frac{1}{3}$ b) 2
c) 3 d) $\frac{1}{2}$

2 Shape Q is enlarged to give shape P. What is the scale factor of the enlargement? (1 mark)

a) $\frac{1}{3}$ b) 2
c) 3 d) $\frac{1}{2}$

3 What are the coordinates of the centre of enlargement in both cases? (1 mark)

a) (3, −2) b) (−2, 3)
c) (−3, 4) d) (0, 0)

Score / 3

B

Answer all parts of the questions.

1 The diagram shows the position of three shapes, A, B and C.

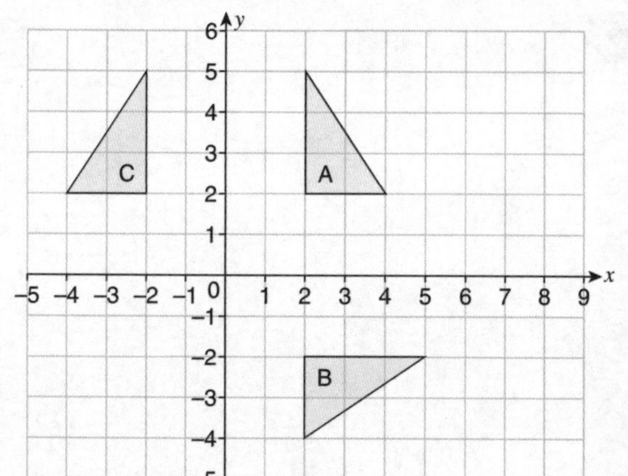

a) Describe the transformation which maps A onto C.

.... (2 marks)

b) Describe the transformation which maps A onto B.

.... (2 marks)

c) Describe the transformation which maps B onto C.

.... (2 marks)

2 On the grid, enlarge triangle PQR by a scale factor of −2 with centre of enlargement (0, 0), and call the image P'Q'R'.

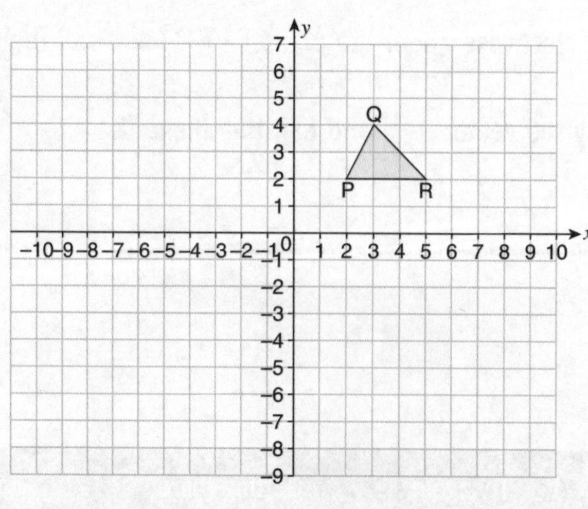

(3 marks)

Score / 9

Letts

GCSE Success

Workbook Answer Booklet

AQA Mathematics Higher

Fiona C. Mapp

GCSE Mathematics Higher AQA Answer Booklet

Answers

NUMBER

Fractions – Page 6

A

1. c
2. a
3. b
4. c
5. a

B

1. a) $\frac{5}{9}$
 b) $\frac{17}{44}$
 c) $\frac{3}{14}$
 d) 3
 e) $1\frac{2}{3}$
 f) $\frac{5}{9}$
 g) $\frac{7}{8}$
 h) $2\frac{34}{49}$
2. a) $\frac{1}{7}$ $\frac{3}{10}$ $\frac{1}{2}$ $\frac{2}{3}$ $\frac{3}{4}$ $\frac{4}{5}$
 b) $\frac{1}{9}$ $\frac{2}{7}$ $\frac{1}{3}$ $\frac{2}{5}$ $\frac{5}{8}$ $\frac{3}{4}$
3. a) true
 b) false
4. 28 students

C

1. Jonathan, since $\frac{2}{3}$ is greater than $\frac{3}{5}$.
2. a) $1\frac{7}{15}$
 b) $1\frac{16}{33}$
 c) $\frac{8}{63}$
 d) $\frac{3}{4}$
3. $\frac{7}{15}$
4. 7 weeks

Percentages 1 – Page 8

A

1. c
2. c
3. a
4. d
5. b

B

1. a) £12
 b) £45
 c) £4
 d) 5 g
2. £26 265
3. 39.3% (3s.f.)
4. 77%
5. £20
6. £225
7. 40%

C

1. a) £30.63
 b) £339.15
2. 20%
3. £70

Percentages 2 – Page 10

A

1. d
2. a
3. c
4. b

B

1. £168.03
2. £75.60
3. £6 969.60
4. £515.88
5. £135 475.20
6. 121.77 pence

C

1. a) £1000 b) £160
2. £1 337.11
3. a) 3.5% b) £757.12
4. £9540.61
5. a) 4.5% b) £59 728.23

Fractions, decimals and percentages – Page 12

A

1. c
2. b
3. d
4. d
5. a

B

1.

Fraction	Decimal	Percentage
$\frac{2}{5}$	0.4	40%
$\frac{1}{20}$	0.05	5%
$\frac{1}{3}$	0.3	$33.\dot{3}$%
$\frac{1}{25}$	0.04	4%
$\frac{1}{4}$	0.25	25%
$\frac{1}{8}$	0.125	12.5%

2. 30% $\frac{1}{3}$ 0.37 $\frac{3}{8}$ $\frac{1}{2}$ 0.62 92%
3. Both will give the same answer because increasing by 20% is the same as multiplying by 1.2. Finding 10% then doubling it gives 20%, which when you add it to 40, is the same as increasing £40 by 20%.

C

1. $\frac{1}{8}$ 25% 0.27 $\frac{1}{3}$ $\frac{2}{5}$ 0.571 72%
2. a) Ed's Electricals: £225
 Sheila's Bargains : £217.38
 Gita's TV shop : £232
 Maximum price = £232
 Minimum price = £217.38
 b) £200
3. 'Rosebushes' is cheaper because $\frac{1}{4}$ = 25% which is greater than the offer at 'Gardens are Us'.
4. $\frac{1}{10}$, $\frac{3}{5}$, $\frac{5}{8}$, $\frac{2}{3}$, $\frac{9}{10}$

Approximations and using a calculator – Page 14

A

1. b
2. d
3. c
4. c
5. d

B

1. a) true
 b) false
 c) false
 d) true
2. a) 100
 b) 90
3. a) 365 (3 s.f.)
 b) 10.2 (3 s.f.)
 c) 6320 (3 s.f.)
 d) 0.0812 (3 s.f.)

C

1. 7.09 (3s.f.)
2. a) 5.937 102 5
 b) $\frac{30 \times 6}{40 - 10} = \frac{180}{30} = 6$
3. a) B
 b) B
 c) B
 d) A
4. 4.5
5. a) 295.3903049
 b) 295

Ratio – Page 16

A

1. c
2. d
3. c
4. d
5. b

B

1. a) 1 : 1.5
 b) 1 : $1.\dot{6}$
 c) 1 : 3
2. 1200 ml
3. a) £10.25
 b) 48 g
4. £25 000
5. 4.5 days

C

1. £206
2. Vicky £6 400
 Tracey £8 000
3. butter 75 g
 sugar 60 g
 eggs 3
 flour 67.5 g
 milk 22.5 ml
4. 6 days

Indices – Page 18

A

1. a
2. c
3. d
4. a
5. b

B

1. a) false b) false
 c) true d) true
 e) false f) true
2. a) 1
 b) $16a^8$
 c) $\frac{3}{4}a^{-3}$
 d) $27a^6b^9$
3. a) $4x^{-2}$
 b) a^2b^{-3}
 c) $3y^{-5}$
4. a) $\pm\frac{1}{5}$
 b) 343
 c) $\frac{25}{16}$
 d) $\frac{1}{27}$

C

1. a) p^7
 b) n^{-4} or $\frac{1}{n^4}$
 c) a^6
 d) $4ab$
2. a) 1
 b) $\frac{1}{81}$
 c) 648
 d) 16
 e) $\frac{1}{5}$
3. a) i) 1
 ii) $\frac{1}{16}$
 iii) $\pm\frac{3}{2} = \pm1\frac{1}{2}$
 b) 5^4
4. a) $\frac{1}{125}$
 b) $\frac{9}{4}$
 c) $\frac{1}{4}$
5. a) 2^{-1}
 b) 2^{20}
 c) $2^{\frac{5}{2}}$
6. a) $125x^3$ b) y^{20} c) $\frac{1}{27y^3}$
 d) $32x^5y^{15}$

Standard index form – Page 20

A

1. b
2. b
3. a
4. b
5. b

B

1. a) true
 b) false
 c) false
 d) false
2. a) 8×10^{15}
 b) 1.4×10^4
 c) 3×10^{16}
 d) 8×10^3
3. a) 8.19×10^3
 b) 7.56×10^2
 c) 6×10^{-7}
 d) 2.225×10^8
4. 1.8×10^{-7} grams

C

1. a) 5.38×10^5
 b) 6.29×10^{-3}
 c) 3.6×10^5
2. a) i) 207 000
 ii) 4.6×10^{-5}
 b) 3.5×10^{12}
3. 2.2×10^{12}
4. 2.6×10^{-6}
5. 1.25×10^{-10}

Recurring decimals and surds – Page 22

A

1. c
2. d
3. a
4. b
5. a

B

1. $0.\dot{3}$ → $\frac{1}{3}$; $0.\dot{7}$ → $\frac{7}{9}$; $0.\dot{2}\dot{4}$ → $\frac{8}{33}$; $0.\dot{7}3\dot{2}$ → $\frac{244}{333}$; $0.4\dot{3}$ → $\frac{13}{30}$
2. $\frac{124}{990} = \frac{62}{495}$
3. a) $2\sqrt{6}$
   b) $5\sqrt{3}$
   c) $6\sqrt{3}$
   d) $6\sqrt{5}$

C

1. a) $\frac{6}{11}$
   b) $\frac{26}{990} = \frac{13}{495}$
2. a) 9
   b) $a = 4$
   c) $\frac{3}{5}$
3. a) $\sqrt{60} = \sqrt{4} \times \sqrt{15}$
   $= 2\sqrt{15}$
   b) $(\sqrt{3}+\sqrt{10})^2 = (\sqrt{3}+\sqrt{10})(\sqrt{3}+\sqrt{10})$
   $= 3 + 2\sqrt{30} + 10$
   $= 13 + 2\sqrt{30}$
4. $\frac{61}{495}$
5. $19 - 8\sqrt{3}$
6. $\frac{\sqrt{125} + \sqrt{50}}{\sqrt{5}}$
   $\frac{5\sqrt{5} + 5\sqrt{2}}{\sqrt{5}}$
   $\frac{5\sqrt{5} + 5\sqrt{2}}{\sqrt{5}} \quad \frac{\sqrt{5}}{\sqrt{5}}$
   $\frac{5(\sqrt{5})^2 + 5\sqrt{10}}{5}$
   $= 5 + \sqrt{10}$
7. $1 + \sqrt{2}$
8. $\frac{25}{33}$
9. $0.\dot{4}\dot{5} = \frac{5}{11}$
   $x = 0.454545....$
   $100x = 45.454545....$
   $99x = 45$
   $x = \frac{45}{99}$
   $x = \frac{5}{11}$

Direct and inverse proportion – Page 24

A

1. d
2. a
3. b
4. c

B

1.

a	**10**	12	30
b	2	**2.4**	6

2.

x	2	4	**3**	**5**
y	12	**48**	27	75

3. a) $z = \frac{k}{v^2}$
   b) i) 62.5
   ii) $\frac{1}{2}$

C

1. 96
2. 9.6
3. $E = kF$
   $6 = k \times 15$
   $\therefore k = \frac{2}{5}$
   $E = \frac{2}{5}F$
   When $F = 80$ N, $E = 32$ cm
4. $V = kh^3$
   $60 = k \times 8$
   $k = 7.5$
   $V = 7.5h^3$
   $V = 937.5 \text{ cm}^3$
5. $I = \frac{k}{d^2}$
   $50 = \frac{k}{4}$
   $\therefore k = 200$
   $I = \frac{200}{d^2}$
   a) $I = 16.3$ (1 d.p.)
   b) $d = 4$
6. $c = \frac{k}{b}$
   $\therefore 4 = \frac{k}{10}$ so $k = 40$
   Daisy is correct.

Upper and lower bounds of measurement – Page 26

A

1. b
2. c
3. c
4. b
5. d

B

1. a) 5.235
   b) 4.5
   c) 0.3245
   d) 8.44
2. Lower bound e
   Upper bound a

C

1. 111.5 grams
2. a) 7.9 cm
   b) 0.642 cm
3. Lower bound 3.9717 cm (5 s.f.)
   Upper bound 3.9738 cm (5 s.f.)
4. $0.1811 \text{ g cm}^{-3} \leqslant$ density $< 0.2 \text{ g cm}^{-3}$
5. 11.25 cm^2
6. 10.5%

ALGEBRA

Algebra – Page 28

A

1. d
2. c
3. d
4. a
5. c

B

1. $T = 6b + 0.67p$
2. a) 4
   b) 5
   c) 8
3. a) $5(2n + 3)$
   b) $12(2 - 3n)$
   c) $(n + 1)(n + 5)$
   d) $(n - 8)(n + 8)$
   e) $(n + 1)(n - 4)$
4. a) $b = \frac{p + 4}{3}$
   b) $b = \pm\sqrt{4y + 6}$
   c) $b = \frac{2 - 5n}{3}$

C

1. $V = 8.9$ (2 s.f.)
2. a) $4x + 7$
   b) i) $6(a + 2)$
   ii) $5a(2a - 3b)$
   c) i) $(n + 2)(n + 3)$
   ii) $\frac{2}{n + 2}$
   d) $(x + y)(x + y + 2)$
3. $(n - 1)^2 + n + (n - 1)$
   $n^2 - 2n + 1 + n + n - 1$
   $= n^2 - 2n + 1 + 2n - 1$
   $= n^2$
4. $\frac{x^2 - 8x}{x^2 - 9x + 8} = \frac{x(x - 8x)}{(x - 8)(x - 1)}$
   $= \frac{x}{(x - 1)}$

Equations – Page 30

A

1. c
2. d
3. b
4. c
5. a

B

1. a) $n = 5$
   b) $n = 36$
   c) $n = 7$
   d) $n = -5.5$
   e) $n = 25$
   f) $n = 4$
2. a) $n = 3$
   b) $n = 5$
   c) $n = 4$
   d) $n = 14$
3. a) $n = 0, n = 4$
   b) $n = -5, n = -1$
   c) $n = 3, n = 2$
   d) $n = -4, n = 7$
4. $2n + (n + 30°) + (n - 10°) = 180°$
   $4n + 20° = 180°$
   $n = 40°$

C

1. a) $m = 3$
   b) $p = \frac{6}{10}$ or $p = \frac{3}{5}$
   c) $x = 6$
   d) $\frac{3w + 2(3w + 2)}{6} = \frac{1}{3}$
   $3w + 6w + 4 = \frac{6}{3}$
   $3w + 6w + 4 = 2$
   $9w + 4 = 2$
   $w = -\frac{2}{9}$
2. a) $y = 2$
   b) $y = \frac{-10}{3}$ or $-3\frac{1}{3}$
3. a) $4y + 4$
   b) Width = 15, Length = 17 cm
4. a) $(x - 1)(x - 3)$
   b) $x = 1$ and $x = 3$
5. i) $k = 3$
   ii) $k = 9$

Equations and inequalities – Page 32

A

1. a
2. d
3. c
4. d
5. c

B

1. a) $a = 2, b = 4$
   b) $a = 3, b = 9$
   c) $a = 5, b = -2$
   d) $a = 3, b = -2$
2. 5.6 and −3.6
3. a) $x < 2$
   b) $x \geqslant 6$
   c) $1 \leqslant x \leqslant 4$
   d) $\frac{1}{3} < x \leqslant 2$

C

1. a) −3 −2 −1 0 1 2
   b) $p \leqslant 2$
2. $x = 2.7$
3. $x = -3, y = 1.5$
4. a) $a = 8, b = 2$
   b) $a = 3, b = 2$

Further algebra and equations – Page 34

A

1. c
2. a
3. d
4. b
5. c

B

1. a) $(x + 6)(x + 5)$
   b) $\frac{4}{(x + 6)} + \frac{4}{(x^2 + 11x + 30)}$
   $= \frac{4}{(x + 6)} + \frac{4}{(x + 6)(x + 5)}$
   $= \frac{4(x + 5) + 4}{(x + 6)(x + 5)}$
   $= \frac{4x + 24}{(x + 6)(x + 5)}$
   $\frac{4}{(x + 5)}$
2. a) $(x + 4)(x - 3) = 2$
   $x^2 + x - 12 = 2$
   $x^2 + x - 14 = 0$
   b) $x = 3.27$ or $x = -4.27$
3. $a = \frac{3(b + c)}{bc}$
   $abc = 3b + 3c$
   $abc - 3c = 3b$
   $c(ab - 3) = 3b$
   $\therefore c = \frac{3b}{ab - 3}$
   Greg is right.

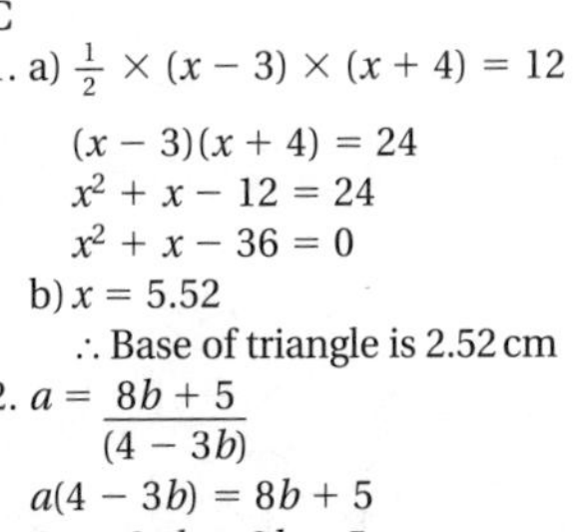

C

1. a) $\frac{1}{2} \times (x - 3) \times (x + 4) = 12$
   $(x - 3)(x + 4) = 24$
   $x^2 + x - 12 = 24$
   $x^2 + x - 36 = 0$
   b) $x = 5.52$
   $\therefore$ Base of triangle is 2.52 cm

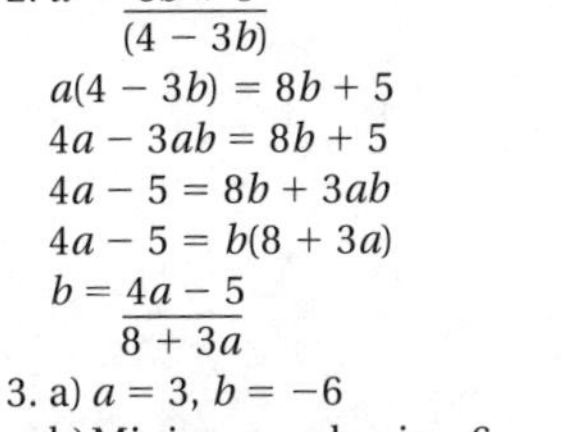

2. $a = \frac{8b + 5}{(4 - 3b)}$
   $a(4 - 3b) = 8b + 5$
   $4a - 3ab = 8b + 5$
   $4a - 5 = 8b + 3ab$
   $4a - 5 = b(8 + 3a)$
   $b = \frac{4a - 5}{8 + 3a}$
3. a) $a = 3, b = -6$
   b) Minimum value is −6.
4. $y = \frac{a(a^2 + b)}{(a - b)}$

Straight line graphs – Page 36

A

1. b
2. d
3. b
4. c
5. a

B

1. a), b) i)

   b) ii) $y = 3x + 2$
   c) (1, 5)
2. $y = 3 - 2x$ and $y = 4 - 2x$

C

1. a) Gradient $= -\frac{2}{3}$
   b) $3y + 2x = 6$ or $y = -\frac{2}{3}x + 2$

c)

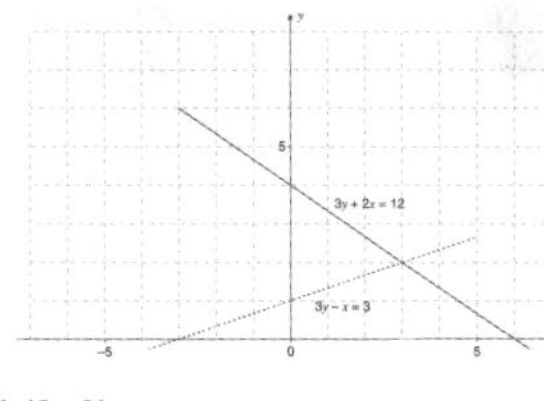

d) (3, 2)
e) $\frac{2}{3}$

Curved graphs – Page 38

A

1. b
2. d
3. c
4. d
5. b

B

1. a)

x	−2	−1	0	1	2	3
y	**6**	**1**	−2	**−3**	**−2**	1

b)

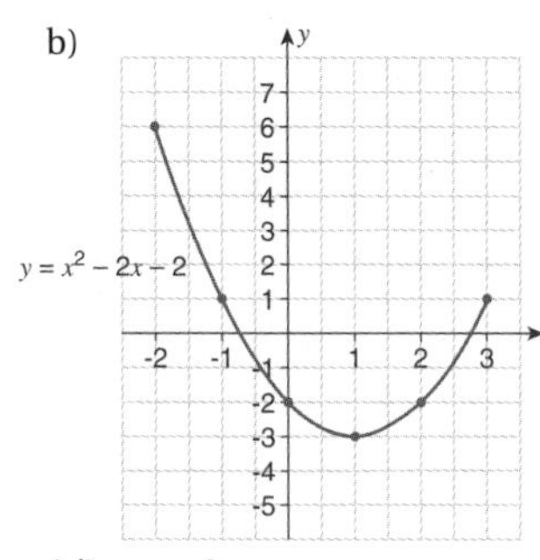

c) i) $y = -3$
ii) $x = 2.7$, $x = -0.62$

C

1. a)

x	−2	−1	0	1	2	3
y	**−12**	−5	**−4**	**−3**	**4**	23

b)

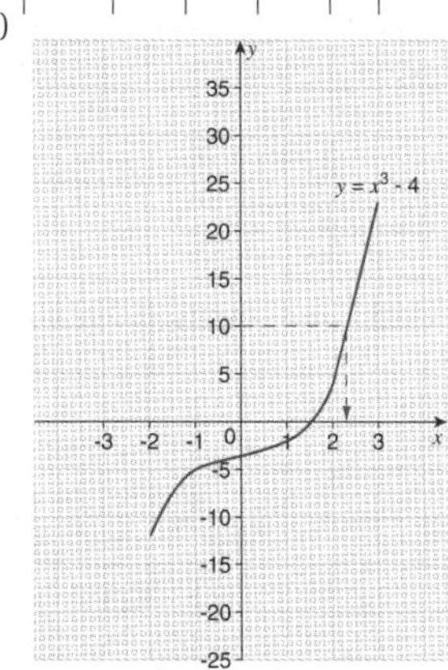

c) i) $x = 1.6$ ii) $x = 2.4$
iii) $x = 1.8$ iv) $x = -1.4$

Harder work on graphs – Page 40

A

1. c
2. a
3. d
4. c

B

1. a) (2, 4)
b) (1, 7)
c) (6, 7)
d) (−2, 7)
e) (1, 7)
2. Statement is true since $x = 1$, $y = -4$ is a simultaneous solution of the two equations: i.e. $2 \times 1 - (-4) = 6$
$1^2 + (-4)^2 = 17$

C

1. a) $x = 3$, $y = -5$ and $x = -5\frac{2}{5}$, $y = -2\frac{1}{5}$
b) They are the coordinates of the points where the line $3y = -12 - x$ intersects with the circle $x^2 + y^2 = 34$.

2. a)

b)

Interpreting graphs – Page 42

A

1. d
2. a
3. d

B

1. Vase A – graph ii.
Vase B – graph i.
Vase C – graph iii.
2. a) Roots are $x = 3$ and $x = -2$ (read where curve crosses x axis)
b) i) Approximately, $x = 3.3$ and $x = -2.3$ (read across where y = 2)
ii) Approximately, $x = -2.7$ and $x = 2.6$ (draw the line $y = 1 - x$ and find the points of intersection with the curve)

C

1. a)

Equation	Graph
$y = x^2 - x - 6$	D
$y = 6 - x^2$	E
$y = x^3$	F
$y = 3x + 2$	B
$y = 5 - x$	A
$y = \frac{2}{x}$	C

2. $a = 2$, $b = 3$

SHAPE, SPACE AND MEASURES

Bearings and scale drawings – Page 44

A

1. c
2. a
3. d
4. b

B

1. 10 km
2. a)

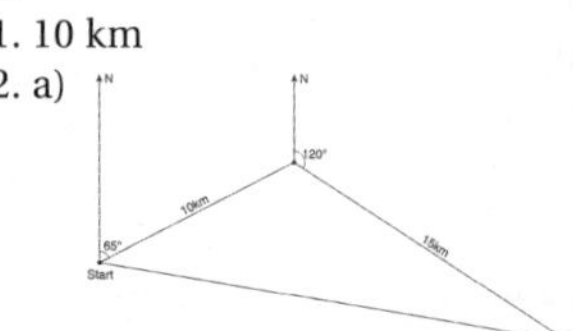

b) 11.1 cm = 22.2 km
c) 099°

3. false

C

1. a) 165 m
b) 210°
c)

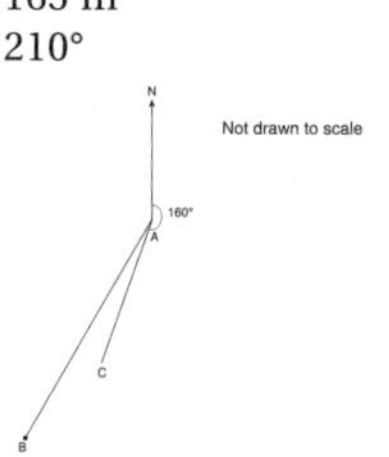

2. Lengths must be ± 2 mm.

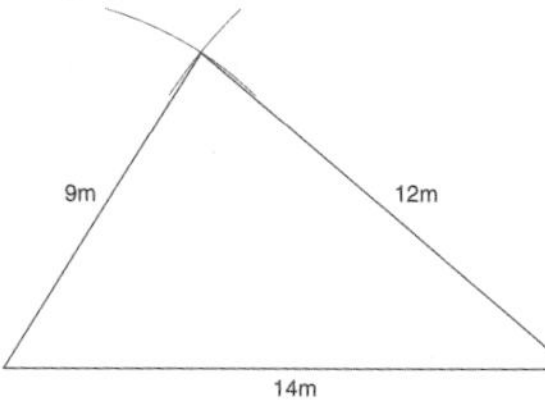

Transformations 1 – Page 46

A

1. a
2. c
3. b
4. b

B

1. a)
b)
c)

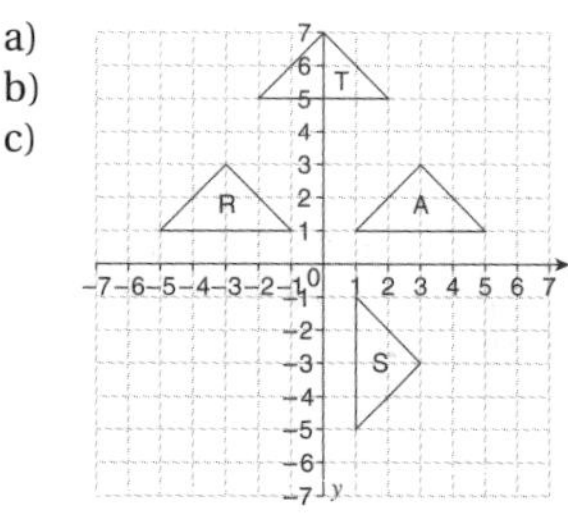

2. a) Translation b) Rotation
c) Translation d) Reflection

C

1. a) Reflection in the x axis.
b) Rotation 90° anticlockwise about (0, 0).
2.

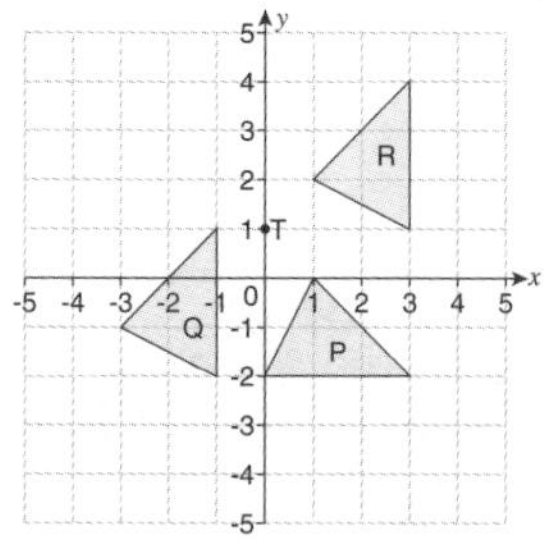

Transformations 2 – Page 48

A

1. d
2. b
3. b

B

1. a) Reflection in the y axis
b) Rotation 90° clockwise about (0, 0)
c) Reflection in the line $y = x$
2.

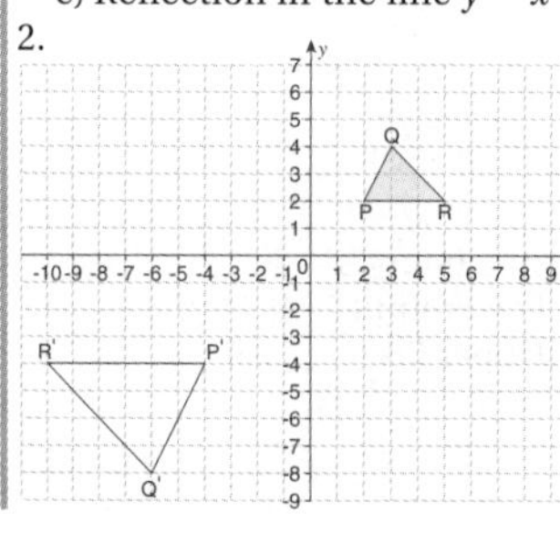

C

1.

2. a) Translation by the vector $\binom{-12}{-7}$
b) Enlargement by a scale factor of $-\frac{1}{2}$, centre of enlargement at (0, 5)
c) Reflection in the line $y = 0$

Similarity and congruency – Page 50

A

1. c
2. b
3. b
4. b

B

1. a) $n = 7.5$ cm
b) $n = 6.5$ cm
c) $n = 6.5$ cm
d) $n = 7.\dot{3}$ cm
2. a) Congruent (RHS)
b) Not congruent
c) Congruent (SSS)

C

1. a) i) angle XMN = 83°
ii) angle XNM = X$\hat{Z}$Y = 68°
Angles in a triangle add up to 180°. Therefore
180° − 68° − 29° = 83°
b) 3.65 cm
c) 11.74 cm
2. a) 225 cm^2
b) 1.08 litres

Loci and coordinates in 3D – Page 52

A

1. c
2. d
3. a
4. d
5. b

B

1.

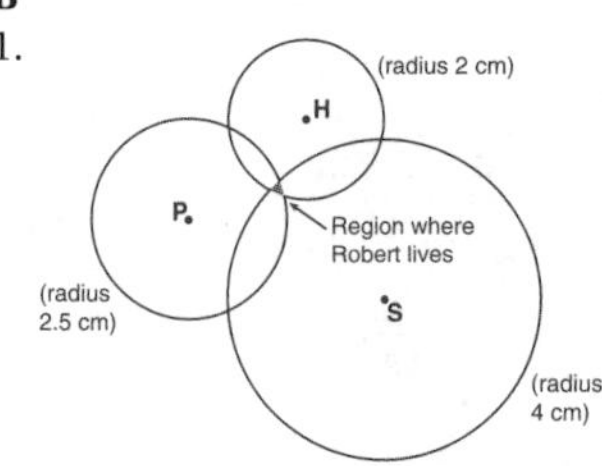

2. R = (3, 3, 0), S = (3, 1, 3), T = (0, 1, 3), U = (0, 1, 1)

C

1.

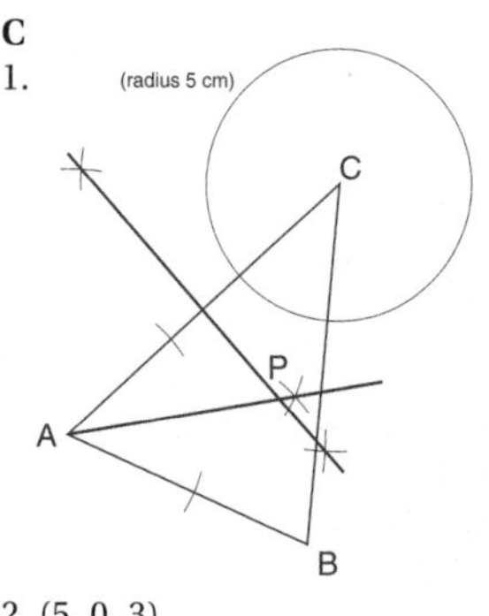

2. (5, 0, 3)

Angle properties of circles – Page 54

A

1. c
2. a
3. d
4. a
5. c

B

1. a) $a = 65°$
   b) $a = 18°$
   c) $a = 60°$
   d) $a = 50°$
   e) $a = 82°$
2. John is correct. Angle a is 42° because angles in the same segment are equal.

C

1. a) 66°
   b) The angle at the centre is twice that at the circumference. Hence $132° \div 2 = 66°$
2. a) angle ROQ = 140°
   b) angle PRQ = 70°
3. A = 63° (alternate segment theorem)
   $p = 180° - 63° - 71°$ (angles in a triangle)
   $p = 46°$

Pythagoras' theorem – Page 56

A

1. d
2. b
3. a
4. c

B

1. a) $n = 15$ cm
   b) $n = 12.6$ cm
   c) $n = 15.1$ cm
   d) $n = 24.6$ cm
2. Since $12^2 + 5^2 = 144 + 25 = 169 = 13^2$, the triangle must be right-angled for Pythagoras' Theorem to be applied.
3. Both statements are true.
   Length of line $= \sqrt{6^2 + 3^2} = \sqrt{45}$ in surd form.
   Midpoint $= \frac{(2+5)}{3}, \frac{(11+5)}{2}$
   $= (3.5, 8)$

C

1. $\sqrt{61}$ cm
2. 10.9 cm
3. 24.1 cm
4. 13.7 cm
5. $\sqrt{41}$ units

Trigonometry 1 – Page 58

A

1. a
2. b
3. d
4. a
5. c

B

1. a) $n = 5$ cm
   b) $n = 6.3$ cm
   c) $n = 13.8$ cm
   d) $n = 14.9$ cm
   e) $n = 6.7$ cm
2. a) 38.7°
   b) 52.5°
   c) 23.6°

C

1. 15 cm
2. a) 9.9 cm b) 65°
3. 18 cm

Trigonometry 2 – Page 60

A

1. c
2. a
3. d
4. c
5. b

B

1. 068°
2. 13.8 cm (1 d.p.)
3. a) i) true
   ii) true
   b) 40.9° (1 d.p.)

C

1. 30.1°
2. 206°
3. a) 389.9 m (1d.p.)
   b) 14.6° (1d.p.)
   c) 22.5° (1 d.p.)

Further trigonometry – Page 62

A

1. c
2. a
3. d
4. c

B

1. a) 13.2 cm (3 s.f.)
   b) 17.3 cm (3 s.f.)
   c) 32.5° (1 d.p.)
   d) 70.9° (1 d.p.)
2. Area $= \frac{1}{2} \times 18 \times 13 \times \sin 37°$
   $= 70.4\ \text{cm}^2$
   Area is approximately $70\ \text{cm}^2$. Isobel is correct.
3. a) A (0°, 1), B (90°, 0), C (270°, 0), D (360°, 1)
   b)

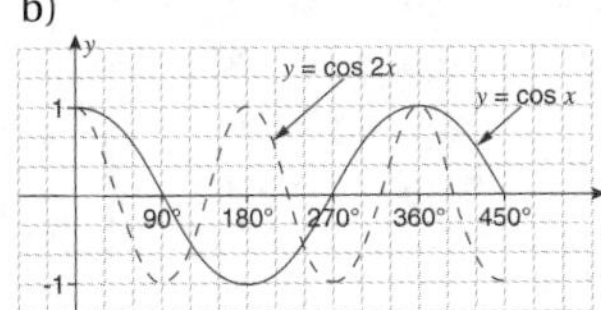

C

1. a) 10.5 cm (3 s.f.)
   b) $12.5\ \text{cm}^2$ (3 s.f.)
   c) $42.5\ \text{cm}^2$ (3 s.f.)
2. 4.13 cm

Measures and measurement – Page 64

A

1. b
2. d
3. a
4. d
5. c

B

1. a) 8000 m
   b) 3.25 kg
   c) 7000 kg
   d) 0.52 m
   e) 2700 ml
   f) 0.002 62 km
2. 12.5 miles
3. 1.32 pounds
4. Lower limit = 46.5 metres
   Upper limit = 47.5 metres
5. $53.\dot{3}$ mph
6. $0.1\ \text{g/cm}^{-3}$

C

1. a) 17.6 pounds
   b) 48 kilometres
2. 80 kg
3. a) 1 hour 36 minutes
   b) $4.\dot{4}$ km/h
4. Length = 12.05 cm, width = 5.5 cm

Area of 2D shapes – Page 66

A

1. c
2. d
3. b
4. d
5. b

B

1. a) false
   b) true
   c) true
   d) false
2. 38.6 cm
3. $84.21\ \text{cm}^2$
4. $70\,000\ \text{cm}^2$

C

1. $81\ \text{cm}^2$
2. $363.6\ \text{cm}^2$
3. 16 cm (to nearest cm)
4. $120.24\ \text{cm}^2$

Volume of 3D shapes – Page 68

A

1. a
2. c
3. a
4. c
5. d

B

1. Emily is not correct. The correct volume is $345.6 \div 2$, i.e. $172.8\ \text{cm}^3$.
2. $170.2\ \text{cm}^3$
3. 9.9 cm
4. $3807\ \text{cm}^3$
5. Volume needs three dimensions.
   $V = 4pr^2$ is only two-dimensional, hence must be a formula for area and not volume.

C

1. $64\ \text{cm}^3$
2. a) $672\ \text{cm}^3$
   b) $0.000\,672\ \text{m}^3$
3. 3.2 cm
4. a)

Expression	Length	Area	Volume	None
A ac		✔		
B $a + bc$				✔
C $ac(b - c)$			✔	
D $\sqrt{b^2}$	✔			

   b) Expression B is none because you cannot add a length (a) to an area (bc).

Further length, area and volume – Page 70

A

1. b
2. a
3. d
4. a
5. c

B

1. Solid A is $314\ \text{cm}^3$
   Solid B is $600\ \text{cm}^3$
   Solid C is $2\,145\ \text{cm}^3$
   Solid D is $68\ \text{cm}^3$
2. The statement is false because:
   Area of segment
   = area of sector − area of triangle
   $= 13.09 - 10.83$
   $= 2.26\ \text{cm}^2$

C

1. 73°
2. $0.0248\ \text{m}^3$ (3 s.f.)
3. 8 mm

Vectors – Page 72

A

1. b
2. c
3. a
4. b
5. b

B

1. a) true
   b) false
   c) true
   d) false
2. $\overrightarrow{OC} = 2\mathbf{a} - 3\mathbf{b}$, $\overrightarrow{OD} = 6(2\mathbf{a} - 3\mathbf{b})$
   Hence the vectors are parallel as one vector is a multiple of the other.
   The vectors lie on a straight line through O.
3.

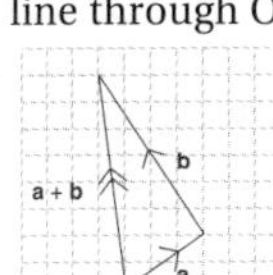

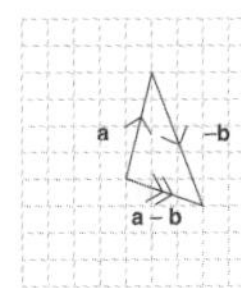

   a) $\mathbf{a} + \mathbf{b} = \binom{-1}{8}$
   b) $\mathbf{a} - \mathbf{b} = \binom{3}{-1}$

C

1. $\binom{2}{4}$
2. $\overrightarrow{AB} = -3\mathbf{a} + 3\mathbf{b}$,
   $\overrightarrow{CD} = -5\mathbf{a} + 5\mathbf{b}$
   Since $\overrightarrow{AB} = \frac{3}{5}\overrightarrow{CD}$, AB and CD are parallel.
3. a) $\overrightarrow{AC} = \mathbf{a} + \mathbf{b}$
   b) $\overrightarrow{BD} = \mathbf{b} + 2\mathbf{b} - \mathbf{a}$
   $= 3\mathbf{b} - \mathbf{a}$
   hence $\overrightarrow{AD} = \overrightarrow{AB} + \overrightarrow{BD}$
   $= \mathbf{a} + 3\mathbf{b} - \mathbf{a}$
   $\overrightarrow{AD} = 3\mathbf{b}$
   $\overrightarrow{AD} = 3\overrightarrow{BC}$ so BC is parallel to AD.
   c) $\overrightarrow{AN} = \overrightarrow{AD} + \overrightarrow{DN}$
   $= 3\mathbf{b} - \frac{1}{2}(2\mathbf{b} - \mathbf{a})$
   $= 3\mathbf{b} - \mathbf{b} + \frac{1}{2}\mathbf{a}$
   $= \frac{1}{2}\mathbf{a} + 2\mathbf{b}$
   d) $\overrightarrow{YD} = \overrightarrow{YA} + \overrightarrow{AD}$
   $= -\frac{3}{4}(\frac{1}{2}\mathbf{a} + 2\mathbf{b}) + 3\mathbf{b}$
   $= -\frac{3}{8}\mathbf{a} - \frac{3}{2}\mathbf{b} + 3\mathbf{b}$
   $= -\frac{3}{8}\mathbf{a} + \frac{3}{2}\mathbf{b}$
   $= \frac{3}{8}(4\mathbf{b} - \mathbf{a})$

HANDLING DATA

Collecting data – Page 74

A

1. b
2. d
3. a
4. b
5. d

B

1. The tick boxes overlap. Which box would somebody who did 2 hours of homework tick? It also needs an extra box with 5 or more hours.

   How much time do you spend, to the nearest hour, doing homework each night?

   0 up to 1 hour
   1 up to 2 hours
   2 up to 3 hours
   4 up to 5 hours
   5 hours or more

2. Year 7: 15 students
   8: 22 students
   9: 20 students
   10: 24 students
   11: 19 students

C

1. From the list below, tick your favourite chocolate bar.
   Mars ☐
   Twix ☐
   Toblerone ☐
   Galaxy ☐
   Bounty ☐
   Snickers ☐
   other ....
2. The key to this question is to break it into subgroups.
   a) On average, how many hours per school day do you watch television?
      0 up to 1 hour ☐
      1 up to 2 hours ☐
      2 up to 3 hours ☐
      3 up to 4 hours ☐
      Over 4 hours ☐
   b) On average, how many hours at the weekend do you watch television?
      0 up to 2 hours ☐
      2 up to 4 hours ☐
      4 up to 6 hours ☐
      6 up to 8 hours ☐
      Over 8 hours ☐
3. a) 30 students
   b) 14 girls

Scatter diagrams and correlation – Page 76

A

1. c
2. a
3. b

B

1. a) Positive correlation
   b) Negative correlation
   c) Positive correlation
   d) No correlation
2. a) Positive correlation
   b)

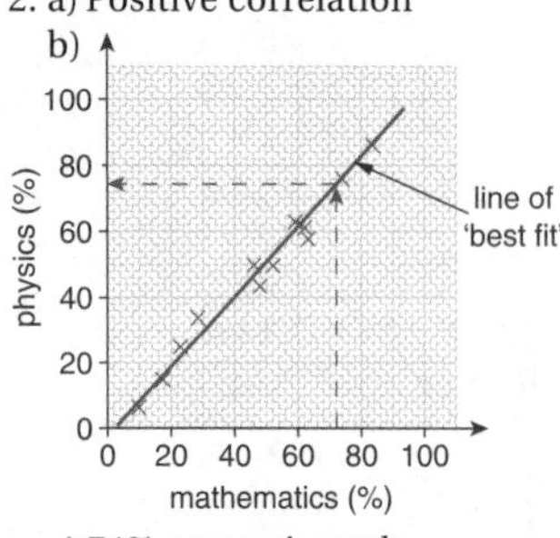

   c) 74% approximately

C

1. a)

   b) Negative correlation – the younger the child, the more hours sleep they needed.
   c) Line of best fit on diagram above.
   d) A four-year-old child needs approximately 14 hours sleep.
   e) This only gives an estimate as it follows the trend of the data. Similarly, if you continued the line it would assume that you may eventually need no hours sleep at a certain age, which is not the case.

Averages 1 – Page 78

A

1. c
2. b
3. d
4. d
5. b

B

1. a) false
   b) true
   c) false
   d) true
2. a) mean = 141.35
   b) The manufacturer is justified in making this claim since the mean is just over 141, and the mode and median are also approximately 141.
3. $x = 17$

C

1. a) 5 b) 3 c) 4.65
2. 81
3. £440
4. $3.\dot{3}$, $4.\dot{6}$, $3.\dot{6}$, 3, $2.\dot{3}$

Averages 2 – Page 80

A

1. c
2. b
3. a
4. a

B

1. 21.5 mm
2. a) 47 b) 35 c) 40

C

1. 1 | 2 4 9 5 7 5 8 8
   2 | 2 7 3 5 7 7
   3 | 1 6 5 2 8
   4 | 1
   Reordering gives this.
   1 | 2 4 5 5 7 8 8 9
   2 | 2 3 5 7 7 7
   3 | 1 2 5 6 8
   4 | 1
   Key: 1|2 means 12
   Stem: 10 minutes
2. a) £31.80
   b) This is only an estimate because the midpoint of the data has been used.
   c) $30 \leqslant x < 40$

Cumulative frequency graphs – Page 82

A

1. c
2. d
3. c
4. a

B

1. a)

Examination mark	Frequency	Cumulative frequency
0–10	4	4
11–20	6	10
21–30	11	21
31–40	24	45
41–50	18	63
51–60	7	70
61–70	3	73

   b)

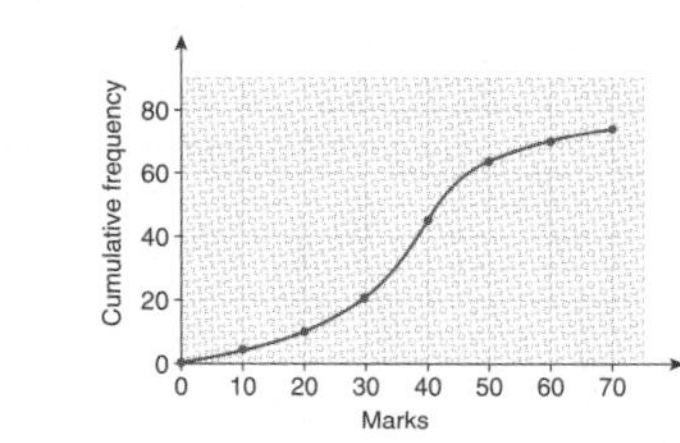

   c) 36.5
   d) 43 − 28 = 15 marks
   e) 45.5 marks

C

1. a)

Time (nearest minute)	Frequency	Cumulative frequency
$120 < t \leqslant 140$	1	1
$140 < t \leqslant 160$	8	9
$160 < t \leqslant 180$	24	33
$180 < t \leqslant 200$	29	62
$200 < t \leqslant 220$	10	72
$220 < t \leqslant 240$	5	77
$240 < t \leqslant 260$	3	80

   b)

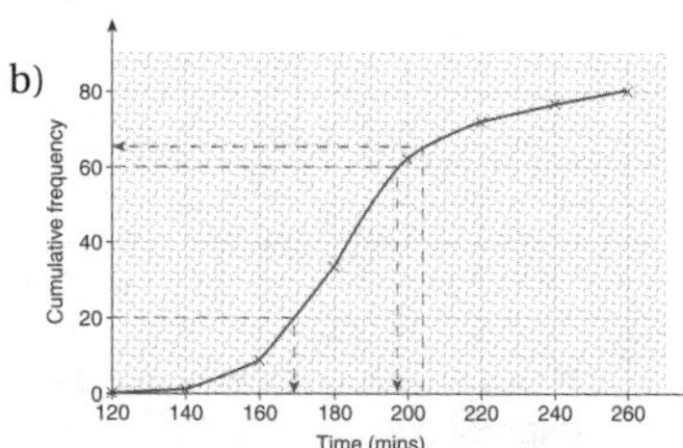

   c) i) Interquartile range = 198 − 169 = 29 minutes
      ii) 80 − 65 = 15 runners
   d)

Histograms – Page 84

A

1. d
2. b
3. b
4. a

B

1. a) $5 < t \leqslant 15$. 26
      $20 < t \leqslant 30$ 14

b)

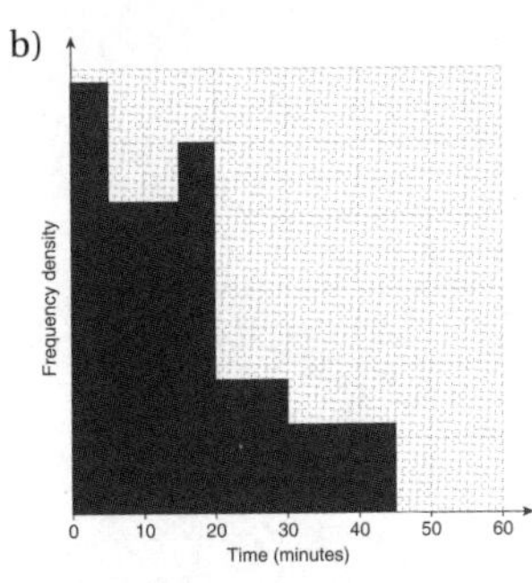

C

1.

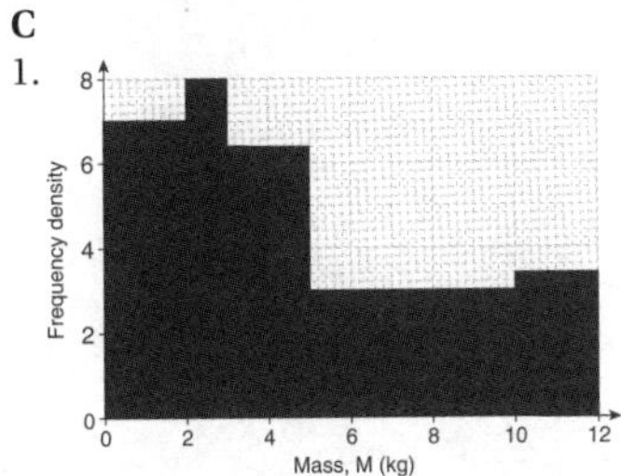

2.

Length S (in seconds)	Frequency
$0 \leqslant S < 10$	2
$10 \leqslant S < 15$	5
$15 \leqslant S < 20$	21
$20 \leqslant S < 40$	28
$S \geqslant 40$	0

Probability – Page 86

A

1. d
2. c
3. b
4. a
5. d

B

1. a)

Spinner 1

Spinner 2	1	2	3	3
1	2	3	4	4
2	3	4	5	5
3	4	5	6	6
6	7	8	9	9

b) i) $\frac{4}{16} = \frac{1}{4}$

ii) $\frac{2}{16} = \frac{1}{8}$

iii) 0

2. 0.09

3. a) $\frac{7}{26}$

b) $\frac{7}{13}$

C

1. a) i) 0.35 ii) 0

b) 50 red beads

2. a) $\frac{6}{36} = \frac{1}{6}$

b) $\frac{4}{36} = \frac{1}{9}$

3. a) Monopoly

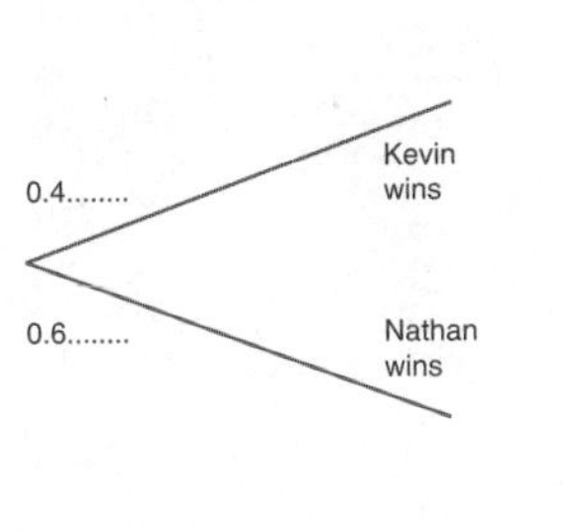

Pool

0.3........ Kevin wins

0.7........ Nathan wins

0.3........ Kevin wins

0.7........ Nathan wins

b) 0.42

c) 0.46

ACKNOWLEDGEMENTS

The author and publisher are grateful to the copyright holders for permission to use quoted materials and images.

Published by Letts Educational Ltd.
An imprint of HarperCollins*Publishers*
77–85 Fulham Palace Road
London W6 8JB

ISBN: 9781906415952

British Library Cataloguing in Publication Data. A CIP record of this book is available from the British Library.

Book concept and development: Helen Jacobs
Author: Fiona C. Mapp
Editorial: Marion Davies, Alan Worth
Project Editor: Katie Galloway
Cover design: Angela English
Inside concept design: Starfish Design
Text design, layout and editorial: Servis Filmsetting, Letts Educational Ltd.

C

These are GCSE-style questions. Answer all parts of the questions. Show your workings (on separate paper if necessary) and include the correct units in your answers.

1 **Enlarge triangle N by scale factor $\frac{1}{3}$ with centre R (−6, 7).** (3 marks)

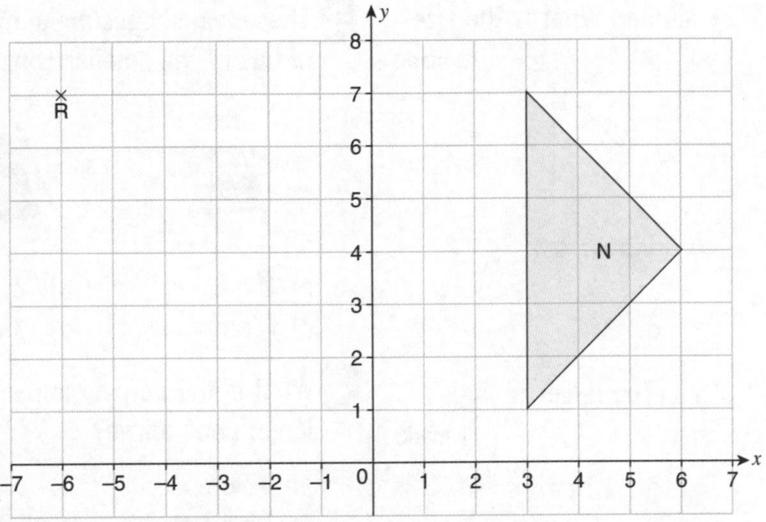

2 **The diagram shows four triangles, T_1, T_2, T_3 and T_4.**

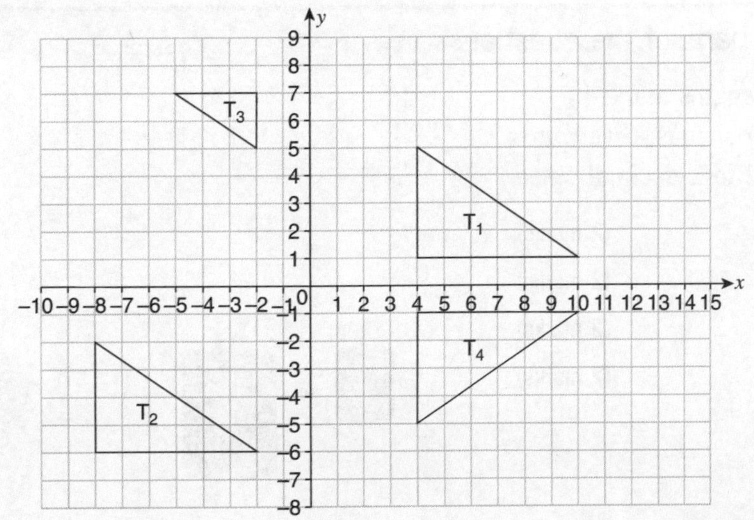

Describe fully the single transformation that maps:

a) T_1 onto T_2 .... (2 marks)

b) T_1 onto T_3 .... (2 marks)

c) T_1 onto T_4 .... (2 marks)

Score /9

How well did you do? ✗ 1–4 Try again 5–9 Getting there 10–16 Good work 17–21 Excellent! ✓

For more information on this topic, see pages 62–63 of your Success Guide.

Similarity & congruency

A Choose just one answer, a, b, c or d.

1 These two shapes are similar. What is the size of angle x? (1 mark)

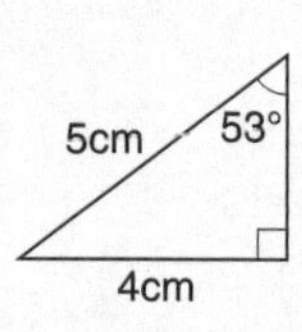

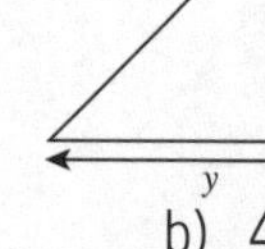

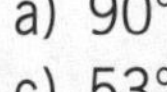

a) 90° b) 47°
c) 53° d) 50°

2 What is the length of y in the larger triangle above? (1 mark)

a) 14 cm b) 12 cm
c) 8 cm d) 16 cm

3 These two shapes are similar. What is the radius of the smaller cone? (C) (1 mark)

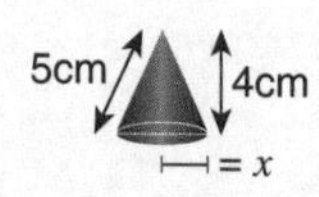

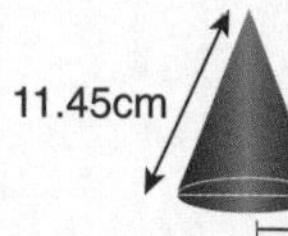

Diagrams not drawn to scale

a) 2 cm b) 3.12 cm
c) 4 cm d) 5 cm

4 What is the perpendicular height of the larger cone above? (C) (1 mark)

a) 12 cm b) 9.16 cm
c) 10.47 cm d) 10 cm

Score / 4

B Answer all parts of the questions.

1 Calculate the lengths marked n in these similar shapes. Give your answers correct to 1 decimal place. (C)

a) n = ... (2 marks)
b) n = ... (2 marks)
c) n = ... (2 marks)
d) n = ... (2 marks)

a)

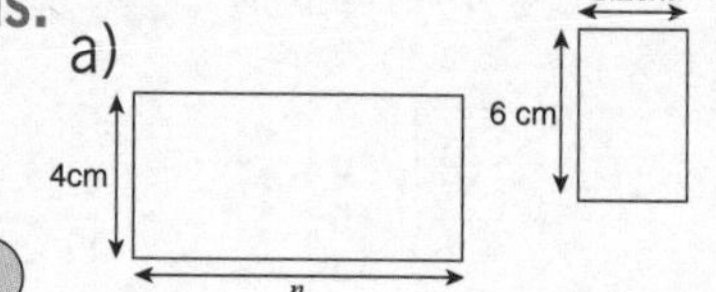

b)

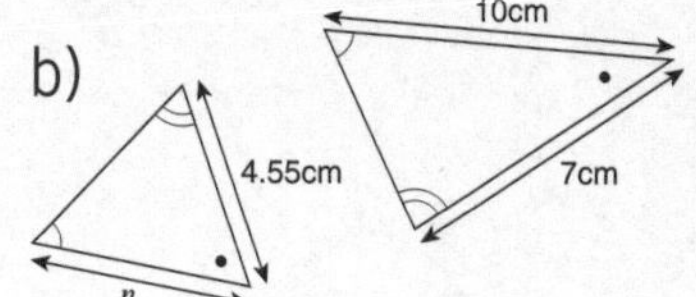

c)

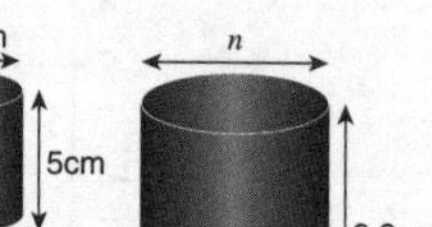

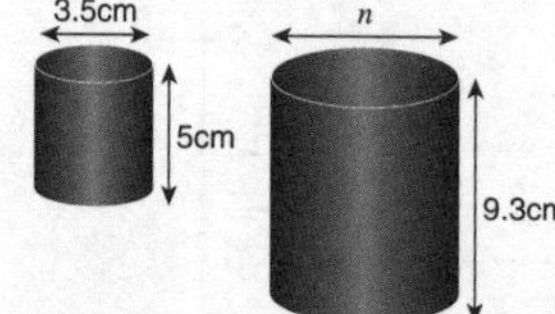

d)

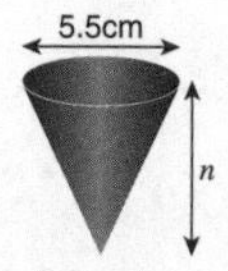

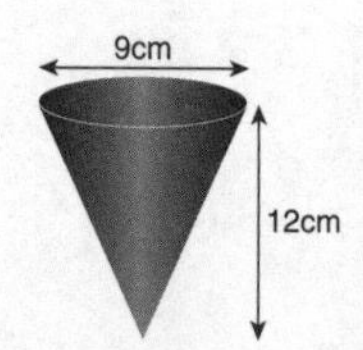

2 Which of the following pairs of triangles, C and D, are congruent? For those that are, state whether the reason is SSS, RHS, SAS or AAS. (3 marks)

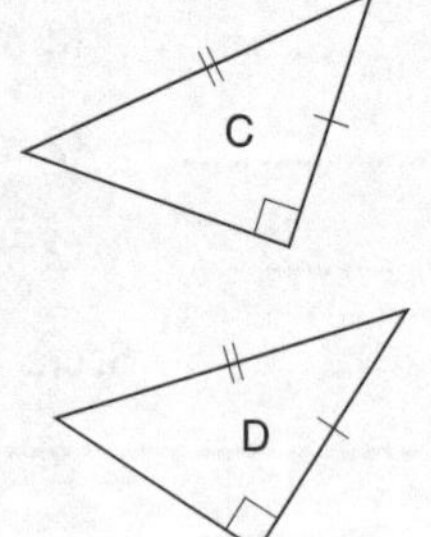

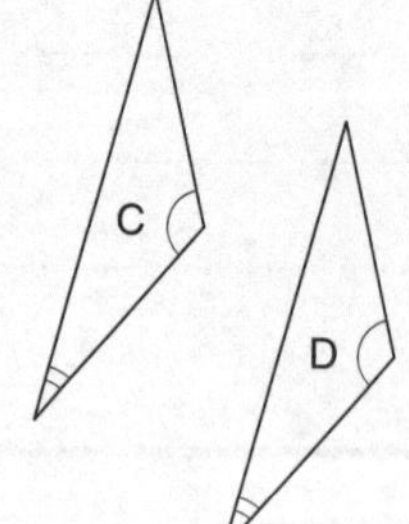

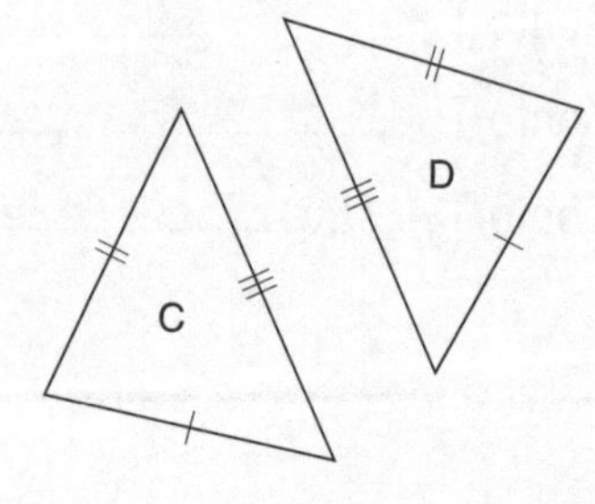

a) .... b) .... c) ....

Score / 11

(C) *Indicates that a calculator may be used*

C These are GCSE-style questions. Answer all parts of the questions. Show your workings (on separate paper if necessary) and include the correct units in your answers.

1 In the diagram MN is parallel to YZ.

YMX and ZNX are straight lines.

XM = 5.1 cm, XY = 9.5 cm, XN = 6.3 cm, YZ = 6.8 cm

∠YXZ = 29°, ∠XZY = 68°

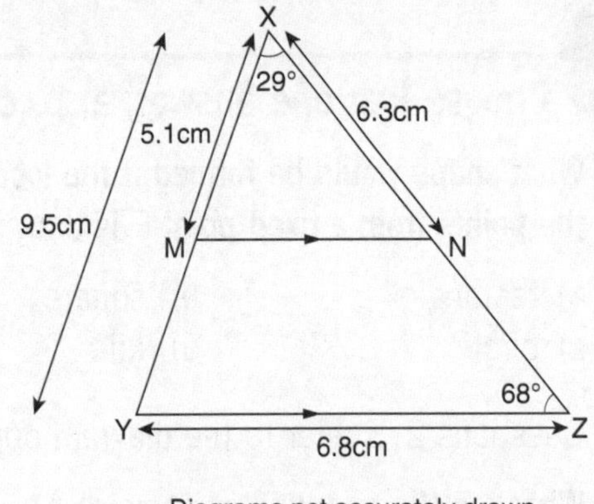

Diagrams not accurately drawn

a) i) Calculate the size of angle XMN. .... ° (1 mark)

ii) Explain how you obtained your answer. (C) (1 mark)

....

....

b) Calculate the length of MN. (C) .... (2 marks)

.... cm

c) Calculate the length of XZ. (C) .... (2 marks)

.... cm

2 Soup is sold in two similar cylindrical cans.

a) The area of the label on the smaller can is 81 cm^2.

Calculate the area of the label on the larger can. (The labels are also similar and in the same proportion as the height of the cans.) (C) (2 marks)

....

b) The capacity of the larger can of soup is 5 litres.

Calculate the capacity of the smaller can of soup. (C) (2 marks)

....

Score / 10

How well did you do? 1–6 Try again 7–12 Getting there 13–18 Good work 19–25 Excellent!

For more information on this topic, see pages 64–65 of your Success Guide.

Loci & coordinates in 3D

A Choose just one answer, a, b, c or d.

1 What shape would be formed if the locus of all the points from a fixed point P is drawn? (1 mark)

a) rectangle b) square
c) circle d) kite

Questions 2–5 refer to the diagram opposite.

2 What are the coordinates of point A? (1 mark)

a) (4, 3, 1) b) (4, 3, 0)
c) (0, 3, 1) d) (4, 0, 1)

3 What are the coordinates of point B? (1 mark)

a) (0, 3, 1) b) (0, 0, 0)
c) (4, 3, 0) d) (0, 3, 0)

4 What are the coordinates of point C? (1 mark)

a) (0, 3, 1) b) (4, 3, 1)
c) (4, 0, 0) d) (4, 3, 0)

5 What are the coordinates of point D? (1 mark)

a) (4, 3, 0) b) (4, 3, 1)
c) (0, 0, 0) d) (0, 3, 0)

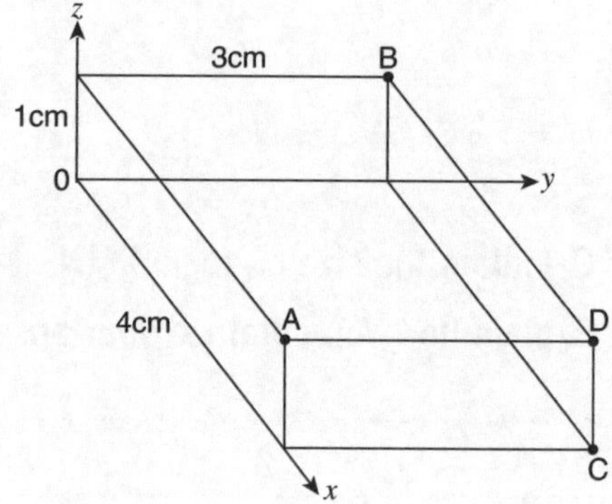

Score / 5

B Answer all parts of the questions.

1 The diagram shows the position of the post office (P), the hospital (H) and the school (S). Robert lives less than 4 miles away from the hospital, less than 5 miles away from the post office and less than 8 miles away from the school.

Show by shading the area where Robert can live. Use a scale of 1 cm = 2 miles. (4 marks)

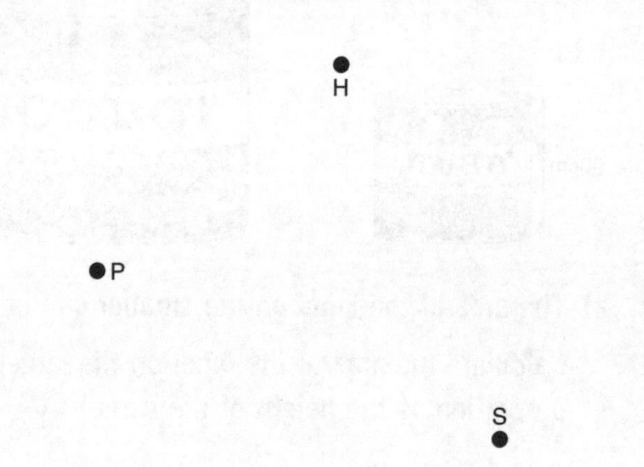

2 The diagram shows a solid. Complete the coordinates for each of the vertices listed below. (4 marks)

R = (.... , ... , ...)

S = (.... , ... , ...)

T = (.... , ... , ...)

U = (.... , ... , ...)

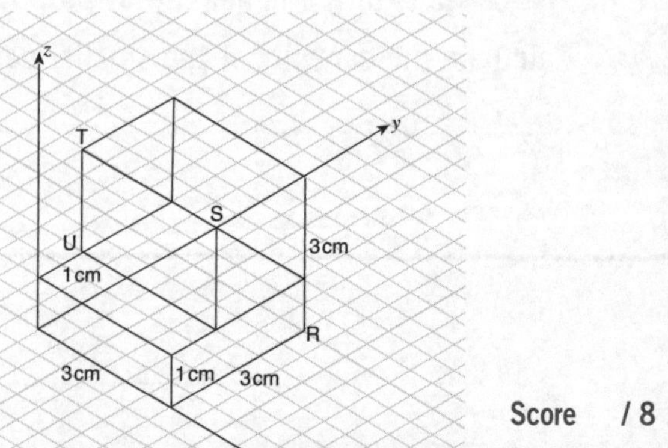

Score / 8

C These are GCSE-style questions. Answer all parts of the questions. Show your workings (on separate paper if necessary) and include the correct units in your answers.

1 In this question you should use ruler and compasses only for the constructions.

Triangle ABC is the plan of an adventure playground, drawn to a scale of 1 cm to 20 m.

a) On the diagram, draw accurately the locus of the points which are 100 m from C. (2 marks)

b) On the diagram, draw accurately the locus of the points which are the same distance from A as they are from C. (2 marks)

c) P is an ice cream kiosk inside the adventure playground.

P is the same distance from A as it is from C.

P is the same distance from AC as it is from AB.

On the diagram, mark the point P clearly with a cross.

Label it with the letter P. (3 marks)

2 A cuboid lies on the coordinate axes.

The point R has coordinates (5,4,3).

Write down the coordinates of point S. (1 mark)

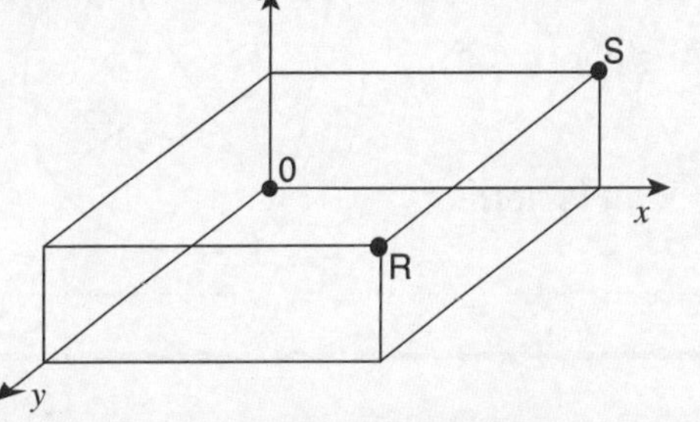

....

Score / 8

How well did you do? 1–4 Try again 5–9 Getting there 10–15 Good work 16–21 Excellent!

For more information on this topic, see page 66 of your Success Guide.

Angle properties of circles

A

Choose just one answer, a, b, c or d.

Questions 1–5 refer to the diagrams drawn below.

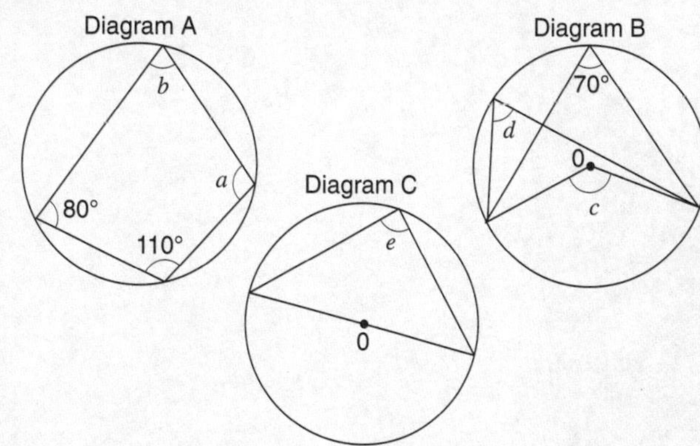

1 In diagram A, what is the size of angle a?

a) 80° b) 110° **(1 mark)**
c) 100° d) 70°

2 In diagram A, what is the size of angle b?

a) 70° b) 110° **(1 mark)**
c) 100° d) 80°

3 In diagram B, what is the size of angle c?

a) 35° b) 70° **(1 mark)**
c) 100° d) 140°

4 In diagram B, what is the size of angle d?

a) 70° b) 35° **(1 mark)**
c) 100° d) 140°

5 In diagram C, what is the size of angle e?

a) 100° b) 45° **(1 mark)**
c) 90° d) 110°

Score / 5

B

Answer all parts of the questions.

1 Some angles are written on cards. Match the missing angles in the diagrams below with the correct card. O represents the centre of the circle. **(5 marks)**

50°	60°	82°	65°	18°

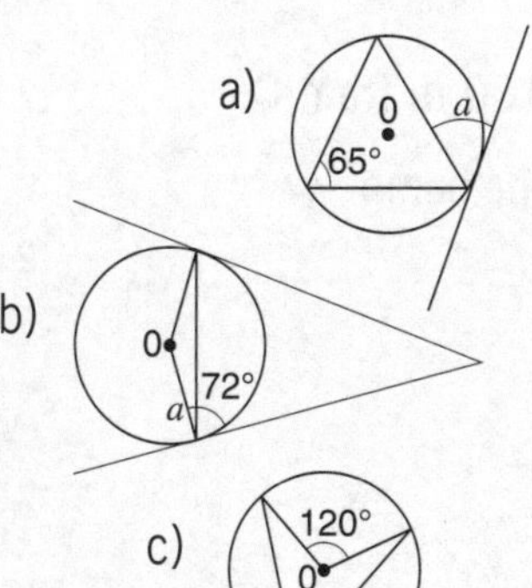

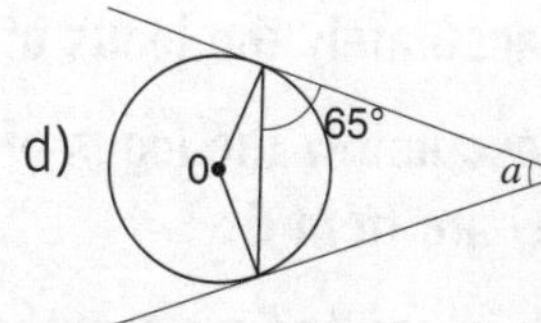

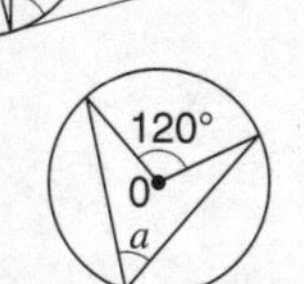

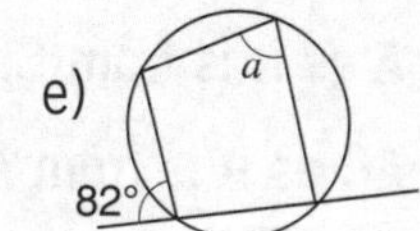

2 John says that 'Angle a is 42°.' **(1 mark)**

42°
a

Explain whether John is correct.

....

Score / 6

C **These are GCSE-style questions. Answer all parts of the questions. Show your workings (on separate paper if necessary) and include the correct units in your answers.**

1

Diagram not accurately drawn

R, S and T are points on the circumference of a circle with centre O.

a) Find angle RST. **(1 mark)**

.... °

b) Give a reason for your answer. **(2 marks)**

....

....

....

....

2 **PQ and PR are tangents to a circle centre O.**

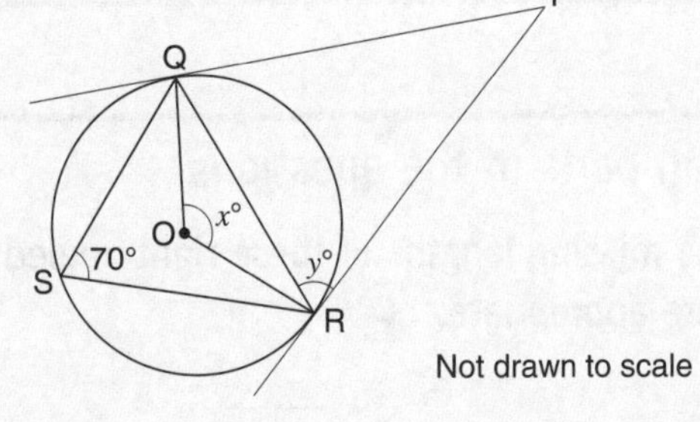

Point S is a point on the circumference.

Angle RSQ is 70°.

a) Find the size of angle ROQ, marked $x°$ in the diagram. **(2 marks)**

.... °

b) Find the size of angle PRQ, marked $y°$ in the diagram. **(4 marks)**

.... °

3 **A, B and C are points on the circumference of a circle.**

MBN is the tangent to the circle at B. **(3 marks)**

Calculate the value of p.

Give a reason for your answer.

Not drawn to scale

.... °

....

Score / 12

How well did you do?  **1–3 Try again** **4–8 Getting there** **9–15 Good work** **16–23 Excellent!**

For more information on this topic, see page 67 of your Success Guide.

Pythagoras' theorem

A

Choose just one answer, a, b, c or d.

1 What is the name of the longest side of a right-angled triangle? (1 mark)

a) hypo b) hippopotamus
c) crocodile d) hypotenuse

2 Calculate the missing length y of this triangle.

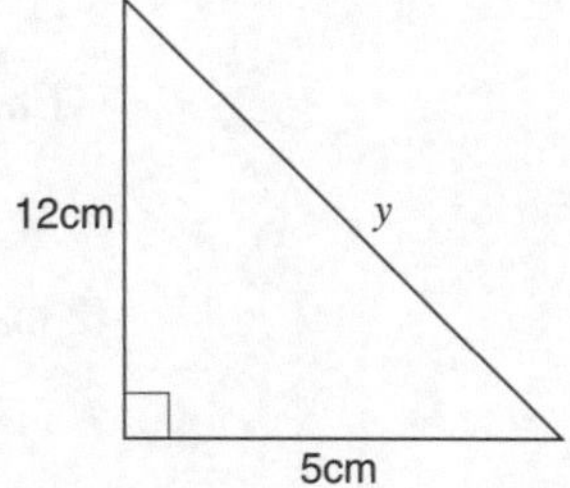

a) 169 cm b) 13 cm (1 mark)
c) 17 cm d) 84.5 cm

3 Calculate the missing length y of this triangle.

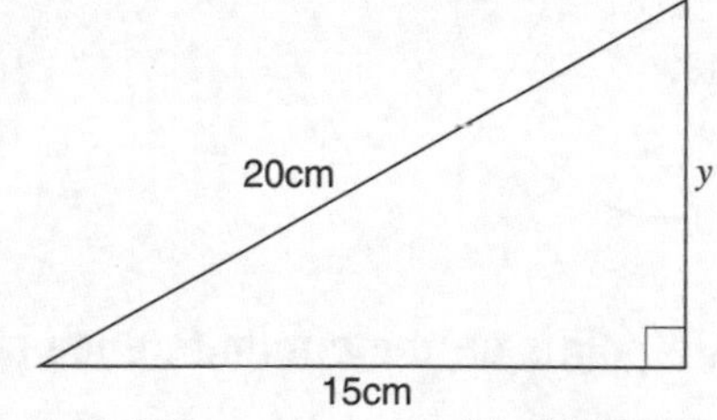

a) 13.2 cm b) 5 cm C (1 mark)
c) 25 cm d) 625 cm

4 Point A has coordinates (1, 4), point B has coordinates (4, 10). What are the coordinates of the midpoint of the line AB? (1 mark)

a) (5, 14) b) (3, 6)
c) (2.5, 7) d) (1.5, 3)

Score / 4

B

Answer all parts of the questions.

1 Calculate the missing lengths of these right-angled triangles. Give your answer to 3 significant figures, where appropriate. C

a)

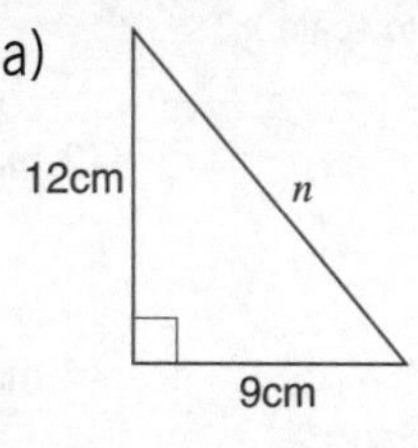

$n =$ ....cm

(2 marks)

b)

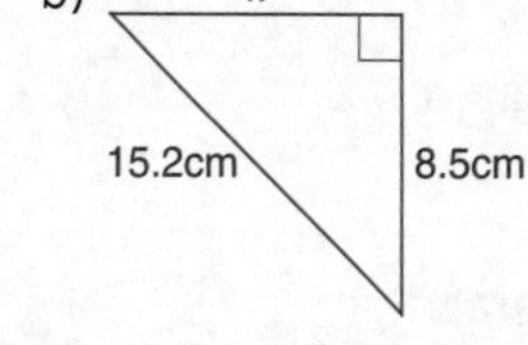
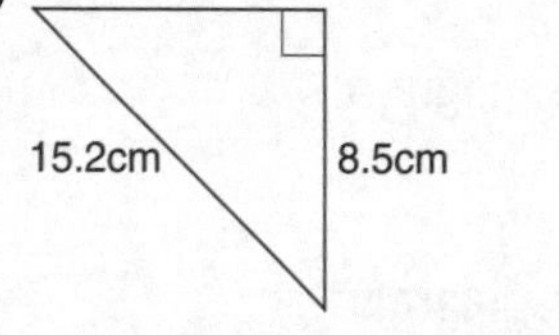

$n =$ ....cm

(2 marks)

c)

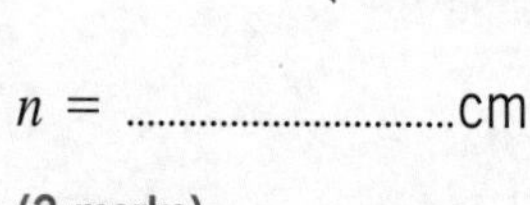

$n =$ ....cm

(2 marks)

d)

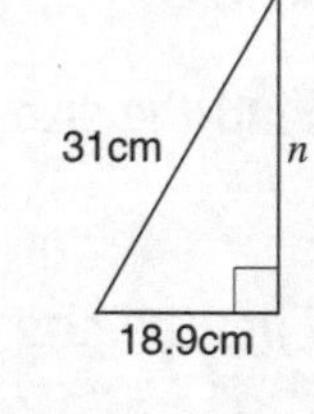

$n =$ ....cm

(2 marks)

2 Molly says, 'The angle $x°$ in this triangle is 90°.'

Explain how Molly knows this without measuring the size of the angle. (2 marks)

12cm 13cm $x°$ 5cm

....

....

3 Colin says, 'The length of this line is $\sqrt{45}$ units and the coordinates of the midpoint are (3.5, 8).'

Decide whether these statements are true or false. Give an explanation for your answer. (2 marks)

....

....

Score / 12

C *Indicates that a calculator may be used*

C

These are GCSE-style questions. Answer all parts of the questions. Show your workings (on separate paper if necessary) and include the correct units in your answers.

1 **ABC is a right-angled triangle. AB = 5 cm, BC = 6 cm**

Calculate the length of AC.

Leave your answer in surd form. (3 marks)

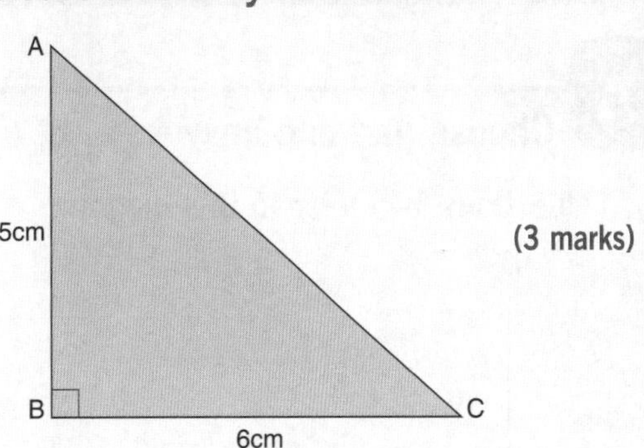

.... cm

2 **PQR is a right angled triangle. PR = 12 cm. RQ = 5cm.** (C)
Calculate the length of PQ. Give your answer to one decimal place. (3 marks)

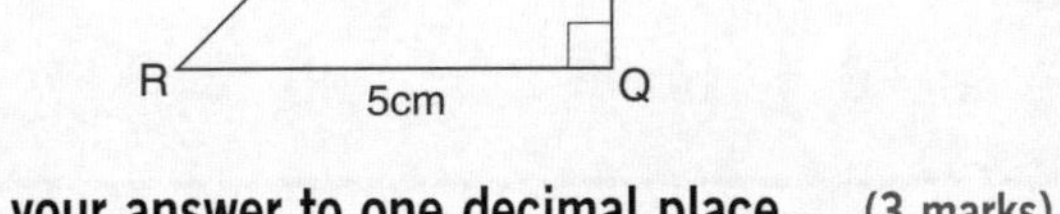

.... cm

3 **Calculate the length of the diagonal of this rectangle. Give your answer to one decimal place.** (3 marks)

.... cm (C)

4 **Calculate the perpendicular height of this isosceles triangle. Give your answer to one decimal place.** (C)

(3 marks)

.... m

5 **Calculate the length of AB in this diagram. Leave your answer in surd form.** (3 marks)

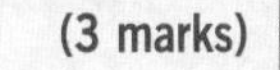

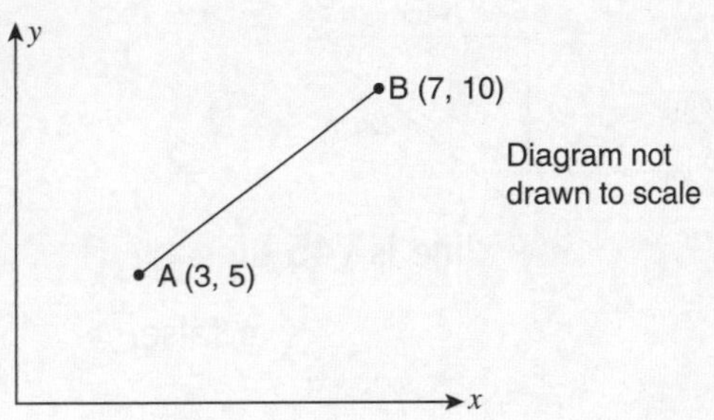

....

Score / 15

How well did you do? 1–7 Try again 8–14 Getting there 15–23 Good work 24–31 Excellent!

For more information on this topic, see pages 68–69 of your Success Guide.

Trigonometry 1

A Choose just one answer, a, b, c or d.

Questions 1–5 refer to this diagram.

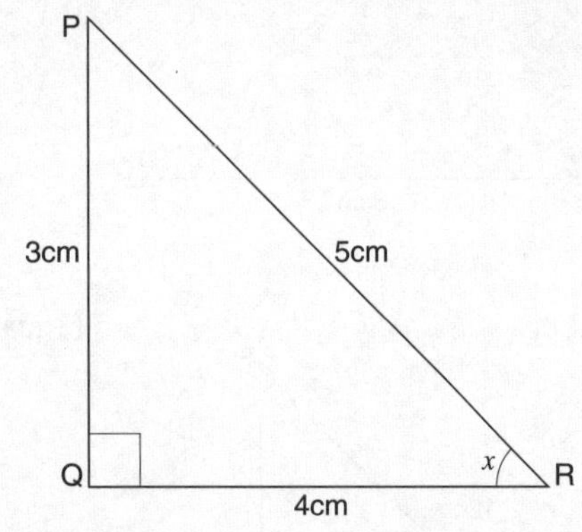

1 Which length is opposite angle x? **(1 mark)**

a) PQ b) PR c) QR d) RX

2 Which length of the triangle is the hypotenuse? **(1 mark)**

a) PQ b) PR c) QR d) RX

3 Which fraction represents tan x? **(1 mark)**

a) $\frac{3}{5}$ b) $\frac{4}{3}$ c) $\frac{4}{5}$ d) $\frac{3}{4}$

4 Which fraction represents sin x? **(1 mark)**

a) $\frac{3}{5}$ b) $\frac{4}{3}$ c) $\frac{5}{3}$ d) $\frac{4}{5}$

5 Which fraction represents cos x? **(1 mark)**

a) $\frac{3}{5}$ b) $\frac{3}{4}$ c) $\frac{4}{5}$ d) $\frac{5}{4}$

Score / 5

B Answer all parts of the questions.

1 Choose a card for each of the missing lengths n on the triangles. The lengths have been rounded to 1 decimal place. Ⓒ

6.3 cm	6.7 cm	13.8 cm	5 cm	14.9 cm

(5 marks)

a)

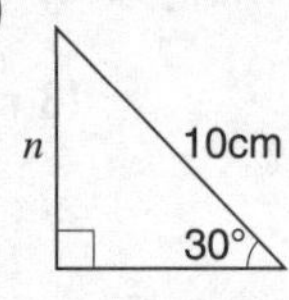

b) n, 12.5cm, 60°

c)

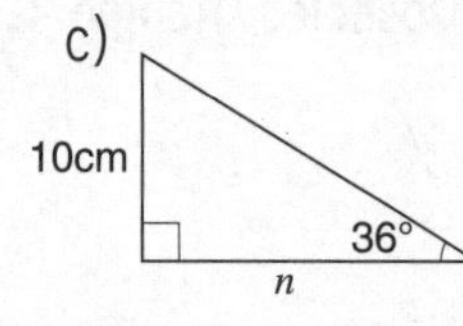

d) 14cm, 20°, n

e)

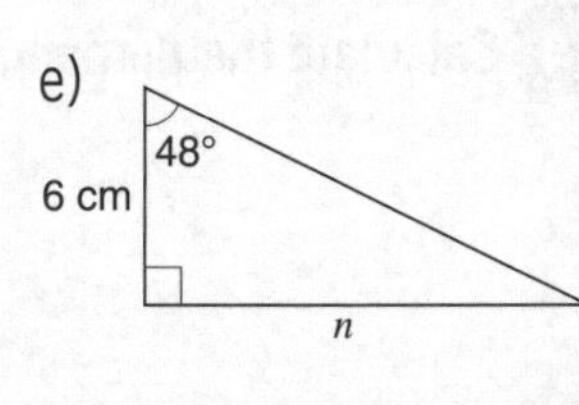

$n =$ .... cm $n =$ .... cm $n =$ .... cm $n =$ .... cm $n =$ .... cm

2 Work out the missing angle x in the diagrams below.

Give your answers to 1 decimal place. Ⓒ

a)

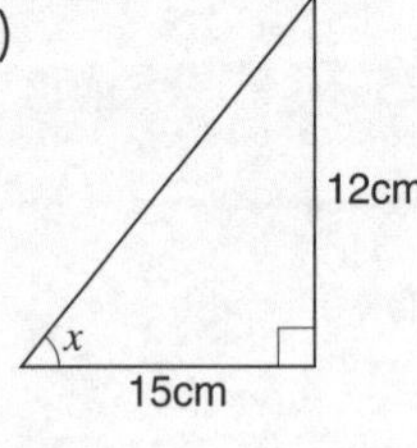

b)

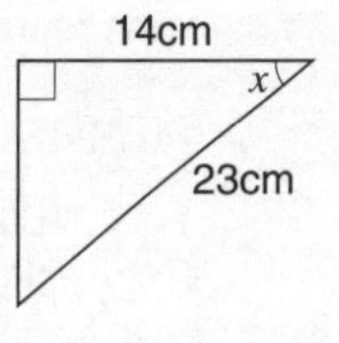

c)

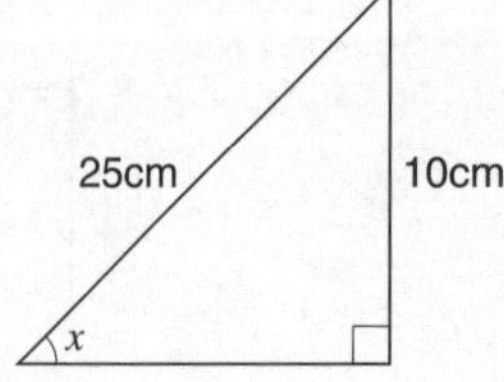

$x =$ .... ° $x =$ .... ° $x =$ .... °

(2 marks) **(2 marks)** **(2 marks)**

Score / 11

Ⓒ *Indicates that a calculator may be used*

C These are GCSE-style questions. Answer all parts of the questions. Show your workings (on separate paper if necessary) and include the correct units in your answers.

1 RS and SU are two sides of a rectangle.

T is a point on SU.

SU is 50 cm.

ST is 18 cm.

Angle STR is 40°.

Calculate the width of the rectangle. (C)

Give your answer correct to the nearest centimetre.

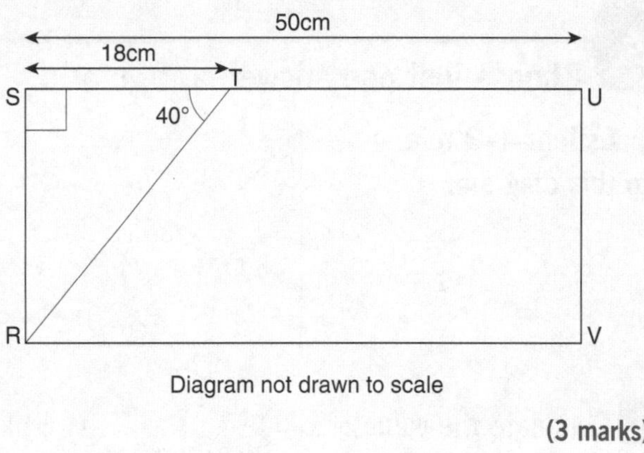

Diagram not drawn to scale

(3 marks)

.... cm

2 The diagram shows two triangles, PQR and QRS.

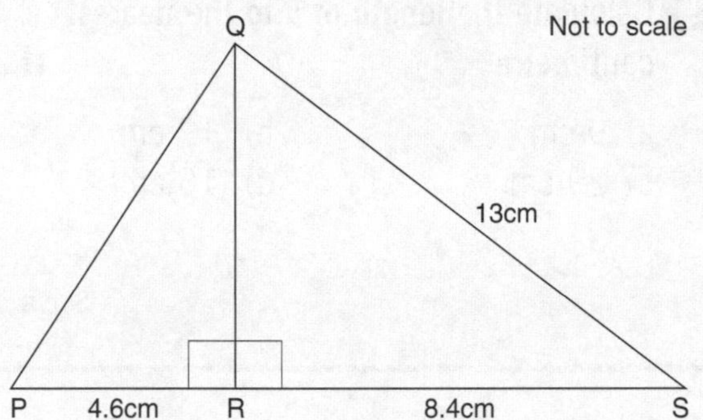

a) Calculate the length of QR. (C) (2 marks)

.... cm

b) Calculate angle QPR. (C) (3 marks)

.... °

3 The diagram shows a right-angled triangle ABC.

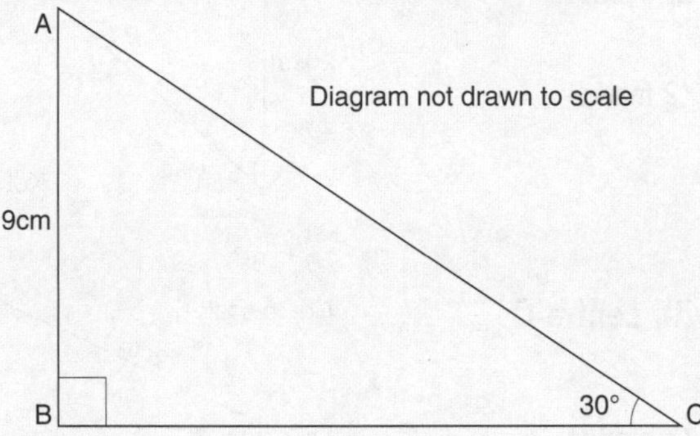

Diagram not drawn to scale

Calculate the length of AC. (C) (3 marks)

.... cm

Score /11

How well did you do? 1–7 Try again 8–12 Getting there 13–19 Good work 20–27 Excellent!

Trigonometry 2

A Choose just one answer, a, b, c or d.

Questions 1–3 refer to this diagram.

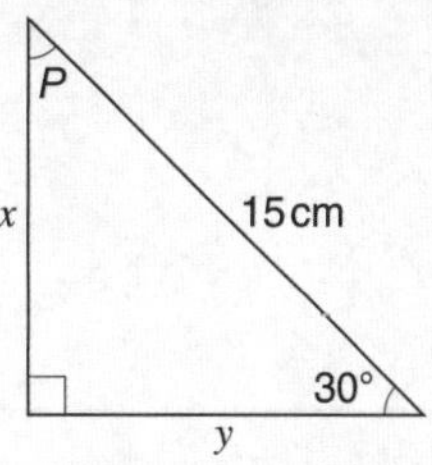

1 **Calculate the value of x.** (C) **(1 mark)**

a) 13 cm b) 8.7 cm
c) 7.5 cm d) 10 cm

2 **Calculate the value of y.** (C) **(1 mark)**

a) 13 cm b) 8.7 cm
c) 7.5 cm d) 10 cm

3 **Which fraction represents cos P?** (C) **(1 mark)**

a) $\frac{13}{15}$ b) $\frac{3}{4}$
c) $\frac{3}{5}$ d) $\frac{1}{2}$

Questions 4 and 5 refer to this diagram.

15cm
a
12cm
b
Not to scale

4 **Calculate the size of angle a to the nearest degree.** (C) **(1 mark)**

a) 53° b) 45° c) 39° d) 37°

5 **Calculate the length of b to the nearest centimetre.** (C) **(1 mark)**

a) 9 cm b) 19 cm
c) 29 cm d) 16 cm

Score / 5

B Answer all parts of the questions.

1 **A ship sails 20 km due north and then 50 km due east. What is the bearing of the finishing point from the starting point?** (C) **(2 marks)**

50km
finish
20km
start
Not to scale

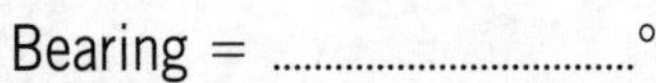

Bearing = ... °

2 **The diagram represents the sector of a circle with centre O and radius 12 cm. Angle POR equals 70°.**

Calculate the length of the straight line PR. (C) **(3 marks)**

Not to scale
P
12cm
O
70°
R

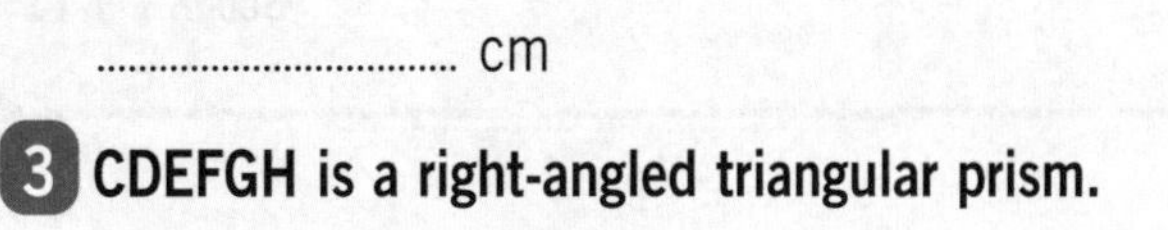

.... cm

3 **CDEFGH is a right-angled triangular prism.**

N is the midpoint of DE.

25cm
G
H
Not to scale
15cm
F
C
E
12cm
N
D

a) Decide whether the following statements are true or false.

i) The length HD is 19.2 cm, correct to 3 s.f. ....

ii) The size of angle HDC is 51.3°, correct to 1 decimal place. .... **(2 marks)**

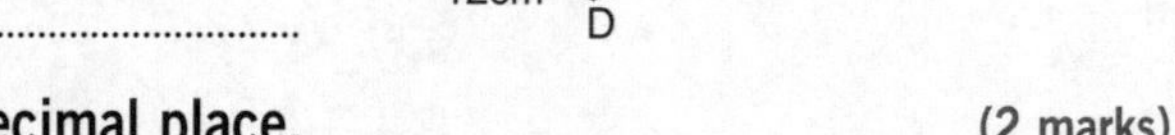

b) Calculate the size of angle HNC. .... ° (C) **(3 marks)**

Score / 10

Indicates that a calculator may be used

C

These are GCSE-style questions. Answer all parts of the questions. Show your workings (on separate paper if necessary) and include the correct units in your answers.

1 The diagram shows a triangle PQR.

PS = 6.5 cm, QR = 12.7 cm and angle QRS = 62°.

Calculate the size of the angle marked x°.

Give your answer correct to 1 decimal place. (C) (5 marks)

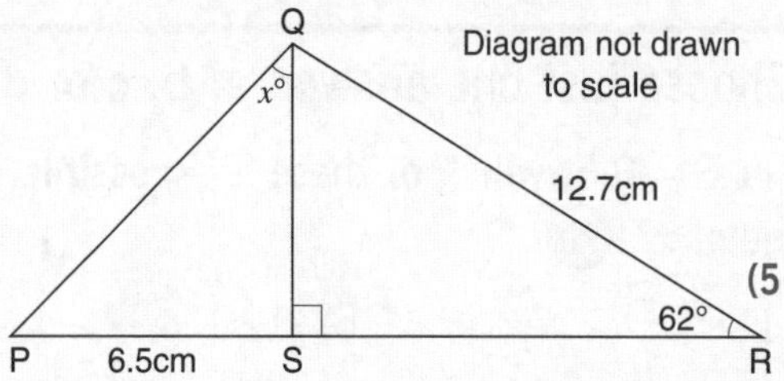

Q
Diagram not drawn to scale
x°
12.7cm
62°
P 6.5cm S R

....

.... °

2 In the diagram P Q and R represent three ships. Work out the bearing of P from Q.

Give your answer to 3 significant figures. (C) (3 marks)

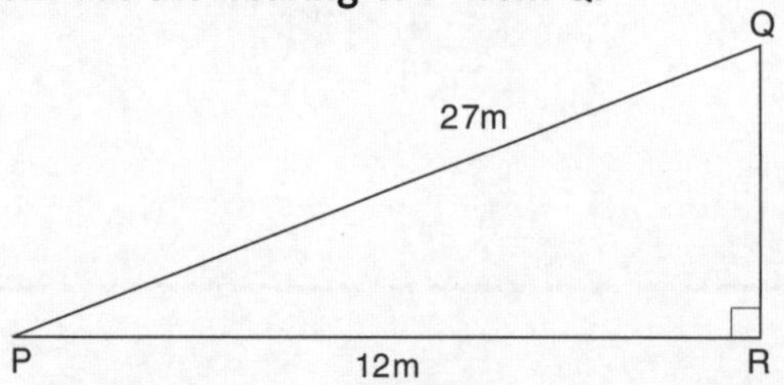

Q
27m
P 12m R

....

3 The angle of elevation of P from T is 18°.

R is 1500 m due west of S and
T is 1200 m due south of S.
SP is a vertical tower.

R, S and T are three points on horizontal ground.

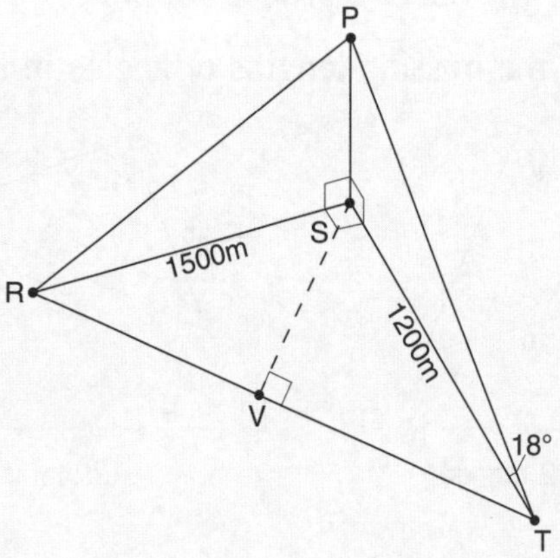

P
S
R
1500m
1200m
V
18°
T

a) Calculate the height of the tower. (C) (2 marks)

....

.... m

b) Find the angle of elevation of P from R. (2 marks)

....

.... °

c) V is a point on RT which is nearest to S.

Calculate the angle of elevation of P from V. (5 marks)

....

....

....

.... °

Score / 17

How well did you do? 1–8 Try again 9–15 Getting there 16–23 Good work 24–32 Excellent!

For more information on this topic, see pages 70–73 of your Success Guide.

Further trigonometry

A

Choose just one answer, a, b, c or d.

1 **If $\sin x = 0.5$, which of these is a possible value of x?** (C) (1 mark)

a) 180° b) 120°
c) 150° d) 90°

2 **If $\cos x = 0.5$, which of these is a possible value of x?** (C) (1 mark)

a) 300° b) 150°
c) 65° d) 120°

3 **If $\sin x = \frac{\sqrt{3}}{2}$, which of these is a possible value of x?** (C) (1 mark)

a) 320° b) 400°
c) 360° d) 420°

4 **Which of these is the correct formula for the cosine rule?** (1 mark)

a) $a^2 = b^2 - c^2 + 2bc \cos A$
b) $b^2 = a^2 + c^2 - 2bc \cos B$
c) $a^2 = b^2 + c^2 - 2bc \cos A$
d) $c^2 = b^2 + a^2 - 2ab \cos A$

Score / 4

B

Answer all parts of the questions.

1 **Calculate the missing lengths or angles in the diagrams below.** (C)

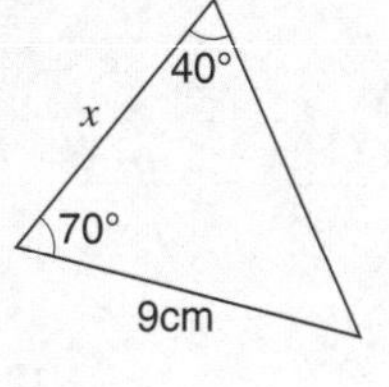

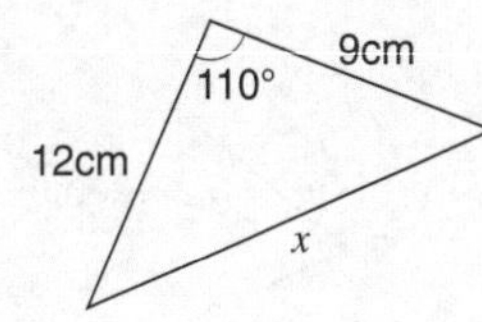

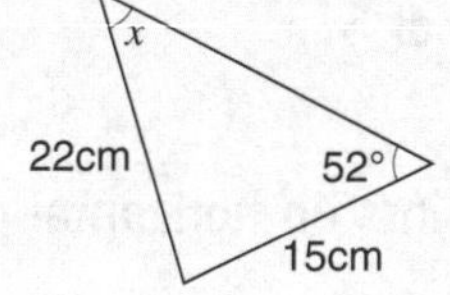

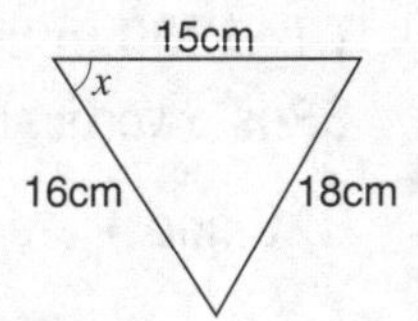

a) $x =$ .... cm (2 marks)
b) $x =$ .... cm (2 marks)
c) $x =$ .... ° (2 marks)
d) $x =$ .... ° (2 marks)

2 **Isobel says, 'The area of this triangle is 70 cm².'**

Decide, with working to justify your answer, whether this statement is true or false. (C) (2 marks)

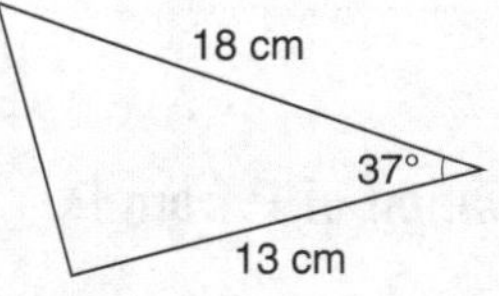

....

....

3 **The diagram shows a sketch of part of the curve $y = f(x)$, where $f(x) = \cos x°$.**

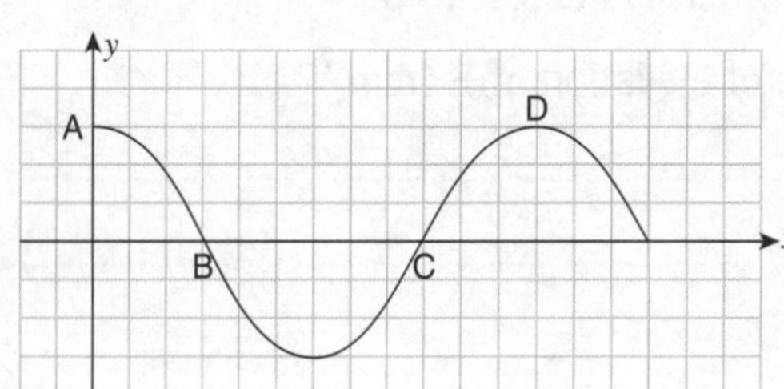

a) Write down the coordinates of the points:

A (.........., ...) B (.........., ...) C (.........., ...) D (.........., ...) (4 marks)

b) On the same diagram, sketch the graph of $y = \cos 2x$ (3 marks)

Score / 17

(C) *Indicates that a calculator may be used*

C These are GCSE-style questions. Answer all parts of the questions. Show your workings (on separate paper if necessary) and include the correct units in your answers.

1 The diagram shows a quadrilateral PQRS.

PS = 4.3 cm, PQ = 5.8 cm, SR = 7.3 cm

Angle PSR = 127°, angle PQR = 54°

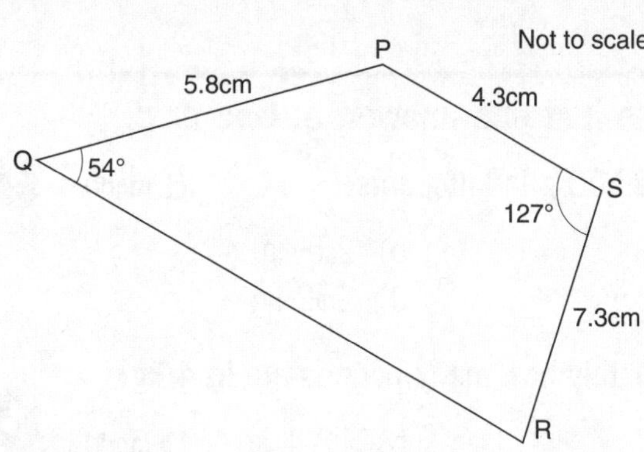

a) Calculate the length of PR. (C)
Give your answer correct to 3 significant figures. .... **(3 marks)**

.... cm

b) Calculate the area of triangle PRS. (C)
Give your answer correct to 3 significant figures. .... **(2 marks)**

.... cm^2

c) Calculate the area of the quadrilateral PQRS. (C)
Give your answer correct to 3 significant figures. .... **(6 marks)**

....

.... cm^2

2

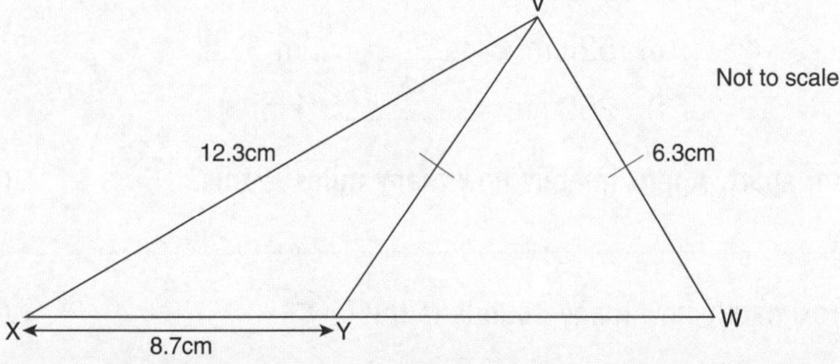

In triangle VWX, Y is the point on WX such that VW = VY.

VW = 6.3 cm, VX = 12.3 cm, XY = 8.7 cm

Calculate the length of WY. (C) **(5 marks)**

....

.... cm

Score / 16

How well did you do? ✗ 1–10 Try again 11–19 Getting there 20–27 Good work 28–37 Excellent! ✓

For more information on this topic, see pages 74–75 & 78 of your Success Guide.

Measures & measurement

A

Choose just one answer, a, b, c or d.

1 **What is 2 500 g in kilograms?** (1 mark)

a) 25 kg b) 2.5 kg
c) 0.25 kg d) 250 kg

2 **Approximately how many pounds are in 4 kg?** (1 mark)

a) 6.9 b) 12.4
c) 7.7 d) 8.8

3 **Jessica is 165 cm tall to the nearest cm. What is the lower limit of her height?** (1 mark)

a) 164.5 cm b) 165.5 cm
c) 165 cm d) 164.9 cm

4 **What is the volume of a piece of wood with density 680 kg m^{-3} and mass 34 kg?** (1 mark)

a) 0.5 m^3 b) 20 m^3 Ⓒ
c) 2 m^3 d) 0.05 m^3

5 **A car travels for two and a half hours at a speed of 42 mph. How far does the car travel?** Ⓒ (1 mark)

a) 96 miles b) 100 miles
c) 105 miles d) 140 miles

Score / 5

B

Answer all parts of the questions.

1 **Complete the statements below.** (6 marks)

a) 8 km = ... m
b) 3 250 g = ... kg
c) 7 tonnes = ... kg
d) 52 cm = ... m
e) 2.7 litres = ... ml
f) 262 cm = ... km

2 **Two towns are approximately 20 km apart. Approximately how many miles is this?** Ⓒ (1 mark)

....

3 **A recipe uses 600 g of flour. Approximately how many pounds is this?** Ⓒ (1 mark)

....

4 **A field is 47 metres long to the nearest metre. Write down the upper and lower limits of the length of the field.** (2 marks)

....

5 **Giovanni drove 200 miles in 3 hours and 45 minutes. At what average speed did he travel?** (2 marks)

.... Ⓒ

6 **What is the density of a toy if its mass is 200 g and its volume is 2000 cm^3?** (2 marks)

....

Score / 14

Ⓒ *Indicates that a calculator may be used*

C

These are GCSE-style questions. Answer all parts of the questions. Show your workings (on separate paper if necessary) and include the correct units in your answers.

1 a) Change 8 kilograms into pounds. (2 marks)

.... pounds (C)

b) Change 30 miles into kilometres. (2 marks)

.... km

2 Two solids each have a volume of $2.5m^3$.

The density of solid A is 320 kg per m^3.

The density of solid B is 288 kg per m^3.

A

B

Calculate the difference in the masses of the solids. (C) .... kg (3 marks)

3 Amy took part in a sponsored walk.

She walked from the school to the park and back.

The distance from the school to the park is 8 km.

a) Amy walked from the school to the park at an average speed of 5 km/h.

Find the time she took to walk from the school to the park. (C) (2 marks)

....

b) Her average speed for the return journey was 4 km/h.

Calculate her average speed for the whole journey. (C) (4 marks)

.... km/h

4 The length of the rectangle is 12.1 cm to the nearest mm.

The width of the rectangle is 6 cm to the nearest cm.

Write down the lower limits for the length and width of the rectangle.

12.1cm

6cm

Length .... cm (2 marks)

Width .... cm

Score / 15

How well did you do? 1–11 Try again 12–19 Getting there 20–27 Good work 28–34 Excellent!

For more information on this topic, see pages 76–77 of your Success Guide.

Area of 2D shapes

A Choose just one answer, a, b, c or d.

1 What is the area of this triangle? **(1 mark)**

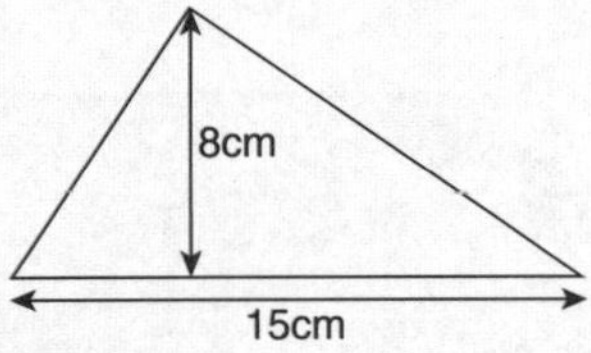

a) 60 mm^2　　b) 120 cm^2
c) 60 cm^2　　d) 46 cm^2

2 What is the approximate circumference of a circle of radius 4 cm? **(1 mark)**

a) 25.1 cm^2　　b) 50.3 cm
c) 12.6 cm　　d) 25.1 cm

3 Change 50 000 cm^2 into m^2. **(1 mark)**

a) 500 m^2　　b) 5 m^2
c) 0.5 m^2　　d) 50 m^2

4 What is the area of this circle? (C) **(1 mark)**

4cm

a) 25.1 cm^2　　b) 55 cm^2
c) 12.6 cm^2　　d) 50.3 cm^2

5 If the area of a rectangle is 20 cm^2 and its width is 2.5 cm, what is the length of the rectangle? **(1 mark)**

a) 9 cm　　b) 8 cm
c) 7.5 cm　　d) 2.5 cm

Score　/5

B Answer all parts of the questions.

1 For each of the diagrams below, decide whether the area (rounded to the nearest whole number) given is true or false.

a)
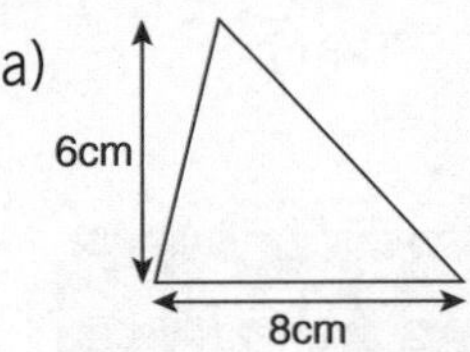

b)
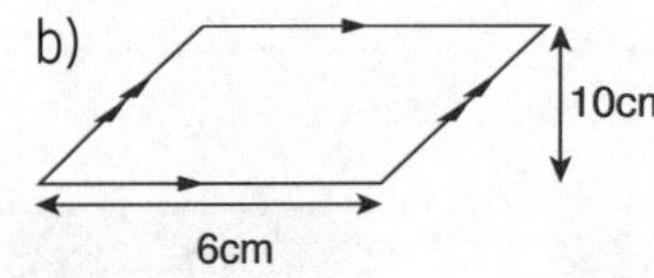

c)
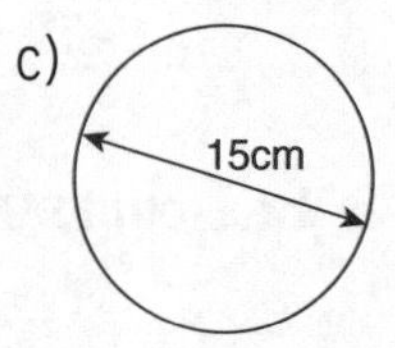

d)
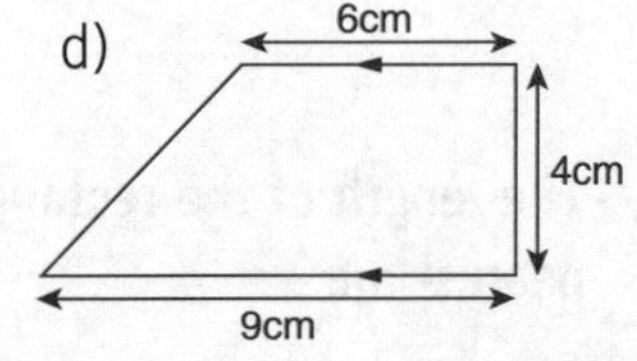

a) Area = 48 cm^2 .... **(1 mark)**

b) Area = 60 cm^2 .... **(1 mark)**

c) Area = 177 cm^2 .... **(1 mark)**

d) Area = 108 cm^2 .... **(1 mark)**

2 Calculate the perimeter of this shape. (C) **(3 marks)**

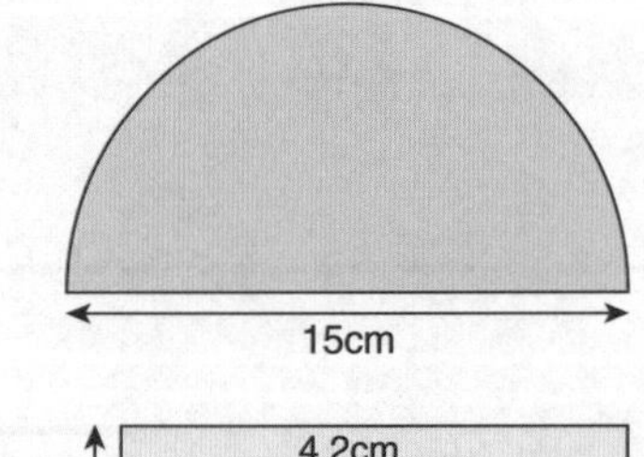

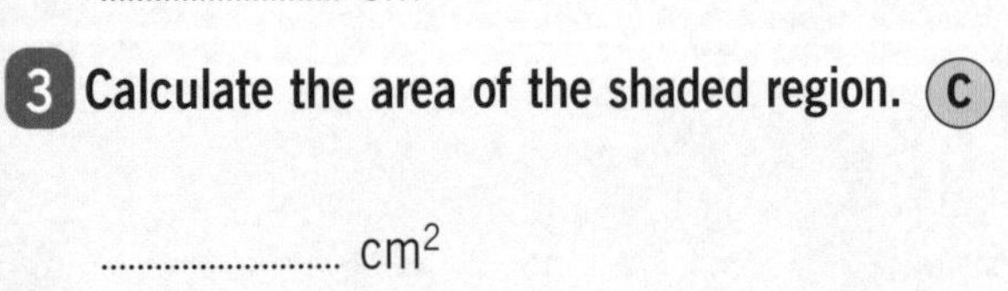

.... cm

3 Calculate the area of the shaded region. (C) **(3 marks)**

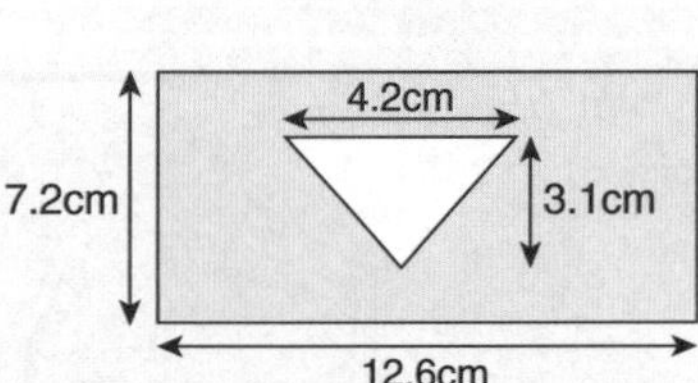

.... cm^2

4 Change 7m^2 to cm^2. .... cm^2 **(2 marks)**

Score　/12

(C) *Indicates that a calculator may be used*

C

These are GCSE-style questions. Answer all parts of the questions. Show your workings (on separate paper if necessary) and include the correct units in your answers.

1 Work out the area of the shape shown in the diagram. (C)

State the units with your answer. **(5 marks)**

15cm
8cm
5cm
9cm
Diagrams not drawn to scale

2 A semicircle is cut from a circle. The circle has a diameter of 25 cm. The semicircle has a diameter of 18 cm

Calculate the area of the shaded area. (C)

Give your answer to 1 decimal place. **(3 marks)**

O

.... cm

3 The area of a circular sewing pattern is 200 cm^2.

Calculate the diameter of the sewing pattern.

Give your answer correct to the nearest centimetre. (C) **(4 marks)**

.... cm

4 Calculate the area of the shape.

State the units with your answer. (C) **(3 marks)**

13.8cm
7.2cm
19.6cm

Score / 15

How well did you do? 1–8 Try again 9–16 Getting there 17–24 Good work 25–32 Excellent!

For more information on this topic, see pages 78–79 of your Success Guide.

Volume of 3D shapes

A

Choose just one answer, a, b, c or d.

1 What is the volume of this cuboid? (1 mark)

a) 30 cm^3
b) 16 cm^3
c) 300 mm^3
d) 15 cm^3

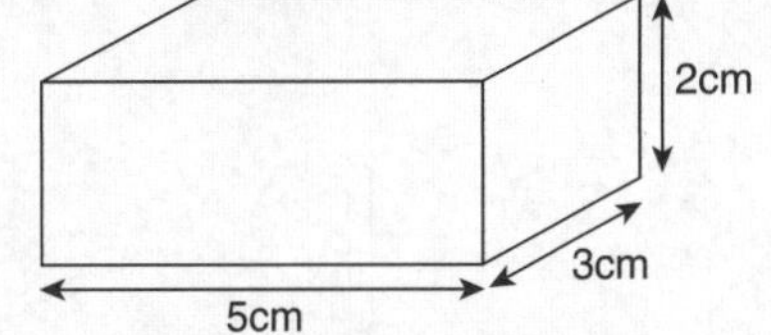

2 What is the volume of this prism? (1 mark)

a) 64 cm^3
b) 240 cm^3
c) 120 cm^3
d) 20 cm^3

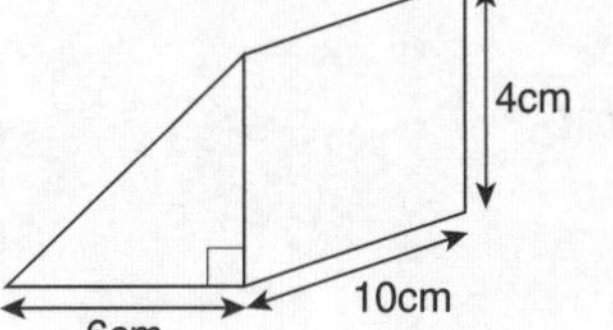

3 The volume of a cuboid is 20 cm^3. If its height is 1 cm and its width is 4 cm, what is its length? (1 mark)

a) 5 cm
b) 10 cm
c) 15 cm
d) 8 cm

4 A cube of volume 2 cm^3 is enlarged by a scale factor of 3. What is the volume of the enlarged cube? (1 mark)

a) 6 cm^3
b) 27 cm^3
c) 54 cm^3
d) 18 cm^3

5 If p and q represent lengths, decide what the formula $\frac{3}{5}\pi p^2 q$ shows. (1 mark)

a) circumference
b) length
c) area
d) volume

Score / 5

B

Answer all parts of the questions.

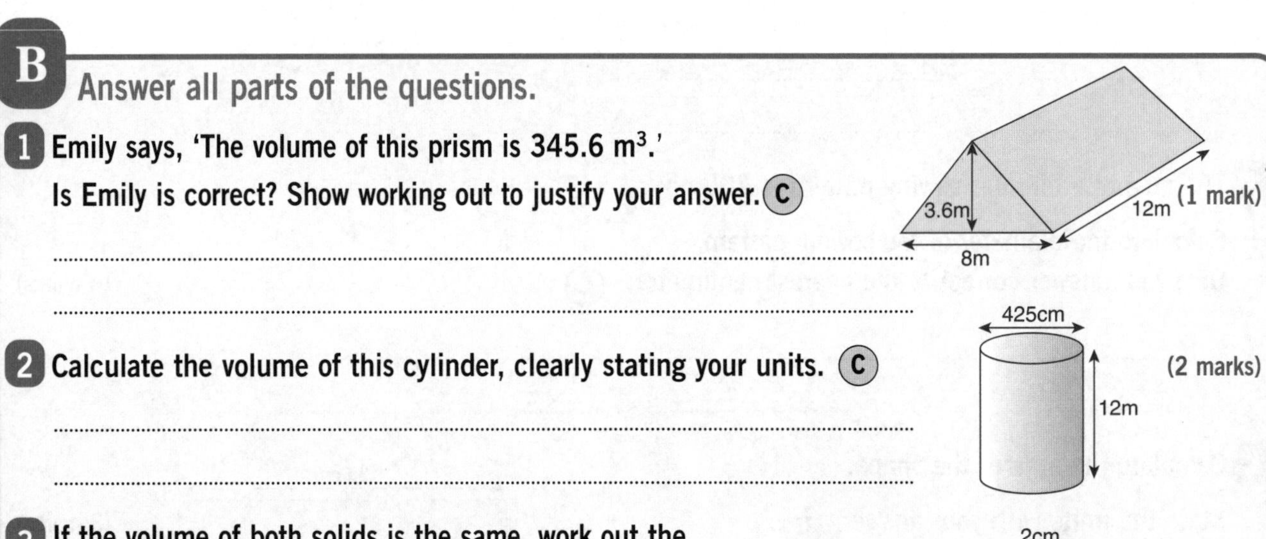

1 Emily says, 'The volume of this prism is 345.6 m^3.'
Is Emily is correct? Show working out to justify your answer. (C) (1 mark)

....

....

2 Calculate the volume of this cylinder, clearly stating your units. (C) (2 marks)

....

....

3 If the volume of both solids is the same, work out the height of the cylinder to 1 decimal place. (C) (4 marks)

....cm

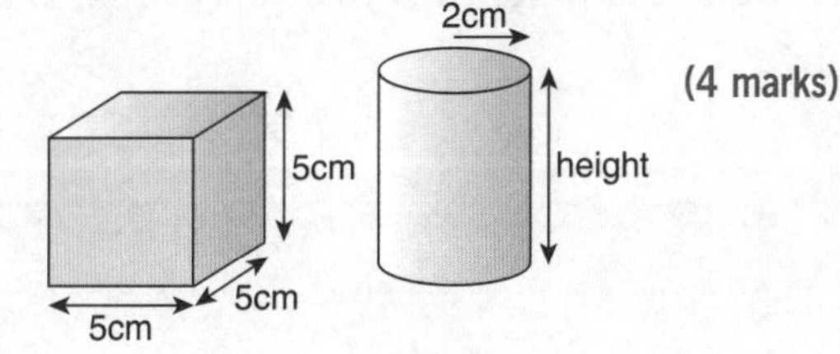

4 The volume of a cube is 141 cm^3.

Each length of the cube is enlarged by a scale factor of 3.
What is the volume of the enlarged cube? (C) (2 marks)

.... cm^3

5 Lucy says that 'The volume of a sphere is given by the formula $V = 4\pi r^2$'.
Explain why she cannot be correct. (C) (1 mark)

....

Score / 10

(C) *Indicates that a calculator may be used*

C

These are GCSE-style questions. Answer all parts of the questions. Show your workings (on separate paper if necessary) and include the correct units in your answers.

1 A cube has a surface area of 96 cm^2. Work out the volume of the cube. (4 marks)

....

2 A door wedge is in the shape of a prism with cross section VWXY.

VW = 7 cm, VY = 15 cm, WX = 9 cm.

The width of the door wedge is 0.08 m.

a) Calculate the volume of the door wedge. (C) (3 marks)

.... cm^3

b) What is the volume of the door wedge in m^3? (C) (1 mark)

.... m^3

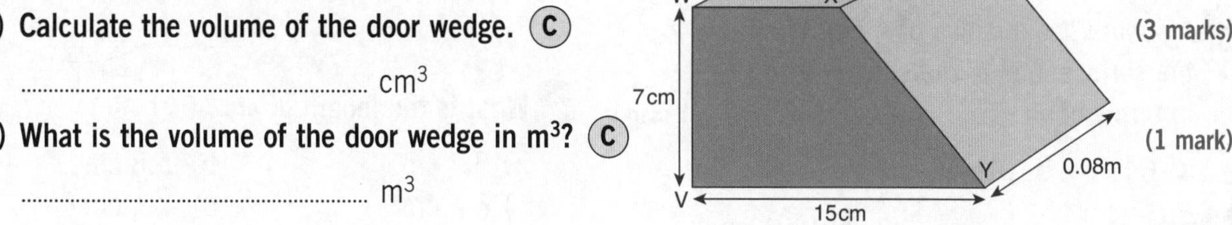

3 The volume of this cylinder is 250 cm^3.

The height of the cylinder is 8 cm.

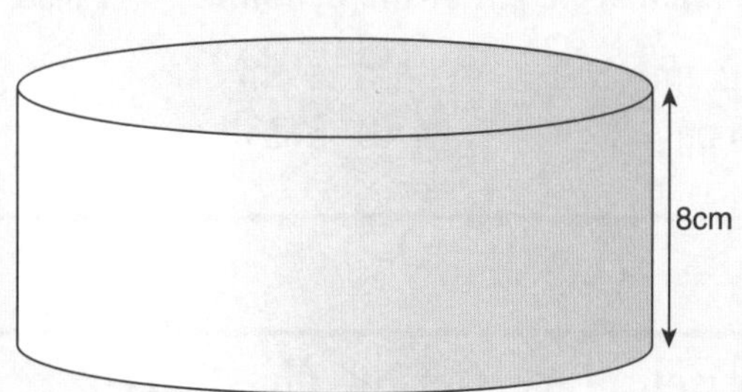

Calculate the radius of the cylinder giving your answer to 1 decimal place. (C) (3 marks)

.... cm

4 In the expressions in the table, a, b and c represent lengths.

	Expression	Length	Area	Volume	None
A	ac				
B	$a + bc$				
C	$ac(b-c)$				
D	$\sqrt{b^2}$				

a) Complete the table to show whether each expression could represent a length, an area, a volume or none of these. (3 marks)

b) Explain your answer for expression B. (1 mark)

....

....

Score / 15

How well did you do? ✗ 1–7 Try again 8–15 Getting there 16–23 Good work 24–30 Excellent! ✓

For more information on this topic, see pages 80–81 & 62 of your Success Guide.

Further length, area & volume

A

Choose just one answer, a, b, c or d.

1 **A sphere has a radius of 3 cm. What is the volume of the sphere given in terms of π?** **(1 mark)**

a) 12π b) 36π c) 42π d) $\frac{81}{4}\pi$

2 **A sphere has a radius of 4 cm. What is the surface area of the sphere, given in terms of π?** **(1 mark)**

a) 64π b) 32π c) $\frac{256}{3}\pi$ d) 25π

3 **The volume of a pyramid is 25 cm^3. The area of the base is 12 cm^2. What is the perpendicular height of the pyramid?** **(1 mark)**

a) 7.2 cm b) 4 cm
c) 25 cm d) 6.25 cm

Questions 4 and 5 refer to this circle diagram

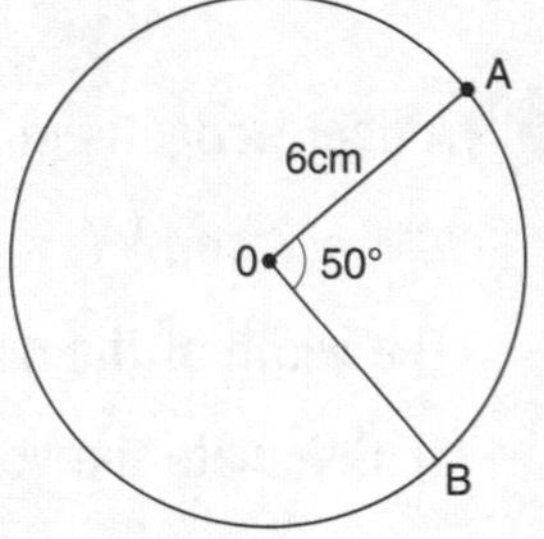

4 **What is the length of arc AOB?** Ⓒ **(1 mark)**

a) 5.2 cm b) 5.8 cm
c) 6.2 cm d) 7.4 cm

5 **What is the area of sector AOB?** Ⓒ **(1 mark)**

a) 15.2 cm^2 b) 25.3 cm^2
c) 15.7 cm^2 d) 16.9 cm^2

Score /5

B

Answer all parts of the questions.

1 **The volumes (to the nearest whole number) of the solids below have been calculated. Match each solid with its correct volume.** Ⓒ

A

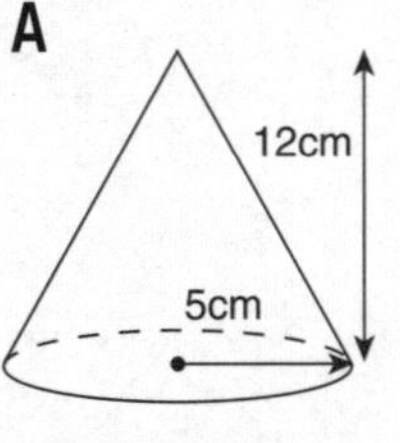

B

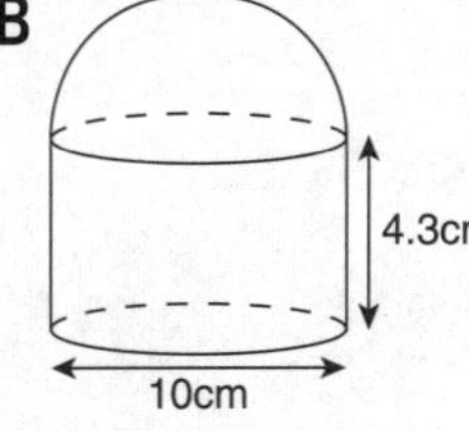

C

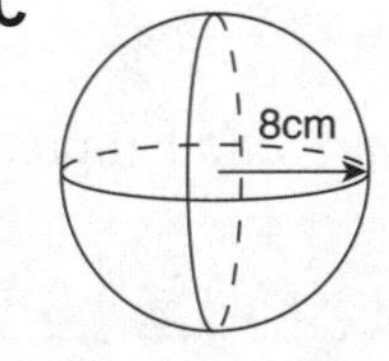

D

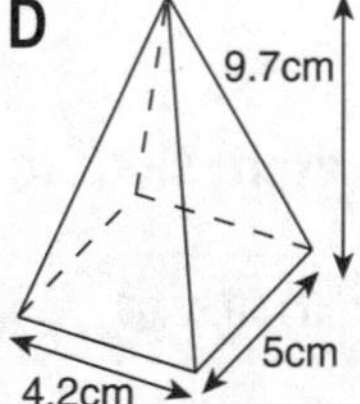

600 cm^3 .... **(2 marks)**

68 cm^3 .... **(2 marks)**

314 cm^3 .... **(2 marks)**

2145 cm^3 .... **(2 marks)**

2 **Decide whether this statement is true or false.** Ⓒ

You must show sufficient working in order to justify your answer.

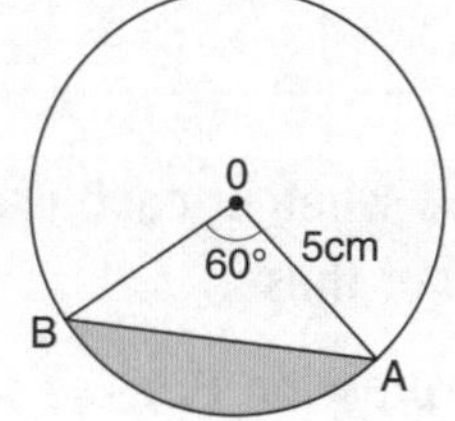

'The area of the shaded segment is 3.26 cm^2.' **(3 marks)**

....

....

....

Score /11

Ⓒ *Indicates that a calculator may be used*

C These are GCSE-style questions. Answer all parts of the questions. Show your workings (on separate paper if necessary) and include the correct units in your answers.

1 The sector area of a circle is 51.6 cm^2.

The radius of the circle is 9 cm.

Work out the size of the angle θ of the sector. (C)

Give your answer to the nearest degree. **(3 marks)**

....

....

....

.... °

2 The diagram shows a plastic container.

The container is formed by joining a cylindrical tube to a hemisphere.

The diameter of the cylinder and hemisphere is 26 cm.

The total height of the container is 51 cm.

Work out the volume of the container. (C)

Give your answer correct to 3 significant figures. **(4 marks)**

....

....

....

.... m^3

3 The volume of a ball bearing is 268 mm^3.

Work out the diameter of the ball bearing, giving your answer to the nearest whole number. (C) **(3 marks)**

....

....

....

.... mm

Score / 10

How well did you do? ✗ 1–7 Try again 8-12 Getting there 3–19 Good work 20–26 Excellent! ✓

For more information on this topic, see pages 82–83 of your Success Guide.

Vectors

A Choose just one answer, a, b, c or d.

1 **If vector $\underline{a} = \begin{pmatrix}2\\3\end{pmatrix}$ and vector $\underline{b} = \begin{pmatrix}-5\\-2\end{pmatrix}$, what is $\underline{a} + \underline{b}$?** (1 mark)

a) $\begin{pmatrix}1\\-3\end{pmatrix}$ b) $\begin{pmatrix}-3\\1\end{pmatrix}$

c) $\begin{pmatrix}7\\-5\end{pmatrix}$ d) $\begin{pmatrix}-10\\-6\end{pmatrix}$

2 **If vector $\underline{c} = \begin{pmatrix}-4\\2\end{pmatrix}$ and vector $\underline{d} = \begin{pmatrix}-6\\-5\end{pmatrix}$, what is $\underline{c} - \underline{d}$?** (1 mark)

a) $\begin{pmatrix}8\\-14\end{pmatrix}$ b) $\begin{pmatrix}-6\\-5\end{pmatrix}$

c) $\begin{pmatrix}2\\7\end{pmatrix}$ d) $\begin{pmatrix}-6\\5\end{pmatrix}$

3 **If vector $\underline{p} = \begin{pmatrix}7\\-2\end{pmatrix}$ and vector $\underline{r} = \begin{pmatrix}-9\\2\end{pmatrix}$, what is $4\underline{p} + \underline{r}$?** (1 mark)

a) $\begin{pmatrix}19\\-6\end{pmatrix}$ b) $\begin{pmatrix}38\\0\end{pmatrix}$

c) $\begin{pmatrix}-6\\19\end{pmatrix}$ d) $\begin{pmatrix}20\\-3\end{pmatrix}$

4 **Which vector is parallel to $\begin{pmatrix}2\\5\end{pmatrix}$?** (1 mark)

a) $\begin{pmatrix}10\\20\end{pmatrix}$ b) $\begin{pmatrix}6\\15\end{pmatrix}$

c) $\begin{pmatrix}20\\45\end{pmatrix}$ d) $\begin{pmatrix}1\\2\end{pmatrix}$

5 **Which vector is parallel to vector $\underline{r} = \begin{pmatrix}-4\\6\end{pmatrix}$?** (1 mark)

a) $\begin{pmatrix}-8\\6\end{pmatrix}$ b) $\begin{pmatrix}-16\\24\end{pmatrix}$

c) $\begin{pmatrix}-4\\12\end{pmatrix}$ d) $\begin{pmatrix}-8\\18\end{pmatrix}$

Score / 5

B Answer all parts of the questions.

1 **The statements below refer to the diagram opposite.**

Decide whether the statements are true or false. (4 marks)

a) $\overrightarrow{OB} = \mathbf{a} + \mathbf{b}$ ....

b) $\overrightarrow{BC} = -\mathbf{a} + \mathbf{b} + \mathbf{c}$ ....

c) $\overrightarrow{AC} = -\mathbf{a} + \mathbf{c}$ ....

d) If N is the midpoint of OC then $\overrightarrow{AN} = -\frac{1}{2}\mathbf{c} + \mathbf{a}$ ....

2 **If $\overrightarrow{OC} = 2\underline{a} - 3\underline{b}$ and $\overrightarrow{OD} = 12\underline{a} - 18\underline{b}$, write down two geometrical facts about the vectors $\overrightarrow{OC}$ and $\overrightarrow{OD}$.** (2 marks)

....

....

3 **On grid paper, draw the vectors $\underline{a}$ and $\underline{b}$, then complete the statements.** (4 marks)

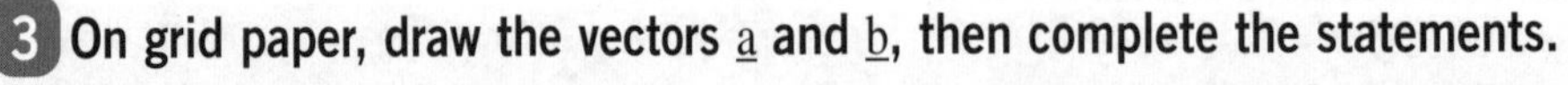

a) $\mathbf{a} = \begin{pmatrix}3\\2\end{pmatrix}$, $\mathbf{b} = \begin{pmatrix}-4\\6\end{pmatrix}$, $\mathbf{a} + \mathbf{b} = \begin{pmatrix} \\ \end{pmatrix}$ b) $\mathbf{a} = \begin{pmatrix}1\\4\end{pmatrix}$, $\mathbf{b} = \begin{pmatrix}-2\\5\end{pmatrix}$, $\mathbf{a} - \mathbf{b} = \begin{pmatrix} \\ \end{pmatrix}$

Score / 10

C **These are GCSE-style questions. Answer all parts of the questions. Show your workings (on separate paper if necessary) and include the correct units in your answers.**

1 **The diagram is a sketch.** **(2 marks)**

A is the point (4,3)

B is the point (6,7)

Write down the vector AB as a column vector $\begin{pmatrix} x \\ y \end{pmatrix}$

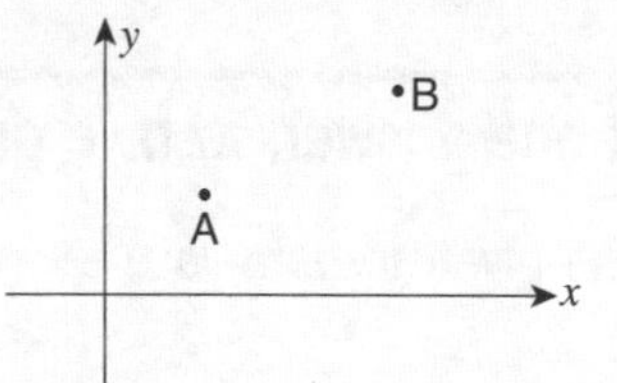

....

2

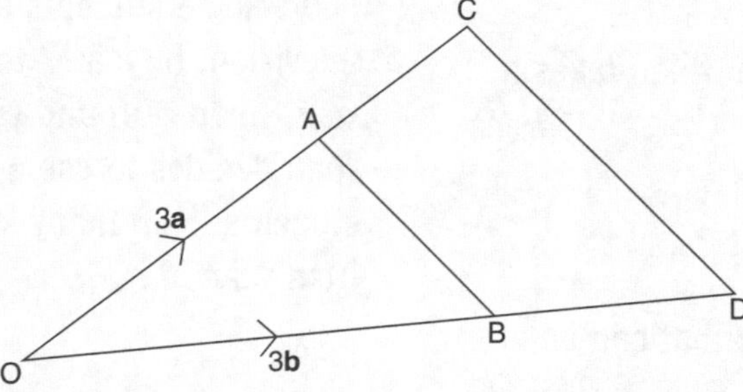

$\overrightarrow{OA} = 3\mathbf{a}$, $\overrightarrow{OB} = 3\mathbf{b}$, $\overrightarrow{OC} = 5\mathbf{a}$, $\overrightarrow{BD} = 2\mathbf{b}$

Prove that AB is parallel to CD. **(3 marks)**

....

....

3

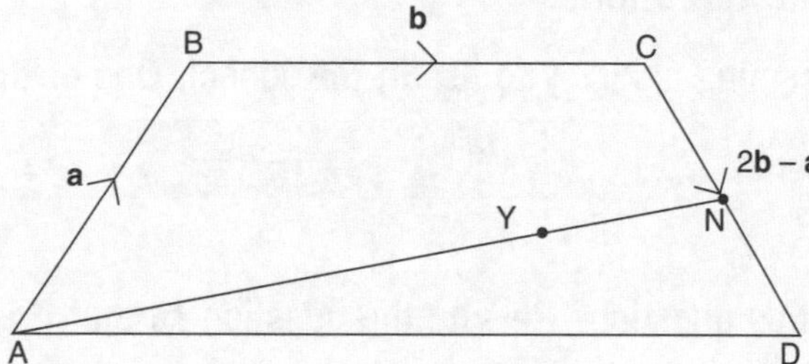

ABCD is a quadrilateral with $\overrightarrow{AB} = \mathbf{a}$, $\overrightarrow{BC} = \mathbf{b}$, and $\overrightarrow{CD} = 2\mathbf{b} - \mathbf{a}$.

a) Express $\overrightarrow{AC}$ in terms of **a** and **b**. .... **(1 mark)**

b) Prove that BC is parallel to AD. .... **(2 marks)**

c) N is the midpoint of CD.

Express $\overrightarrow{AN}$ in terms of **a** and **b**. **(2 marks)**

....

d) Y is the point on AN such that AY : YN = 3 : 1.

Show that $\overrightarrow{YD} = \frac{3}{8}(4\mathbf{b} - \mathbf{a})$.

....

.... **(3 marks)**

Score / 13

How well did you do? 1–6 Try again 7–12 Getting there 13–19 Good work 20–28 Excellent!

For more information on this topic, see pages 84–85 of your Success Guide.

Collecting data

A

Choose just one answer, a, b, c or d.

1 What is the name given to data you collect yourself? (1 mark)

a) continuous b) primary
c) secondary d) discrete

2 What is the name given to data which takes a set of values? (1 mark)

a) continuous b) primary
c) secondary d) discrete

3 What is the name given to data that can be a value in a range? (1 mark)

a) continuous b) primary
c) secondary d) discrete

4 This type of data does not give a value. (1 mark)

a) quantitative b) qualitative
c) continuous d) discrete

5 A survey is being carried out on the number of hours some students spend watching television. In year 7 there were 240 students, year 8 had 300 and year 9 460 students. John decides to use a stratified sample of 100 students. How many students should he ask from year 7? (1 mark)

a) 46 b) 30
c) 48 d) 24

Score / 5

B

Answer all parts of the questions.

1 Jim and Annabelle are designing a survey to use in the school. One of their questions is shown below.

How much time do you spend doing homework per night?

0–1 h	1–2 h	2–3 h	3–4 h

What is the problem with this question? Rewrite the question so that it is improved. (2 marks)

....

....

....

2 Laura conducts a survey of the students in her school. She decides to interview 100 students.

Calculate the number of students she should choose from each year group to provide a representative sample. Complete the table below. (C) (3 marks)

Year group	Number of students	Number of students in sample
7	120	
8	176	
9	160	
10	190	
11	154	

Score / 5

(C) *Indicates that a calculator may be used*

C These are GCSE-style questions. Answer all parts of the questions. Show your workings (on separate paper if necessary) and include the correct units in your answers.

1 Mrs Robinson is going to sell chocolate bars at the school tuck shop. She wants to know what type of chocolate bars pupils like.
Design a suitable questionnaire she could use.

(2 marks)

2 Robert is conducting a survey into television habits. One of the questions in his survey is:
'Do you watch a lot of television?'.
His friend Jessica tells him that it is not a very good question.
Write down two ways in which Robert could improve the question. (2 marks)

....

....

....

....

3 The table shows the gender and number of students in each year group.

Year group	Number of boys	Number of girls	Total
7	160	120	280
8	108	132	240
9	158	117	275
10	85	70	155
11	140	110	250

Mark is carrying out a survey about how much pocket money students are given.
He decides to take a stratified sample of 150 students from the whole school.
Calculate how many in the stratified sample should be:  (4 marks)

a) students from Year 8 .... students

b) girls from Year 11 .... girls

Score /8

How well did you do? ✗ 1–4 Try again 5–9 Getting there 10–13 Good work 14–18 Excellent! ✓

For more information on this topic, see pages 88–89 of your Success Guide.

Scatter diagrams and correlation

A

Choose just one answer, a, b, c or d.

1 **A scatter diagram is drawn to show the height and weight of some students. What type of correlation is shown?** (1 mark)

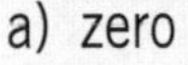

a) zero b) negative
c) positive d) scattered

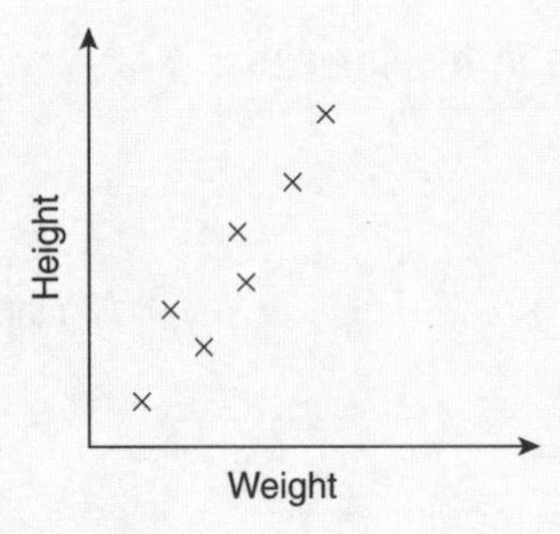

2 **A scatter diagram is drawn to show the maths scores and heights of a group of students. What type of correlation is shown?** (1 mark)

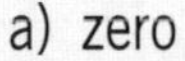

a) zero
b) negative
c) positive
d) scattered

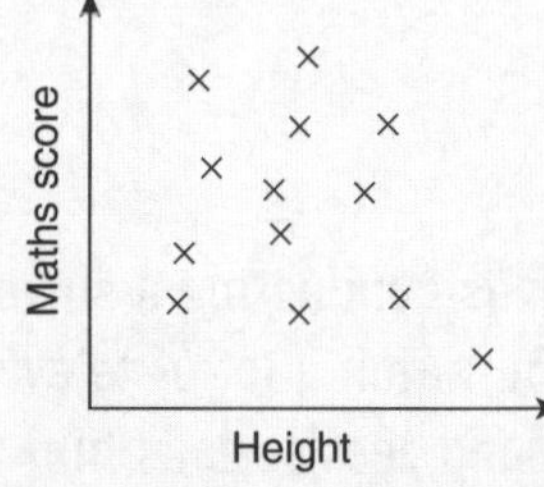

3 **A scatter diagram is drawn to show the age of some cars and their values. What type of correlation would be shown?** (1 mark)

a) zero b) negative
c) positive d) scattered

Score /3

B

Answer all parts of the questions.

1 **Some statements have been written on cards:**

Positive Correlation | Negative Correlation | No Correlation

Decide which card best describes these relationships.

a) The temperature and the sales of ice lollies .... (1 mark)
b) The temperature and the sales of woollen gloves .... (1 mark)
c) The mass of a person and his/her waist measurement .... (1 mark)
d) The height of a person and his/her IQ .... (1 mark)

2 **The scatter diagram shows the marks scored in a Mathematics and Physics examination.**

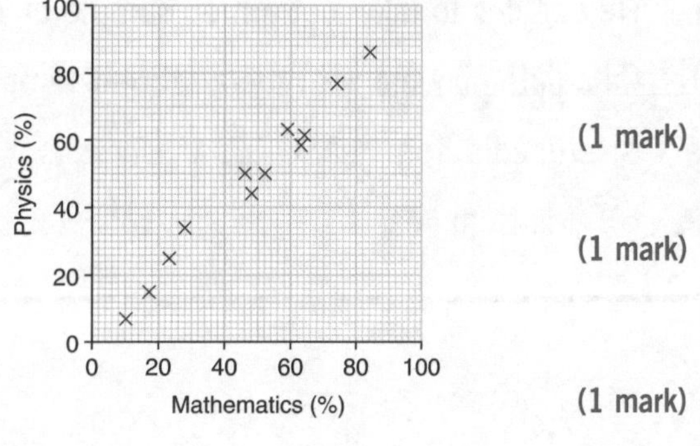

a) Describe the relationship between the Mathematics and Physics scores. (1 mark)

....

b) Draw a line of best fit on the scatter diagram. (1 mark)

c) Use your line of best fit to estimate the Mathematics score that Jonathan is likely to obtain if he has a Physics score of 75%. (1 mark)

....

Score /7

C

These are GCSE-style questions. Answer all parts of the questions. Show your workings (on separate paper if necessary) and include the correct units in your answers.

1 The table shows the ages of some children and the total number of hours sleep they had between noon on Saturday and noon on Sunday.

Age (years)	2	6	5	3	12	9	2	10	5	10	7	11	12	3
No. of hours sleep	15	13.1	13.2	14.8	10.1	11.8	15.6	11.6	13.5	11.8	12.8	10.2	9.5	14

a) On the scatter diagram, plot the information from the table. (4 marks)

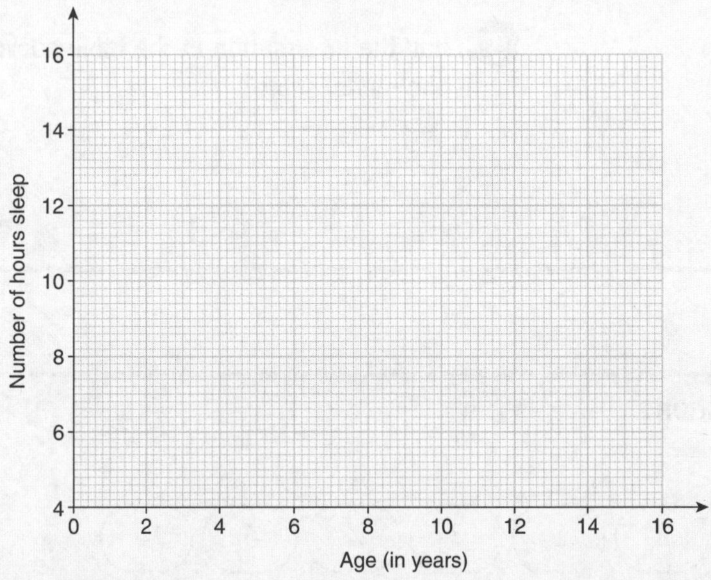

b) Describe the correlation between the age of the children in years and the total number of hours sleep they had. (2 marks)

....

....

c) Draw a line of best fit on your diagram. (1 mark)

d) Estimate the total number of hours sleep for a 4-year-old child. (2 marks)

....

e) Explain why the line of best fit only gives an estimate for the number of hours slept. (2 marks)

....

....

Score / 11

How well did you do? 1–4 Try again 5–10 Getting there 11–15 Good work 16–21 Excellent!

For more information on this topic, see pages 92–93 of your Success Guide.

Averages 1

A

Choose just one answer, a, b, c or d.

1 **What is the mean of this set of data?**
2, 7, 1, 4, 2, 6, 2, 5, 2, 6 (1 mark)

a) 4.2 b) 3.6
c) 3.7 d) 3.9

2 **What is the median value of the set of data used in question 1?** (1 mark)

a) 2 b) 3
c) 4 d) 5

3 **What is the range of this set of data?**
2, 7, 1, 4, 11, 9, 6 (1 mark)

a) 1 b) 6
c) 11 d) 10

4 **A dice is thrown and the scores are noted. The results are shown in the table below. What is the mean dice score?** Ⓒ (1 mark)

Dice score	1	2	3	4	5	6
Frequency	12	15	10	8	14	13

a) 5 b) 3
c) 4 d) 3.5

5 **Using the information in the table above, what is the modal score?** (1 mark)

a) 15 b) 2
c) 4 d) 8

Score / 5

B

Answer all parts of the questions.

1 **Here are some number cards:**

8 7 11 4 2 1 3 12 4 4

Decide whether the following statements, which refer to the number cards above, are true or false.

a) The range of the number cards is 1–11. .... (1 mark)

b) The mean of the number cards is 5.6. .... (1 mark)

c) The median of the number cards is 5. .... (1 mark)

d) The mode of the number cards is 4. .... (1 mark)

2 **A baked beans factory claims that 'On average, a tin of baked beans contains 141 beans.'**

In order to check the accuracy of this claim, a sample of 20 tins was taken and the number of beans in each tin counted. Ⓒ

Number of beans	137	138	139	140	141	142	143	144
Number of tins	1	1	1	2	5	4	4	2

a) Calculate the mean number of beans per tin. .... (2 marks)

b) Explain briefly whether you think the manufacturer is justified in making its claim. (1 mark)

....

3 **The mean of 7, 9, 10, 18, x and 17 is 13. What is the value of x?** .... Ⓒ (2 marks)

Score / 9

Ⓒ *Indicates that a calculator may be used*

C These are GCSE-style questions. Answer all parts of the questions. Show your workings (on separate paper if necessary) and include the correct units in your answers.

1 Some students took a test. The table gives information about their marks in the test.

Mark	Frequency
3	2
4	5
5	11
6	2

a) Write down the modal mark. .... (1 mark)

b) Work out the range of the marks. .... (1 mark)

c) Work out the mean mark. (C) (3 marks)

....

....

2 Simon sat three examinations. His mean score is 65. To pass the unit, he needs to get an average of 69. What score must he get in the fourth and final examination to pass the unit? (C) (3 marks)

....

....

3 A company employs 3 women and 7 men.

The mean weekly wage of the 10 employees is £464.

The mean weekly wage of the 3 women is £520.

Calculate the mean weekly wage of the 7 men. (C) (4 marks)

....

....

4 Find the three-point moving average for the following data: (C)

2 5 3 6 2 1 4 (5 marks)

....

....

....

....

Score /17

How well did you do? 1–10 Try again 11–17 Getting there 18–24 Good work 25–31 Excellent!

For more information on this topic, see pages 94–95 of your Success Guide.

Averages 2

A

Choose just one answer, a, b, c or d.

The following questions are based on the information given in the table below about the time taken in seconds to swim 50 metres.

Time (seconds)	Frequency (f)
$0 \leqslant t < 30$	1
$30 \leqslant t < 60$	2
$60 \leqslant t < 90$	4
$90 \leqslant t < 120$	6
$120 \leqslant t < 150$	7
$150 \leqslant t < 180$	2

1 How many people swam 50 metres in less than 60 seconds? (1 mark)

a) 2 b) 4
c) 3 d) 6

2 Which of the intervals is the modal class? (1 mark)

a) $60 \leqslant t < 90$ b) $120 \leqslant t < 150$
c) $30 \leqslant t < 60$ d) $90 \leqslant t < 120$

3 Which of the class intervals contains the median value? (1 mark)

a) $90 \leqslant t < 120$ b) $150 \leqslant t < 180$
c) $120 \leqslant t < 150$ d) $60 \leqslant t < 90$

4 What is the estimate for the mean time taken to swim 50 metres? (C) (1 mark)

a) 105 seconds b) 385 seconds
c) 100 seconds d) 125 seconds

Score /4

B

Answer all parts of the questions.

1 The length of some seedlings are shown in the table below.

Length (mm)	Number of seedlings
$0 \leqslant L < 10$	3
$10 \leqslant L < 20$	5
$20 \leqslant L < 30$	9
$30 \leqslant L < 40$	2
$40 \leqslant L < 50$	1

Calculate an estimate for the mean length of the seedlings. (4 marks)

Mean = ... mm

2 The stem-and-leaf diagram shows the marks gained by some students in a mathematics examination.

Stem	Leaf
1	2 5 7
2	6 9
3	4 5 5 7
4	2 7 7 7 7
5	2

Stem = 10 marks
Key: 1 | 2 = 12 marks

Using the stem-and-leaf diagram, calculate:

a) the mode. .... (1 mark)

b) the median. .... (1 mark)

c) the range. .... (1 mark)

Score /7

AVERAGES 2

Handling Data

(C) *Indicates that a calculator may be used*

C

These are GCSE-style questions. Answer all parts of the questions. Show your workings (on separate paper if necessary) and include the correct units in your answers.

1 A psychologist records the times, to the nearest minute, taken by 20 students to complete a logic problem.

Here are the results.

12	22	31	36	35	14	27	23	19	25
15	17	15	27	32	38	41	18	27	18

Draw a stem-and-leaf diagram to show this information. (4 marks)

2 John asks 100 people how much they spent last year on newspapers. The results are given in the table below.

Amount £ (x)	Frequency
$0 \leqslant x < 10$	12
$10 \leqslant x < 20$	20
$20 \leqslant x < 30$	15
$30 \leqslant x < 40$	18
$40 \leqslant x < 50$	14
$50 \leqslant x < 60$	18
$60 \leqslant x < 70$	3

a) Calculate an estimate of the mean amount spent on newspapers. (C) (4 marks)

....

b) Explain briefly why this value of the mean is only an estimate. (1 mark)

....

c) Calculate the class interval in which the median lies. (C) (2 marks)

....

Score / 11

How well did you do? 1–6 Try again 7–11 Getting there 12–16 Good work 17–22 Excellent!

For more information on this topic, see pages 96–97 of your Success Guide.

Cumulative frequency graphs

A Choose just one answer, a, b, c or d.

The data below show the number of letters delivered to each of the 15 houses in Whelan Avenue (arranged in order of size).

0, 0, 1, 1, 1, 1, 1, 1, 2, 2, 2, 3, 4, 5, 5

Use the information above to answer these questions.

1 What is the median number of letters delivered? (1 mark)

a) 0 b) 2 c) 1 d) 5

2 What is the lower quartile for the number of letters delivered? (1 mark)

a) 0 b) 2 c) 3 d) 1

3 What is the upper quartile for the number of letters delivered? (1 mark)

a) 0 b) 2
c) 3 d) 1

4 What is the interquartile range for the number of letters delivered? (1 mark)

a) 2 b) 3
c) 4 d) 5

Score / 4

B Answer all parts of the questions.

1 The table shows the examination marks of some year 10 pupils in their end-of-year mathematics examination.

Examination mark	Frequency	Cumulative frequency
0–10	4	
11–20	6	
21–30	11	
31–40	24	
41–50	18	
51–60	7	
61–70	3	

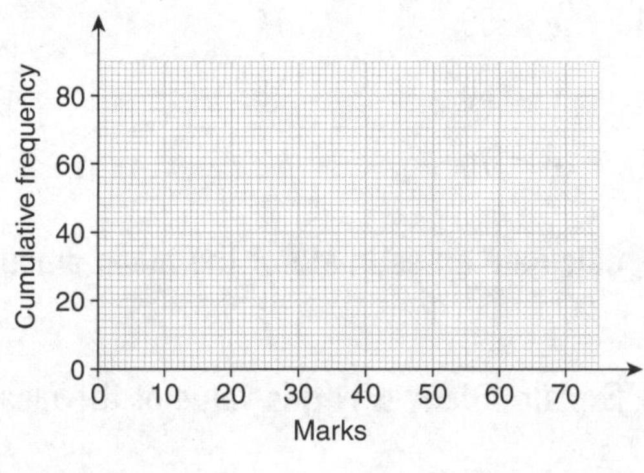

a) Complete the cumulative frequency column in the table above. (2 marks)

b) Draw the cumulative frequency graph. (3 marks)

c) From your graph, find the median mark. .... (1 mark)

d) From your graph, find the interquartile range. .... (2 marks)

e) If 16 pupils were given a grade A in the examination, what is the minimum score needed for a grade A? (2 marks)

.... marks Score / 10

C

These are GCSE-style questions. Answer all parts of the questions. Show your workings (on separate paper if necessary) and include the correct units in your answers.

1 The table gives information about the time, to the nearest minute, taken to run a marathon.

Time (mins)	Frequency	Cumulative frequency
$120 < t \leqslant 140$	1	
$140 < t \leqslant 160$	8	
$160 < t \leqslant 180$	24	
$180 < t \leqslant 200$	29	
$200 < t \leqslant 220$	10	
$220 < t \leqslant 240$	5	
$240 < t \leqslant 260$	3	

a) Complete the table to show the cumulative frequency for this data. **(2 marks)**

b) Draw the cumulative frequency graph for these data. **(3 marks)**

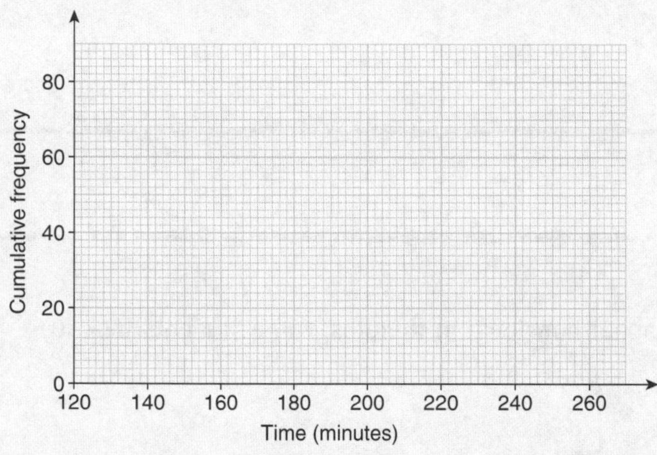

c) Use your graph to work out an estimate for:

i) the interquartile range. .... minutes **(2 marks)**

ii) the number of runners with a time of more than 205 minutes. **(1 mark)**

.... runners

d) Draw a box plot for this data. **(3 marks)**

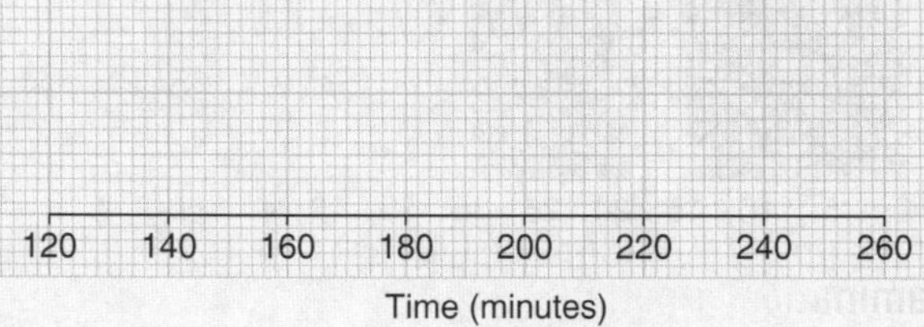

Score / 11

How well did you do? 1–6 Try again 7–12 Getting there 13–18 Good work 19–25 Excellent!

For more information on this topic, see pages 98–99 of your Success Guide.

Histograms

A Choose just one answer, a, b, c or d.

The table shows the distance travelled to work by some employees. Use the information in the table to answer the questions below.

Distance (km)	Frequency
$0 \leq d < 5$	8
$5 \leq d < 15$	20
$15 \leq d < 20$	135
$20 \leq d < 30$	47
$30 \leq d < 50$	80

1 Which class interval has a frequency density of 4.7? (1 mark)

a) $0 \leq d < 5$ b) $5 \leq d < 15$
c) $15 \leq d < 20$ d) $20 \leq d < 30$

2 The frequency density for one of the class intervals is 4. Which one? (1 mark)

a) $5 \leq d < 15$ b) $30 \leq d < 50$
c) $0 \leq d < 5$ d) $15 \leq d < 20$

3 Which class interval has the highest frequency density? (1 mark)

a) $0 \leq d < 5$ b) $15 \leq d < 20$
c) $20 \leq d < 30$ d) $5 \leq d < 15$

4 Which class interval has the lowest frequency density? (1 mark)

a) $0 \leq d < 5$ b) $5 \leq d < 15$
c) $15 \leq d < 20$ d) $30 \leq d < 50$

Score /4

B Answer all parts of the questions.

1 The table and histogram give information about how long, in minutes, some students took to complete a maths problem.

Time t (in minutes)	Frequency
$0 < t \leq 5$	19
$5 < t \leq 15$	....
$15 < t \leq 20$	16
$20 < t \leq 30$	....
$30 < t \leq 45$	12

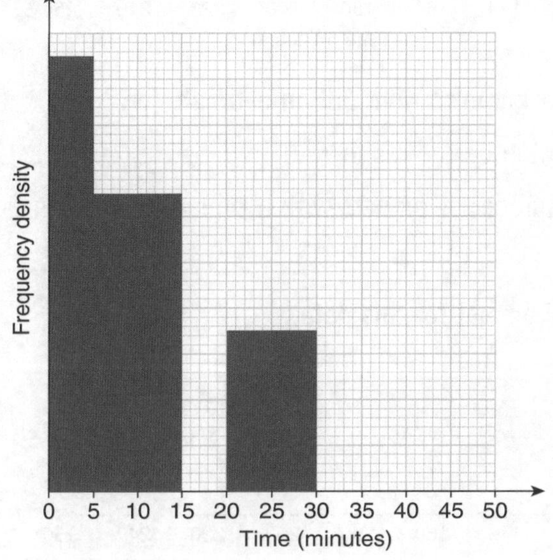

a) Use the information in the histogram to complete the table. (2 marks)
b) Use the table to complete the histogram. (2 marks)

Score /4

HISTOGRAMS
Handling Data

C These are GCSE-style questions. Answer all parts of the questions. Show your workings (on separate paper if necessary) and include the correct units in your answers.

1 The masses of some objects are given in the table below.

Mass M (kg)	Frequency
$0 \leqslant M < 2$	14
$2 \leqslant M < 3$	8
$3 \leqslant M < 5$	13
$5 \leqslant M < 10$	14
$10 \leqslant M < 12$	7
$M \geqslant 12$	0

Draw a histogram to show the distribution of the masses of the objects. Use a scale of 1 cm to 2 kg on the mass axis. (3 marks)

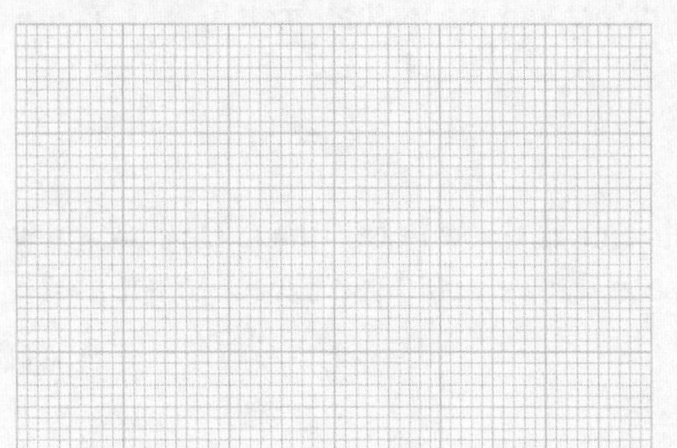

2 Pierre recorded the length, in seconds, of some advertisements shown on television in a week.

His results are shown in the histogram.

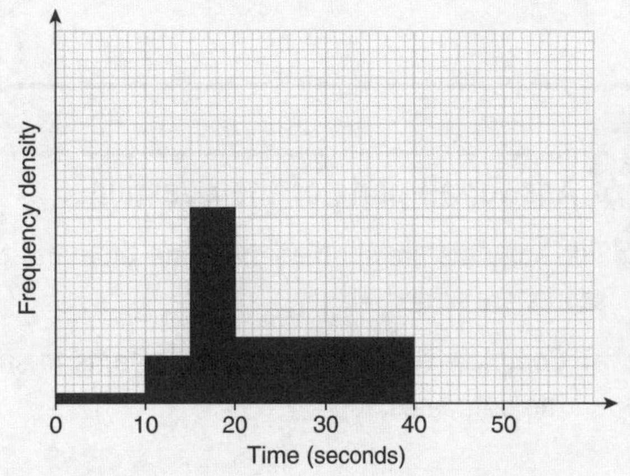

Use the information in the histogram to complete the table. (3 marks)

Length S (in seconds)	Frequency
$0 \leqslant S < 10$	....
$10 \leqslant S < 15$	....
$15 \leqslant S < 20$	21
$20 \leqslant S < 40$	....
$S \geqslant 40$	0

Score / 6

How well did you do? 1–2 Try again 3–6 Getting there 7–10 Good work 11–14 Excellent!

For more information on this topic, see page 100–101 of your Success Guide.

Probability

A Choose just one answer, a, b, c or d.

1 **The probability that Highbury football club win a football match is $\frac{12}{17}$. What is the probability that they do not win the football match?** **(1 mark)**

a) $\frac{5}{12}$ b) $\frac{17}{29}$

c) $\frac{12}{17}$ d) $\frac{5}{17}$

2 **A fair dice is thrown 600 times. On how many of these throws would you expect to get a 4?** **(1 mark)**

a) 40 b) 600

c) 100 d) 580

3 **A fair dice is thrown 500 times. If a 6 comes up 87 times, what is the relative frequency?** **(1 mark)**

a) $\frac{1}{6}$ b) $\frac{87}{500}$

c) $\frac{10}{600}$ d) $\frac{1}{587}$

4 **The probability that it snows on Christmas Day is 0.2. What is the probability that it will snow on Christmas Day in two consecutive years?** **(1 mark)**

a) 0.04 b) 0.4

c) 0.2 d) 0.16

5 **The probability that Fiona is in the hockey team is 0.7. The probability that she is picked for the netball team is 0.3. What is the probability that she is picked for both teams?** **(1 mark)**

a) 1.0 b) 0.1

c) 0.12 d) 0.21

Score /5

B Answer all parts of the questions.

1 **Two spinners are spun at the same time and their scores are added.**

Spinner 1

3	3
2	1

Spinner 2

6	2
3	1

a) Complete the sample space diagrams to show the outcomes. **(2 marks)**

Spinner 1 (across), Spinner 2 (down)

	1	2	3	3
1	2			
2		4		
3		5		
6		8		9

b) Find the probability of: **(3 marks)**

i) a score of 4 .... ii) a score of 9 .... iii) a score of 1 ....

2 **The probability that Michelle finishes first in a swimming race is 0.3. Michelle swims two races. Work out the probability that Michelle wins both races.** .... **(2 marks)**

3 **There are 13 counters in a bag: 7 are red and the rest are white. A counter is picked at random, its colour noted and it is not replaced. A second counter is then chosen. What is the probability of choosing:**

a) two red counters? .... **(2 marks)**

b) a red and a white counter? .... **(3 marks)**

Score /12

C

These are GCSE-style questions. Answer all parts of the questions. Show your workings (on separate paper if necessary) and include the correct units in your answers.

1 A bag contains different coloured beads.

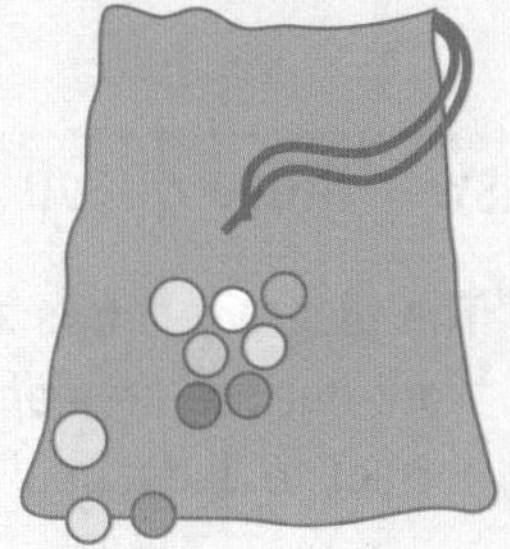

The probability of taking a bead of a particular colour at random is as follows.

Colour	Red	White	Blue	Pink
Probability	0.25	0.1		0.3

Jackie is going to take a bead at random and then put it back in the bag.

a) i) Work out the probability that Jackie will take out a blue bead. .... (1 mark)

ii) Write down the probability that Jackie will take out a black bead. .... (1 mark)

b) Jackie will take out a bead from the bag at random 200 times, replacing the bead each time. Work out an estimate for the number of times that Jackie takes a red bead. (2 marks)

....

2 Two fair dice are thrown together and their scores are added.

a) Work out the probability of a score of 7. .... (2 marks)

b) Work out the probability of a score of 9. .... (2 marks)

3 Kevin and Nathan challenge each other to a game of Monopoly and a game of pool. A draw is not possible in either game.

The probability that Kevin wins at Monopoly is 0.4

The probability that Nathan wins at pool is 0.7

a) Draw a probability tree diagram in the space below. (3 marks)

b) What is the probability that Nathan wins both games? .... (2 marks)

c) What is the probability that they win a game each? .... (3 marks)

Score / 16

How well did you do? 1–11 Try again 12–21 Getting there 22–27 Good work 28–33 Excellent!

For more information on this topic, see pages 102–105 of your Success Guide.

Mixed GCSE-style Questions

Answer these questions. Show full working out

1 **The diagram shows a circle of diameter 2.7m. Work out the area of the circle. Give your answer correct to 1 decimal place.** (C)

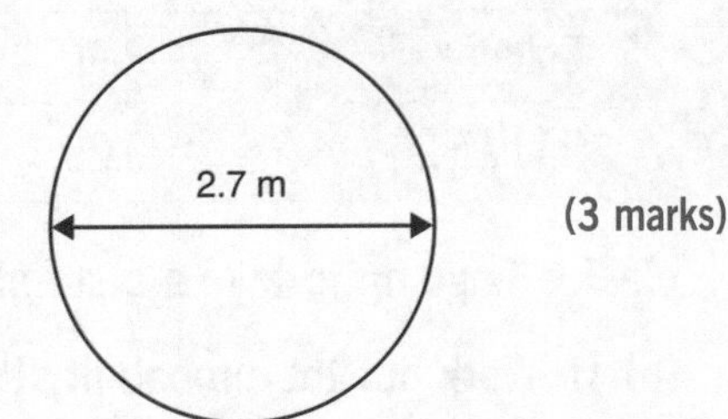

(3 marks)

.... m^2

2 Katy sells CDs, she sells each CD for £9.20 plus VAT at 17.5%. She sells 127 CDs.

Work out how much money Katy receives. (C) (4 marks)

....

3 **Estimate the value of** $\frac{8.9 \times 5.2}{(10.1)^2}$ .... (2 marks)

4 Here are the ages in years of the members of a golf club.

9	42	37	28	36	44	47	43	62	19	17	36	40
56	58	32	18	41	52	42	54	38	27	29	32	51

In the space provided draw a stem and leaf diagram to show these ages. (3 marks)

5 The lines PQ and RS are parallel

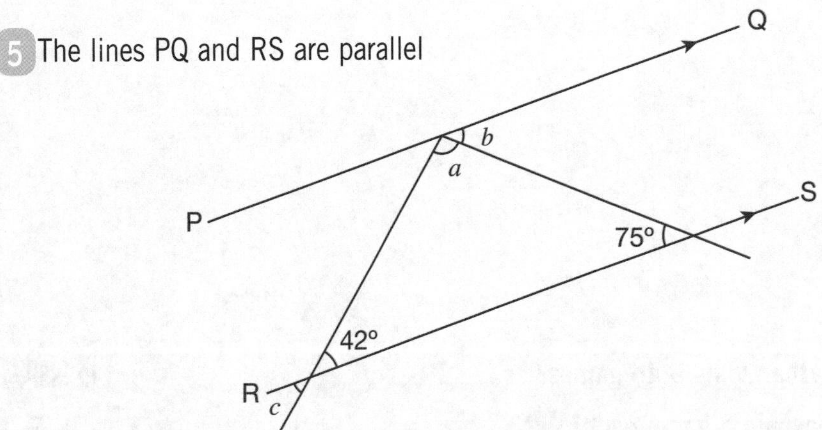

a) Write down the value of b. Give a reason for your answer. (2 marks)

....

b) Write down the value of c. Give a reason for your answer. (2 marks)

....

c) Write down the value of a. (2 marks)

....

(C) *Indicates that a calculator may be used*

6 Here are the first four terms of an arithmetic sequence:

5, 9, 13, 17

Find an expression, in terms of n, for the nth term of the sequence. (2 marks)

....

7 The diagram shows the position of three towns, A, B and C. Town C is due east of towns A and B. Town B is due east of A.

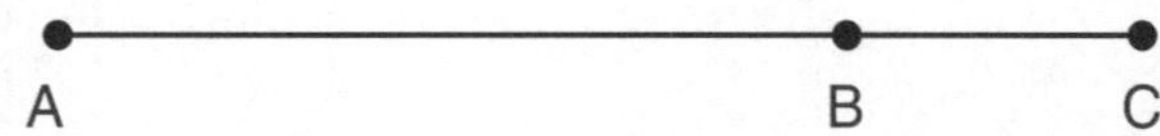

Town B is $3\frac{1}{3}$ miles from town A.

Town C is $1\frac{1}{4}$ miles from town B.

Calculate the number of miles between town A and town C. (3 marks)

....

8 **a) Solve $5x - 2 = 3(x + 6)$** $x =$ .... (2 marks)

b) Solve $\frac{3 - 2x}{4} = 2$ $x =$ .... (2 marks)

c) i) Factorise $x^2 - 10x + 24$ .... (2 marks)

ii) Hence solve $x^2 - 10x + 24 = 0$ .... (2 marks)

d) Simplify $\frac{x^2 + 2x}{x^2 + 5x + 6}$ .... (3 marks)

e) Simplify these.

i) $p^4 \times p^6$ .... (1 mark)

ii) $\frac{p^7}{p^3}$ .... (1 mark)

iii) $\frac{p^4 \times p^5}{p}$ .... (1 mark)

iv) $(p^{-\frac{1}{2}})^4$ .... (1 mark)

9 The times, in minutes, taken to finish an assault course are listed in order.

8, 12, 12, 13, 15, 17, 22, 23, 23, 27, 29

a) Find: **(2 marks)**

i) the lower quartile ....

ii) the interquartile range ....

b) Draw a box plot for this data. **(3 marks)**

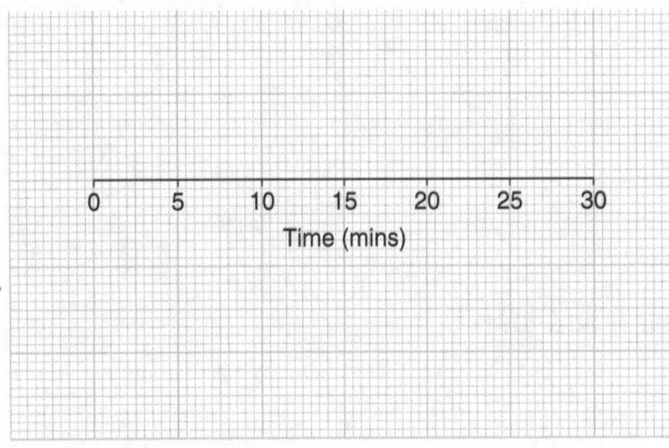

10 a) Megan bought a TV for £700. Each year the TV depreciated by 20%.

Work out the value of the TV two years after she bought it. (C) **(3 marks)**

....

b) In a '20% off' sale, William bought a DVD player for £300.
What was the original price of the DVD player before the sale? **(3 marks)**

....

11 The diagram shows a right-angled triangle.

PQ = 14.2 cm.

Angle PRQ = 90°.

Angle RPQ = 38°.

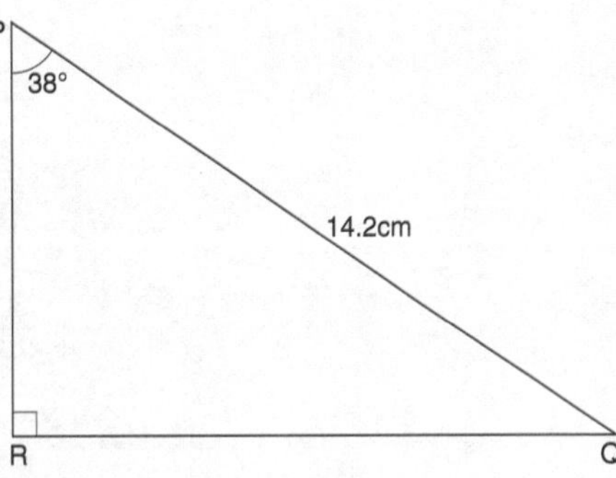

Find the length of the side QR. Give your answer to 3 significant figures.  **(3 marks)**

....

12 The table gives the times to the nearest minute to complete a puzzle.

Time t (mins)	Frequency
$0 \leqslant t < 10$	5
$10 \leqslant t < 20$	12
$20 \leqslant t < 30$	8
$30 \leqslant t < 40$	5

Calculate an estimate for the mean number of minutes taken to complete the puzzle. (C) **(4 marks)**

....

13 **a)** $b = \dfrac{a + c}{ac}$ $\quad a = 3.2 \times 10^5 \quad c = 5 \times 10^6$

Calculate the value of b. (C) **(2 marks)**

Give your answer in standard form. ....

b) Rearrange the formula to make a the subject. .... **(2 marks)**

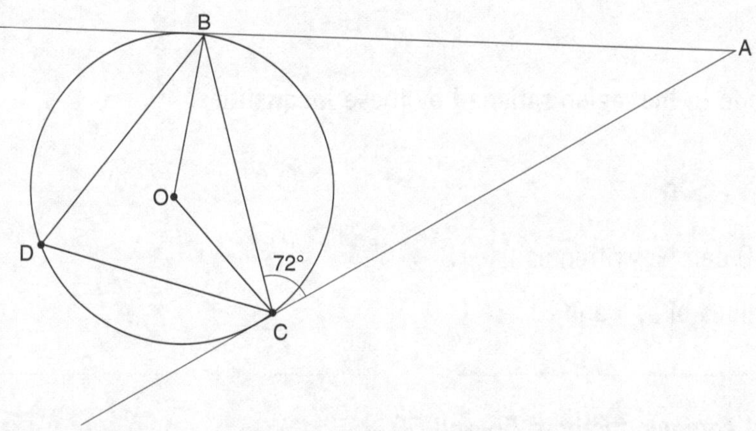

D, B and C are points on a circle with centre O.
AB and AC are tangents to the circle. Angle ACB = 72°.

a) Explain why angle OCB is 18°. **(1 mark)**

....

....

b) Calculate the size of angle BDC. Give reasons for your answer. **(3 marks)**

....

....

....

15 The diagram shows the graphs of these equations:

$x + y = 4$

$y = x - 2$

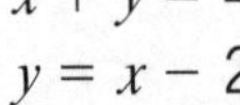

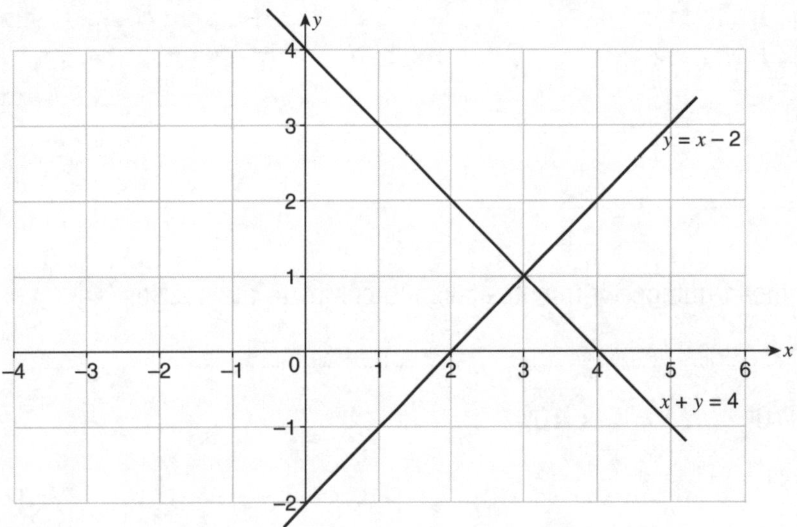

a) **Use the diagram to solve the simultaneous equations.** **(4 marks)**

$\boldsymbol{x + y = 4}$ $\quad x =$ ....

$\boldsymbol{y + 2 = x}$ $\quad y =$ ....

b) **On the grid, shade in the region satisfied by these inequalities.** **(2 marks)**

$\boldsymbol{x + y \leqslant 4}$

$\boldsymbol{y \geqslant x - 2}$ $\quad \boldsymbol{x \geqslant 0}$

16 a) The number 360 can be written as $2^a \times 3^b \times 5^c$. **(3 marks)**

Calculate the values of a, b and c.

....

b) **Find the highest common factor of 56 and 60.** **(2 marks)**

....

c) **Find the lowest common multiple of 56 and 60.** **(2 marks)**

....

17 a) p is an integer such that $0 < 4p \leqslant 13$. **(1 mark)**

List all the possible values of p.

....

b) **Solve the inequality $\dfrac{t + 1}{4} \leqslant t - 3$** **(2 marks)**

....

18 $a = 2 + \sqrt{7}$ and $b = 2 - 3\sqrt{7}$

Simplify the following, giving your answer in the form $p + q\sqrt{7}$, where p and q are integers.

a) $a + b$ .... **(3 marks)**

b) a^2 .... **(3 marks)**

c) ab .... **(3 marks)**

19

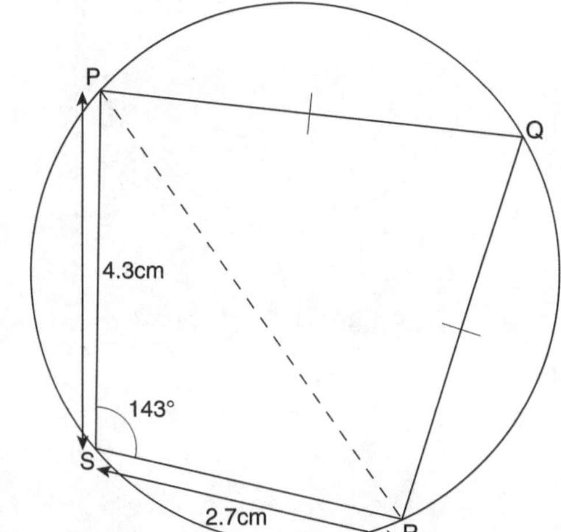

PQRS is a cyclic quadrilateral.
PS = 4.3 cm, SR = 2.7 cm, angle PSR = 143° and PQ = QR.

a) Calculate the length of PR. ....cm **(3 marks)**

b) Calculate the length of QR. ....cm **(3 marks)**

c) Calculate the area of triangle PQR. ....cm^2 **(3 marks)**

20 **Solve the equation** $\frac{x-4}{x^2-16} + \frac{2}{2x-4} = 1$ **(5 marks)**

Leave your answers in surd form. $x =$ ....

21 The diagram shows a child's toy, which is hollow. The height of the cone is 4 cm. The base radius of cone and hemisphere is 3 cm.

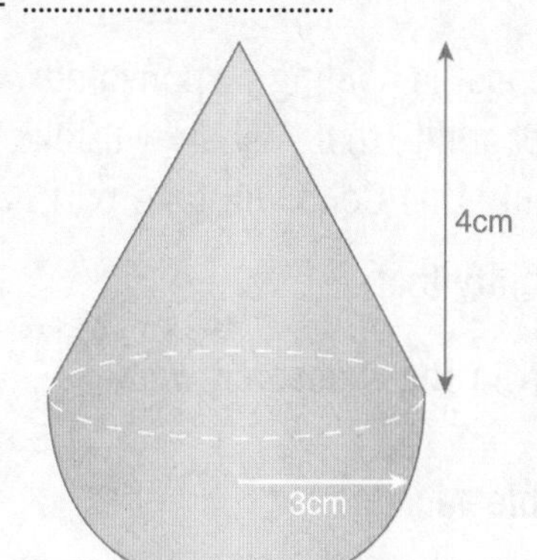

a) Work out the total surface area of the toy. **(4 marks)**
Give your answer as a multiple of π.

....cm^2

b) The toy is made in two sizes. The large toy is three times the size of the toy above.
What is the total surface area of the large toy? Give your answer as a multiple of π. **(3 marks)**

....cm^2

22

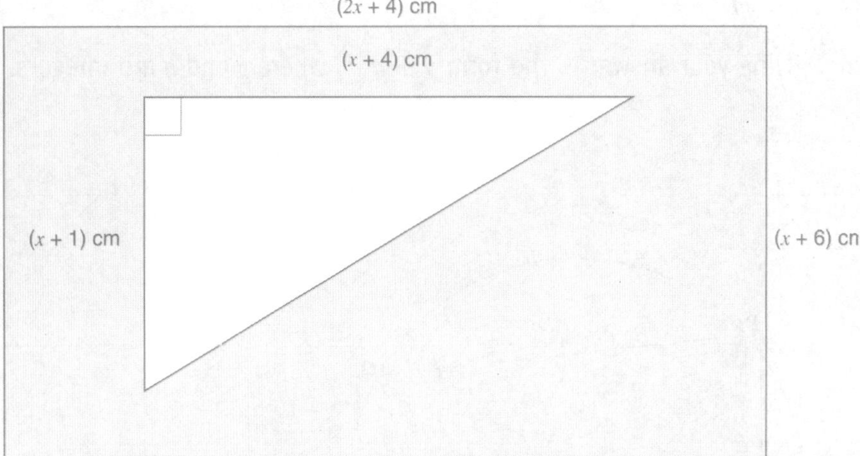

A triangular piece of metal is cut out of a rectangular piece of metal.

The length of the rectangle is $(2x + 4)$ cm

The width of the rectangle is $(x + 6)$ cm

The height of the triangle is $(x + 4)$ cm

The base of the triangle is $(x + 1)$ cm

The shaded region in the diagram shows the metal remaining.

The area of the shaded region is 38.5 cm^2.

a) Show that $x^2 + 9x - 11 = 0$. **(4 marks)**

....

....

b) i) Solve the equation $x^2 + 9x - 11 = 0$.
Give your answer correct to 3 significant figures. **(3 marks)**

....

ii) Hence find the area of the triangle. **(1 mark)**

....

23 Riddlington High School is holding a sponsored walk. The pupils at the school decide whether or not to take part. The probability that Afshan will take part is $\frac{2}{3}$. The probability that Bethany will take part is $\frac{4}{5}$ and the probability that Colin will take part is $\frac{1}{4}$.

Calculate the probability that:

a) all three take part in the sponsored walk **(2 marks)**

....

b) exactly two of them take part in the sponsored walk **(3 marks)**

....

Answers to mixed questions

1 Area $= \pi r^2$
$= \pi \times 1.35^2$
$= 5.7\ \text{cm}^2$

2 $9.20 \times 1.175 = £10.81$
with VAT for each CD.
$127 \times £10.81$
$= £1372.87$

3 $\frac{8.9 \times 5.2}{(10.1)^2}$

$\approx \frac{9 \times 5}{100}$ or $\approx \frac{10 \times 5}{100}$

$= 0.45$ $= 0.5$

4

0	9
1	7 8 9
2	7 8 9
3	2 2 6 6 7 8
4	0 1 2 2 3 4 7
5	1 2 4 6 8
6	2

Key: 1|7 means 17 years
stem = 10 years

5 a) $b = 75°$ since angle b and 75° are alternate angles.
b) $c = 42°$ since c and 42° are vertically opposite
c) $a = 63°$

6 $4n + 1$

7 $4\frac{7}{12}$ miles

8 a) $x = 10$
b) $x = -2.5$
c) i) $(x - 4)(x - 6)$
ii) $x = 4$ and $x = 6$
d) $\frac{x(x+2)}{(x+2)(x+3)} = \frac{x}{x+3}$
e) i) p^{10} ii) p^4 iii) p^8 iv) $p^{-2} = \frac{1}{p^2}$

9 a) i) lower quartile = 12
ii) interquartile range = 11

9 b)

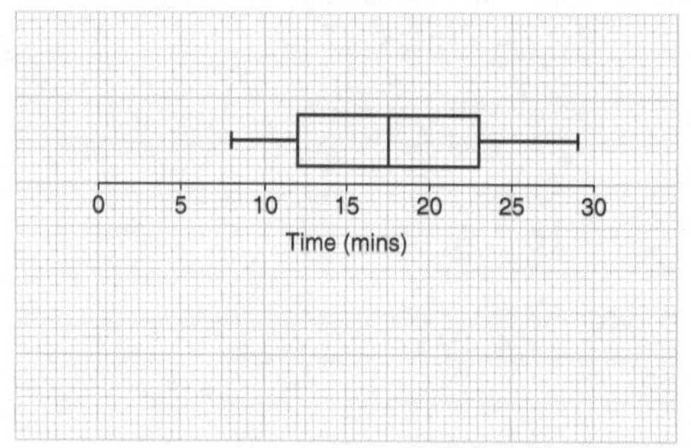

10 a) £448 b) £375

11 8.74 cm

12 $19.\dot{3}$ minutes

13 a) 3.325×10^{-6} b) $a = \frac{c}{bc - 1}$)

14 a) The radius and tangent meet at 90°. Since angle ACB = 72° then angle OCB = 90° − 72° = 18°.

b) Angle OCB = angle OBC = 18°. Angle BOC = 180° − (2 × 18°) = 144°.
Angle BDC = 144° ÷ 2 = 72°, since the angle subtended at the centre is twice the angle at the circumference.

15 a) $x = 3$, $y = 1$

b)

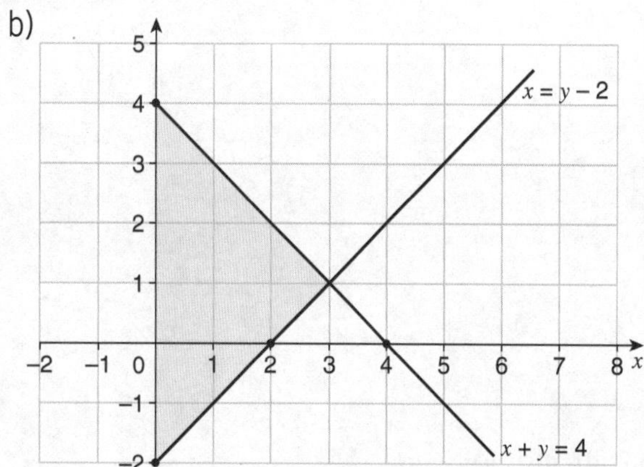

16 a) $a = 3$, $b = 2$, $c = 1$ b) 4 c) 840

17 a) 1, 2, 3 b) $t \geqslant \frac{13}{3}$

18 a) $4 - 2\sqrt{7}$ b) $11 + 4\sqrt{7}$
c) $-17 - 4\sqrt{7}$

19 a) 6.66 cm (3 s.f.)
b) 10.49 cm (3 s.f.)
c) 33.1 cm^2 (3 s.f.)

20 $\frac{x-4}{x^2-16}+\frac{2}{2x-4}=1$

$\frac{x-4}{(x-4)(x+4)}+\frac{2}{2(x-2)}=1$

$\frac{1}{(x+4)}+\frac{1}{(x-2)}=1$

$x-2+x+4=1\ (x+4)(x-2)$
$2x+2=x^2+2x-8$
$x^2+2x-8-2x-2=0$
$x^2-10=0$
$x=\pm\sqrt{10}$
$x=+\sqrt{10}$ or $x=-\sqrt{10}$

21 a) Curved surface area of cone = πrl
$\pi \times 3 \times 5 = 15\pi$
Curved surface area of hemisphere = $\frac{4\pi r^2}{2}$
$2\pi \times 9 = 18\pi$
Total curved surface area = 33π

b) Linear scale factor = 3
Area scale factor = $3^2 = 9$
Curved surface area of larger toy = 297π

22 a) $(2x+4)(x+6)-\frac{1}{2}\times(x+1)(x+4)=38.5$

$2x^2+16x+24-\frac{(x^2+5x+4)}{2}=38.5$

$4x^2+32x+48-x^2-5x-4=77$
$3x^2+27x+44=77$
$3x^2+27x-33=0$
$(\div 3)\ \therefore x^2+9x-11=0$

b) i) $x = 1.09$ or $x = -10.09$, but $x > 0$
ii) Area of triangle = $\frac{1}{2}\times 2.09 \times 5.09$
$= 5.319\ 05$
$= 5.32$ cm^2 (3 s.f.)

23 a) $\frac{2}{15}$ b) $\frac{1}{2}$